At Twice Thirty

Edward W. Bok

TWICE THIRTY

SOME SHORT AND SIMPLE ANNALS OF THE ROAD

BY

EDWARD W. BOK

AUTHOR OF "THE AMERICANIZATION OF EDWARD BOK"
"TWO PERSONS," "A MAN FROM MAINE"
EDITOR OF "GREAT HOLLANDERS"

CHARLES SCRIBNER'S SONS
NEW YORK · LONDON
1925

THE CONTENTS OF THIS BOOK

TWICE THIRTY

TWICE THIRTY

ONE:

WHY THIS BOOK WAS WRITTEN

"To see a thing and tell it in plain words is the greatest thing a soul can do"

JOHN RUSKIN

———

"The author who succeeds in his work is he who describes the interesting and significant things which it has been given him to observe and experience in his own life"

TOLSTOI

WHY THIS BOOK WAS WRITTEN

This book is written for and addressed to:—

my sons
William Curtis Bok
(at twenty-seven)
and
Cary William Bok
(at twenty)

I

YOUR mother has proposed that I should put down for you some of my more significant experiences. This will be different from my book *The Americanization of Edward Bok*, which is largely narrative. There I refrained from expressing opinions. This means that in this book I may here and there become "preachy," as it is called,— something that the public, as a rule, so dislikes, and which those who review books delight to condemn. But you cannot very well proclaim a thought, or draw a conclusion, or "point a moral or adorn a tale," without falling into the category of the preacher, can you?

II

The time seems opportune to adopt your mother's suggestion, because, as I write this, I am completing the circle of my twice-thirty period, and I recall an incident which may be of interest to you.

One evening, nearly forty years ago, I was trying to

3

help Henry Ward Beecher with his mail. There were no scheduled engagements, the mail was light and Mr. Beecher was enjoying that rare thing in his life: a brief period of leisure. He was sitting at his desk, the end of the quill-pen balanced between his lips, as was his wont, —a habit which, when there was ink on the end of the pen, gave Mrs. Beecher many a moment of bewildered wonder at the presence of ink spots in the most unlikely places.

Suddenly he turned in his swivel chair, and, taking the pen from his mouth, asked, "How old are you now, Edward?"

"Twenty-two, sir," I replied.

"Full of hopes and plans as to what you are going to do with your life, I suppose?" he asked.

"More hopes than plans, I think, sir," I answered.

"That is right," he returned. "The first thirty years *should* be full of hopes. The imagination should then be at its liveliest."

"And full of learning?" I asked.

"In a way," he mused. "A certain kind of learning, that is, school and book learning. But actual lessons come only from Life itself, and we begin to learn intelligently only at thirty. Then you begin to take in and pack away."

"And give out?" I ventured.

"We do, yes, of course," was the answer, "but not wisely. Wisdom does not come so easily nor so quickly as that."

"When does wisdom come, sir?" my curiosity prompted.

"At sixty," was the prompt response. "Not before. Then if you have listened intently and lived carefully, and learned from living, you have stored up a background of wisdom from which you begin to draw for ripe and correct decision. Yes, it takes sixty years to reach wisdom. It seems a long road, doesn't it? But wisdom is a rare quality, my boy, just like a rare orchid. It takes years to cultivate it. and, like the orchid, it feeds on the unseen."

"You feel then, Mr. Beecher, that you have experienced only thirteen years of wisdom in all your seventy-three years of life?" I asked.

"Just about, my boy, just about," he mused, and once more the quill went between the lips as he sat looking into space. "Certainly not any more," he concluded.

III

The little talk always remained with me: in fact, I noted it down at the time. I felt as if it would stay with me. And as the road has been travelled and has fallen behind, year after year, the truth of the great preacher's words has often come home, and always with increasing force. It will be difficult for you boys to believe this at twenty-seven and twenty. It was for me at twenty-two. But it became interesting at thirty: it had become easy of acceptance at fifty, and now, standing at the threshold of the beginning of the age of wisdom, experience has crystallized it into a conviction.

It has been a fascinating pastime of the last ten years to watch the mental processes and discerning power of

more comfortable third person. This would not fit so well in the case of this book, and so you must make allowances, as we shall go along, for the frequent appearance of the obtrusive pronoun. One thing is certain: it cannot be more offensive to you as readers than it is to me as writer.

VI

You will, perhaps, feel conscious, too, of a certain naïve note in these pages. But that, to me, goes with these annals, which, if told at all, must be set down with an obvious simplicity. They are simple of themselves: therefore a simple method in the telling of them is logical: in fact—is called for. I remember a critic (curious how we believe in the existence of such a person!) said of my last book that it was written with "a simple naïveness almost childlike." He objected to it. I can imagine the unpleasant time in store for this young man in the pages ahead if he is given this volume to criticize. What that wise censor of the output of the book world overlooks—or rather what he does not know, since his years are on the sunny side of four decades, and his background is thus very near—is that after one has written for a while he no longer writes to a public, but to friends, friends whom he has made by personal contact, by letter, or through the printed page. By virtue of the fact that they have gone with him through his previous pages they are prepared for the note of naïveté in his further work. They understand. It is not like a first book, a first meeting, a first experience; the acquaintance has been made, the relation created—fixed, if you please. Experience can only be told, as I see it, by the use of a naïve simplicity. But one has to turn the corner of fifty or a few corners beyond before this understanding of the relation of a writer with his reader comes. So if you are conscious of this note of naïveté in what follows, be assured that I was conscious of it before you.

VII

You boys have been told in commencement addresses and baccalaureate sermons that the path of Life which lies before you is difficult. My experience has taught me that Life is only difficult if we think it so or make it so. Of itself, Life is really not so difficult as it is at times perplexing. Here and there, in spots, it seems to wind itself into a tangle, and we become confused. But Life in itself is really not so. It is we who make it so, we who fail to keep it simple. Man creates his own complications. The skeins of Life as they are given us are all very simple and are laid apart. The trouble comes when we begin to weave them in and out according to faulty finite knowledge, and we get them at times into a tangled mess. We become confused and finally bewildered by snarls of our own making. It is "a tangled web we weave!" It is so easy to leave the direct and simple road, and so difficult to find it again. You will find as you go along that few indeed there are who have the marvelous gift of keeping their lives simple and avoiding the snares that lie in wait on each side of the middle of the road.

VIII

Life, too, would be simpler of grasp and fuller of enjoyment if we more firmly believed that it has its compensations at each stage. You boys are very apt to think of the period through which you are passing as the best in your lives. It is only natural that youth should strongly feel this. There is a stage in life when you turn first to the sporting page of the newspaper, and then there is also a time, not so very much later as time goes, when you read first the obituary notices. Those at the first stage can never understand the habit of those at the other stage—until they arrive there themselves! You think of maturity and certainly of old age as a time to be dreaded. I did. When my father passed away at fifty-two, he was to me, at seventeen, an old man whose race had been run. When I reached fifty-two, I indulgently smiled at the thought. Life had brought compensations at fifty which I never dreamed of at fifteen. At fifty I found I was still beginning to live. Achievement was ahead, not behind. The best of the road was to come. And now as I am completing the twice-thirty circle, I am keen for the experiences which will come in the age of wisdom. It is a wonderful lure. Experiences will be richer and deeper. It will be a wonderful feeling to have a background. When, at sixty, one takes stock of the things worth while, the deduction is very simple that the two great factors in Life upon which, after all, we can with any safety or surety depend are, at the beginning, the quality of our birth, and, at the finish, the background which we have built.

IX

So, with a keen zest and confidence in the years before me, I am glad to do as your mother thinks I should:
put down here for you these short and simple annals of
the road, hoping that, here and there, I may offer a suggestion upon which you can enlarge and improve in the
twice-thirty years which I hope lie ahead for each of you.

And I think you will agree with me that I should dedi-
cate this book

TO

YOUR MOTHER

without whom the three of us would not have amounted
to much. In fact, two of us would not be here at all,
and with the third the undertakings of the last thirty
years would have failed of achievement.

Your affectionate

FATHER.

MERION
PENNSYLVANIA
October, 1924

TWO:
ON BEING BORN

*"I thank the goodness and the grace
Which on my birth have smiled."*

JANE TAYLOR

ON BEING BORN

I

You and I have heard an occasional one who has muddied the streams of life say: "I wish I had never been born." There is something radically wrong with a person who takes this view of his birth, wrong either of his own mistakes or of wrongs imposed upon him. It is true that we have nothing to do with our coming into the world: we are brought into life unasked. It is this important fact that I think parents are prone to overlook in the handling of their offspring, with the result that the heart often aches at the unfairnesses practiced upon children who are treated as if their presence were a fact for which they are responsible. A child is rarely accepted for what it really is: an invited guest. But by the same token is birth an unequaled privilege. It is an atom of limitless potentialities. Few have pictured the wonder of birth as beautifully as did President Coolidge when he said that no man was ever meanly born. About his cradle is the wondrous miracle of life. He may descend into the depths, he may live in infamy and perish miserably, but he is born great. Men build monuments above the graves of their heroes to mark the end of a great life, but women seek out the birthplace and build their shrine not where a great life had its ending, but where it had its beginning, seeking with a truer instinct the common source of things not in that which is gone forever, but in that which they know will again be manifest. Life may depart, but the source of life is constant.

II

There is nothing for which I am more deeply grateful than for my birth: the marvelous privilege of existence. Perhaps I feel this more than some because of the manner in which I came into the world. For many years I failed to understand why the children who came to my mother after me did not survive. Then I was told one day that I weighed fourteen pounds at my birth, costing my mother a year of her life on crutches. A considerable part of the over-sized child consisted of head, my mother explained to me when I was old enough to understand, and, according to her narrative, the owner of that head lost little time in its use.

It has been pretty well settled by the scientist and biologist, satisfactorily to themselves at least, that the quality of our birth has a greater effect on our characters and lives than the environment under which we find ourselves in life. If this contention be true, that the human race must offer different strata of humanity the same as exist in the animal world, we are dependent largely upon the quality of our heredity. It still remains true, however, that, as parents, we can give our children certain controllable heritages—the priceless heritage of a vigorous constitution, for example, by transmitting a strain of healthy blood to our children.

My parents gave me this precious heritage.

III

I remember one of the first letters I received after the publication of my book, *The Americanization of Edward Bok.* "You say," ran the letter, "there is no such thing as luck. Don't you think it is a great piece of good luck to be born well?"

That "great piece of good luck" has been transmitted to you boys: the English and New England strain on your mother's side: the pure Dutch strain, not crossed for centuries, on your father's side—generations of men and women of careful lives on both sides, ensuring, at least, a combined strain of unsullied blood. This is much: not only to inherit, but to perpetuate, for when we speak of being well-born we mean just that. If your mother and father have succeeded in doing aught in the world, it is largely due to the background which they inherited, and which they have passed on to you boys. As you go along you will realize how much background counts: for it becomes a possession upon which you can always depend.

Hence to be born well is a priceless privilege: not for the purpose of boastfulness; not to be declared by crest or coat-of-arms,—but to be translated into works which will measure up to the quality of the gift. It is a wonderful opportunity which every child is given to perpetuate the standards of his forbears: to carry on the family name so that each generation will be the richer because a member of that family has been of it.

I do not mean by being "well-born" the tracing of a lineage to a royal house or to one of wealth. The mother

ruler. What should have been taught our young by their parents or teachers was left for them to find out through a cataclysm, only to learn these lessons, in some instances, just for a little while before they left behind them a little brown bundle in the grass of France while they went into realms where their souls were to be filled with that beauty which was denied them on earth.

"I never knew the sky was so full of romance," said one of our boys in France as we stood looking up at a sky of wondrous beauty: a companion had pointed out to the young sentry the Pole Star, and had told him why the Great Bear was hanging low in the North at that time while at other times it would be straight overhead, and had traced out for him the Milky Way and the Great Dipper. "They can be your wonderful companions in your vigil," said my friend, while the ardent sentry, with awe in his voice, replied, "They certainly will be from now on." But by morning he knew in another world more than had been explained to him.

How easy it would have been for father or mother or teacher to have opened up to such a boy the richness of a lyric heaven for the nights of lonely vigil, which was his for just those few brief hours before his night of emancipation and the morning of his deliverance!

It is truly a wonderful heritage to be born well.

VII

I had not been in this world many days before I was bundled up and trundled along the dykes of the North Sea. When the salt mists hung heavily, obscuring the sea and almost the path on top of the dykes, I was taken just the same: my governess simply bundled me up a bit more. Through rains she trundled my little coach, and no winds were so high as to keep me indoors.

Young as I was, my governess made an indelible impression upon me. Her name was Antje which, in English, would probably mean Annie. I can see her immaculate white cap now, and, Dutch-like, it was always immaculate: never a ruffle visible in it. On days when the wind was high—and it can be high along those dykes—she would clamp it down with a wide brass clasp on the order of the head-gear worn by the Scheveningen fisherwomen; only Antje's clasp was of a more artistic order. When the sun would strike this brass ornament it would naturally attract my infantile interest, and often would I purposely pull my coverings down, or perform some acrobatic act with my sturdy legs so that Antje would leave her post behind and come to the front of the carriage where I could see the wonderful glistening ornament on her head. I recall that I used to wonder why my mother did not wear so beautiful a thing on her head. But then I noticed that she did not wear a cap like Antje, either. So I figured out, to my satisfaction, that if she didn't wear a cap, there was, of course, no occasion for her to wear a brass clasp to keep it in position on windy days. Antje also wore two dresses of which I was passionately fond. They were both of a very small square check pattern: one was pink and white and the other was blue and white. No matter how cold the day, Antje wore one or the other of these linen dresses. Bundled up as I was under blankets, she looked cold to me. But she certainly looked clean,

and that satisfied my Dutch sense for neatness. It was
not until years afterward that my mother explained to
me that Antje was "very warmly dressed underneath."
But that, of course, I did not know, nor could I see.
Her dresses, too, fairly screamed from the starch in
them—they actually stuck out. But they were as immaculate as was her cap. Over her dress she always
wore a large apron. It was not the apron that interested
me so much as a large pocket in that apron! As I
grew older, I discovered that this pocket always contained something, and once I made this discovery it was
not long before I found out the ways and means which
led to this "something." I had only to become obstrep-
erous, when Antje's hand would find its way instinctively into this pocket, and the something would invariably come forth, and that something was always in
the shape of candy! Of course, this was not according
to Hoyle. In fact, I learned afterward that this little
custom was distinctly against my mother's orders. But
then, why a governess if there do not exist some deep,
dark secrets between her and her charge? And there
was a decided freemasonry between Antje and her
charge. She knew all the signs, and so did I, and the
result was we got along famously together, and to-day
I think of her with a passionate devotion. No, dear
reader, Antje did not wear wooden shoes. That is an
artistic (?) myth which the Dutch leave to American
artists who have either never visited the Netherlands
or who have not the intelligence to understand class-
distinctions in costume. A governess in a Dutch family
of position would as readily think of wearing wooden

shoes as would a governess in an American family of position think of wearing blinders!

My parents believed in fresh air, and any one who knows anything about the North Sea along the Dutch coast knows there is air aplenty and that of its fresh quality there is no doubt. In fact, to be day in and day out exposed to the rigors of the climate of the Northern Dutch coast, as a child, means a wonderful physical start if he survives it. Not only did I survive it, but I throve prodigiously. And if I felt no other debt to my mother and to my native land than the six years in which I laid the foundations of a constitution that was to stand me in such marvellous stead, my obligation, for that precious gift alone, is difficult of fulfillment.

VIII

It was probably my mother's long incapacity which led one of my aunts, Tante Katrien (Aunt Catherine) to come into my baby-life and implant herself there so firmly that she has remained there all these sixty years. It was not long after we began to be able to walk that my brother and I beat a well-worn path to my aunt's house almost every day. "There was a reason!" The moment we appeared, the dear auntie, thoroughly conversant with the nature of children, although she never married, went at once to a magical sideboard, for there would always appear some toothsome sweet, a cookie or a heavenly strawberry-jam sandwich which, strangely enough, was always ready. Naturally, those little attentions go straight to the heart as well as to the stomach of a boy.

I remember on one of our many visits I wore a new velvet suit of which I was very proud: in fact, my visit was purely for the purpose of having her see the wonderful addition to my wardrobe. I received strict injunctions from my mother that I should not sit down in my suit, since a restless boy and a cane chair were not conducive to enhancing the smoothness of a velvet suit, and my governess was cautioned to see that I did not forget. Naturally, to make a visit and stand up all the time does not promote sociability, particularly when a special, delicious drink was added to the regular sweets to celebrate the occasion. I explained to my aunt, corroborated by my governess, why I could not sit down on a chair.

"Of course not," agreed my aunt. "I can well understand that, but you can sit on my lap. That won't hurt your beautiful suit."

We all agreed to that! Dear, wise auntie!

What an institution in a child's life is such an auntie! Think of some one who always believes that what you do is exactly right. And even in those extremely rare moments when you are, well, just a bit naughty—even then, there *must* be always some reason, some excuse. Blessed haven of complete understanding: certain refuge in time of trouble! And there are so many troublesome moments in a child's life when mother simply does not understand. But auntie always does. There is an understanding at once complete and which never fails. Even more dependable is she than a grandmother, and how much that says! Yes, there is a divination of a child in the heart of a favorite auntie that never forsakes: it is always there and always ready to see so clearly and iron out all the big troubles that loom up so terrifyingly in a child's life. Some folk who do not know call it spoiling a child. But it isn't. It is developing a child's trust, a child's love that grows with the years until it ripens into the highest and one of the most beautiful of human relations.

It is the misfortune of you boys that you have never known what it is to have such a favorite aunt. She is a very precious possession, an affectionate memory which never goes out of one's life, even after the physical presence is removed.

Fortunately, in this instance, the dear little auntie is still hale and hearty in the flesh, as graciously gentle as ever, four thousand miles away from this particular loving nephew, but always the centre of a bevy of other adoring nephews and nieces and cousins.

Some women never marry, but what loving children they have and how many of them!

IX

When I came to the United States, and was to learn every phase of hardship and poverty: to have a child's appetite and not be able to satisfy it; to work instead of play—it was then that all the health I had imbibed in my early Dutch environment was to come into use. I went through babyhood and childhood without a single one of the ills or ailments associated with those years: I knew not a day's illness. A cold was an affliction unknown to me. The household errands I ran; the early hours at which I rose to sift the previous day's ashes and build and start a fire, the exercise of washing dishes or scrubbing floors and stairs, the serving of a newspaper route—all those kept my mind active and my body healthy. I had no time to think of ailments. But I always got a night's full sleep: upon that point my mother was adamant, and I thank her now for her vigilance, although at the time I was not so keenly appreciative of her solicitude.

X

It was when I began to strike out for myself, to fill my days and then my evenings and later my nights to overflowing, when my mother's watchful eyes were no longer so lovingly upon me, when the spur of dire necessity prodded, when the desire came strong upon me to repay my mother, so far as I could, for the travail of my birth, and to reinstate her in the position in the world and amid those comforts to which I felt she was entitled, that I began to take liberties with my healthy body.

Yet, save a period or two of nervous exhaustion, when I have been compelled to seek some spot of quiet repose, and an early abuse of the digestive organs impairing my efficiency, which is my keenest regret, I have been blessed with a physical heritage which has always aroused my deepest gratitude. My mother's insistence on sleep has become a gospel of my life, so that to-day I can and do sleep the clock around once and sometimes twice a week.

XI

In sixty years I have spent, under compulsion, exactly three days in bed.

THREE:

THE CHILD WITH THE INQUIRING MIND

"When all the world is new
And things are passing strange."

———

"I cannot tell what you and other men
Think of this life; but, for my single self,
I had as lief not be as live to be
In awe of such a thing as I myself."

SHAKESPEARE

THE CHILD WITH THE INQUIRING MIND

I

The story is told of one of the most beautiful women in England who was deaf and dumb, but so radiant was her beauty that, despite her handicaps, she became the wife of an English Earl of vast estates. In due course of time her first child was laid in her arms. The first day she was permitted to walk she went into the adjoining room where her child lay asleep in its cradle, watched over by a nurse. For some moments the mother gazed at the child with anxious lines on her face, and then going to the window she lifted a huge china vase of inestimable value, carried it to the crib of the child, lifted it above her head and poised it as if to dash it at the child. Stricken dumb with horror at the sight, the nurse sat powerless. She dared not cry out: and she was too far away to throw herself between the upraised vase and the sleeping child. In another moment the vase crashed on the floor, broken into a hundred pieces. The child awoke with a scream of terror, whereupon the delighted mother, convinced that her child had not inherited the absence of speech or hearing, clasped her baby in her arms.

II

No such experiment was necessary in my babyhood. I was evidently endowed to a supreme degree with a quality which makes a child so great a nuisance that it seems often a defect at birth, but certainly tends to equip him for certain lines of activity later,—perhaps that of an editor: the quality of curiosity. A pair of large blue eyes became interested in people and things almost from the moment when they saw the light, and the mind began to follow as soon as it could. The obstruction to a complete enjoyment of the world at that stage seemed to have been an inability to speak. An object or person would catch the eye, the most searching and intent look would follow, lasting sometimes for minutes. Then would come a determined attempt to reach expression; for the lips would become so rigidly tight as to cause alarm to the nurse: the face would grow purple from inner effort: the head would shake in irritating failure, almost audibly saying "it's no use"; the body would relax and settle back, and with an agonizing look I would present a picture of eloquent futility and abject failure. So "little of this great world can I speak!" I tried to reach vocal expression even before I made that most wonderful of all discoveries which is so truly amazing and mystifying to a baby: that its hands really belong to it.

Maybe every man in infancy would reveal to a sufficiently observing eye the qualities that rule his career. In my case they were obvious. They were the two impulses to see and to express, that is to discover and to tell about—or to cause to be told about. However troublesome they must have made me in childhood, and afterward too, I fear, they were the controlling ones in my career. The big-eyed infant, in this particular instance, was certainly the father of the man,—for better or worse.

III

At the age of twenty months I gave what my parents recited as a demonstration, and a rather embarrassing one, of this investigating character of my mind. The last baby in the family is, of course, always a source of interest to visiting friends, and on this occasion the visiting friend was Count von Bismarck. I never ascertained whether the great Chancellor was a guest at my parents' home in the Netherlands or if the occasion was a dinner-party elsewhere. The fact that Bismarck was a friend of my father and that upon this occasion he was at dinner seated at my mother's right leads to the natural conclusion that my parents were the hosts.

At any rate, I was brought down to the dinner-party to be duly admired by the guests, particularly by the guest of honor, and my nurse placed me on the knees of the famous Chancellor. The guests, the lights, and the flowers naturally attracted my interest for a few moments. My eyes swept over the table and guests, and then my gaze rested and distinctly settled on the face of the man on whose knees I was sitting. It was the cursory glance of a child at first, and then something held me. I shifted my position, drew back my little body toward the table, so that I could get all the perspective possible in order to afford a full view of the face. Then I began my scrutiny,—to the intense interest of the one under inspection and the entire party. (My mother is, of course, telling this.) There seemed to be no portion of the face which failed to interest me, and from part to part my intent gaze travelled as I

investigated apparently every inch. Bismarck sat im-
movable during the scrutinizing process. For fully two
minutes my interest seemed riveted, and then with a
deep sigh I turned to the next guest. But only for a
moment. Almost immediately I came back to the face
of Bismarck. Evidently I had not finished my minute
examination. Once more my intent gaze fixed itself on
the face, and then drawing my body back I examined
the right side of the face and throwing my body forward
minutely inspected the left side. Then I came back to
the full face, and again for a full minute I made a further
examination. All this time Bismarck sat like the Sphinx;
not a movement did he make, not a word did he speak.
For fully five minutes—an incredibly long time for a
continued silence at a dinner-party—I had gone on
with my careful examination. Then came another deep
sigh, when, my eye shifting for a moment and resting
on my nurse standing behind Bismarck, I pointed my
little index finger straight into Bismarck's face, and my
face became red with the effort to reach vocal expression.
Then did Bismarck speak for the first time. Turning
to my mother he said: "Never have I been so minutely
and critically scrutinized. I wonder what can be the
child's thoughts." (I wonder, too!)

The tension was now broken, and Bismarck reached
for a wine-glass and proposed a toast to "the health and
future of the child with the inquiring mind." But somehow or other this act did not please me. With a quick
dash of the arm I knocked the glass out of the Chancellor's hand, upsetting the wine on his shirt-front and
over his clothes. I was snatched up by my nurse, while

my mother quickly with her handkerchief (one of those wonderful feminine contrivances which can scarcely absorb a drop, let alone a glassful) attempted to wipe off the great German's shirt-front. That handkerchief with its dark wine stains I still possess.

IV

When I began the collection of autograph letters and documents, some years later, my father, seeing that my interest was genuine, suggested that he might make a distinct contribution to my collection with several documents, one of which was a diplomatic appointment signed by von Bismarck. Accompanying it was a small carte-de-visite photograph of the Chancellor presented by him to my father. It was an excellent likeness, my father explained: the Chancellor's favorite photograph.

"Father," I said, looking at the photograph, "have I ever seen Bismarck?"

I recall that at the question my father looked significantly at my mother.

"Don't you think you would remember it if you ever saw him?" my father asked.

"Yes," was my answer, "I suppose I would."

"And you don't remember?" my mother asked.

"No," I answered.

"Then why do you ask?" urged my father.

"Well, I don't know, but whenever I see a picture of Bismarck there comes from inside of me a sense that somehow or somewhere I have seen that face. Of course, it is a fancy, but isn't it curious how I get that feeling about him and no one else?" I said.

"Not so curious as you think," said my mother. Then she told me, for the first time, the episode of my babyhood. Naturally I did not recall any detail of the occasion; I have never since been able to remember even the slightest incident in connection with it. But back in my baby-head there was unquestionably left an impression of the strong, rugged face which I had studied so minutely and for such an unusually long time; and to-day I never see a photograph of von Bismarck but the same indefinite sense strongly comes to me.

I think this worth setting down here in view of the discoveries of recent psychology which tend to show that nothing is ever forgotten; that every impression is stored away at varying depths in the subconscious mind, even an incident like this that occurred in the early months of infancy.

V

I spoke of an inquiring mind as a precious possession in a protective sense because I have the conviction that the most devastating factor in the human mind, fear, finds no resting-place in a mind that is always busy with the investigating processes.

So far as I can recall, I have never been in fear of anything in my life. I was preserved from fear not by the possession of any special virtue, but by this quality of curiosity, of interest. The result is that I have never had the sense of being afraid of anything to be done or of a decision to be made. And I was put to the test of a fearlessness of decision very early in life.

I was seventeen years of age, when, in the early part

of 1881, my father fell desperately ill. For two weeks the doctors battled with the steadily-gaining disease: for I learned afterward that it was hemorrhagic meningitis. One evening the physicians held a long consultation, and at its close one of them, a close personal friend of my father and the family, called me into the room. The two physicians looked at me kindly, and then our friend spoke: "Eddie," he said, "we have to ask you to make a very important decision. We do not want to ask your mother to make it, nor your brother: we do not want them even to know that we have asked it of you. Your father is very ill. A blood-vessel has burst at the base of the brain. It is just possible that by an operation we may save his life, but we cannot guarantee it. We will try it, however, if you decide that we shall. But if we save him, he will sit at that window for the rest of his life without a mind. We cannot save his reason: that is beyond hope now. The decision is a large one for a boy such as you to make, but we feel you should make it. Do you wish us to operate with the probable result that I have explained, or do you wish that we should let your father's life run out? We are going now, but will be back early to-morrow morning. Do you think you can tell us then?"

I thought I could, and the physicians left.

VI

My eyes wandered to the window at which the doctor had pictured my father as sitting, bereft of his mind for the rest of his days, unable to read or speak intelligently: just idly sitting through the long years. His mind had truly been to him his kingdom. What could life hold out to him without mental capacity? I thought of my mother, not over-strong, having the care of him as of a child. We had little or no means. My brother and I had just barely begun our start in the world. Jointly we were earning a pitifully small sum, inadequate even to support a mother. I thought of the hardships which a reversal of fortune had already brought to my mother.

I went into my father's room. He was partially asleep, but tossing restlessly and muttering as if in pain. I stood there for fully fifteen minutes. Then he opened his eyes and seemed to beckon me. He gave me his hand, and I, his youngest child, with the responsibility of his life within my power of decision, sat there mute. He spoke not a word. I shall never know, of course, whether telepathically he got the thought which filled me, but the occasional look which he gave me, as he turned over restlessly, seemed to me one of supplication that his sufferings might be allowed to come to an end.

All that night I considered every aspect of the matter a hundred times; in the early dawn I went again to my father's room and stood at the foot of the bed. As I stood there I realized clearly that the longer I argued the matter with my judgment the more certain I was, each time, to revert to that first and instinctive decision which came to me at the moment when the physician first proposed the problem.

In the morning when the doctors came I told them, without a question of doubt in my mind, that my father's life should be allowed to run out. And never in all the passing years have I felt that my decision was other than right, considering all the conditions involved.

When, two days afterward, my father passed away, both doctors came to me and assured me of the wisdom of my decision. They said that if I had left it to them, as they felt I might do, they would have decided against the operation.

Only recently, in talking over the matter with a noted physician, he said: "You need never feel the slightest remorse over your decision. Even to-day, with the advance of surgical knowledge and skill, the percentage of successful operations for hemorrhagic meningitis is very small: in 1881 the chances for a favorable outcome would have been almost negligible."

VII

I speak of this incident not so much because of the weightiness of the decision or of the early age at which I was asked to make it, but to present the point that never for a single instant did the element of fear come into my acceptance of my father's condition and the responsibility of reaching a conclusion. At no point was I afraid: I had no anxiety lest I make a wrong decision, for my instinct seemed to have pointed the way perfectly clearly to me from the moment I was asked to reach a decision. The element of fear was absolutely absent, just as completely as it has been in all other questions or situations in my life where fear might naturally be supposed to be present.

When, for instance, our party found itself suddenly

call, and, much to the amazement of my companions, was asked to come up-stairs. To their chagrin I came down an hour later having had a delightful chat with the President and obtaining his autograph in my book and a signed photograph in the bargain.

On another occasion, the same two companions lost heart at the last moment when we called upon King Kalakaua, of the Sandwich Islands, who had come upon a much-heralded visit to New York. My experience with the President of the United States did not seem to my companions to bear any relation to calling upon an actual King! Once more we ventured to the hotel, and once more the courage of my companions failed at the office desk! To my mind, it was inconceivable how an effort could be started by any one without at least the attempt to carry it through. Their reason for being "afraid" was inexplicable to me because the fear-thought was absolutely foreign to a mind dominated by curiosity —the desire to learn. What was there to be afraid of, I argued? Because a man was a monarch, he still remained a simple human being. Besides, it must have crossed my mind that although Kalakaua was undeniably a king, he could hardly be reckoned as one of the important rulers of the earth. My mind, too, was full of some information which I wanted to obtain from His Majesty as to certain postage-stamps of his country which were missing in my collection. I had taken the precaution to bring the page from my book devoted to Hawaiian postage-stamps. It was a perfectly natural thought to a boy that the ruler of a nation should be the one authority as to the postage-stamps of his land! I wrote my usual note, received word to come up-stairs and, followed by the amazed looks of my two companions, I went, and in a few moments I was busily engaged, through an interpreter, in telling my story to the dusky Hawaiian monarch! To him it was no more of an apparent surprise that a boy would wish to talk with him than it was to me that I should ask it. I did not get the information I wanted about the stamps, for the King assured me with a laugh that, apparently, I knew more about the postage-stamps of his own country than he did. But I added "Kalakaua" to my autograph album:

Kalakaua
Hotel Brunswick
Sept 23 - 1881. New York City

He also gave me an autographed photograph of himself, shook me warmly by the hand as I left him,—and I had seen my first King!

X

The decision to let the life of my father pass on had a decisive effect upon me. I left the doctors that morning to go to my job as office-boy in the Western Union Telegraph Company. My mind was naturally full of my experience. My father would pass away within the next few days, the doctors told me, and I realized that the full support of my mother would fall upon my brother and myself. The small amount of insurance on my father's life I figured out would about cover the medical fees and the funeral expenses. There would be practically nothing left. The combined weekly wage of my brother and myself was twelve dollars and a half per week.

As I walked down to the ferry that morning, I looked around at the houses and up and down the streets which I crossed: I looked at the people I met, I remember I looked up at the cloudless sky. Then I lumped them all together and, clinching my fists and setting my teeth, I said (it must have been audibly, for I remember a man passing me at the moment looked at me and stood following me with his eyes): "America, you have *got* to give me a chance,—you have *got* to give me a place." I placed a fiendish emphasis on each "got."

I did not expect to have the chance or the place offered me, for I felt I would have to work for it and find it. But how was I to have the chance? Where was I to begin? I looked at every person I met as if expecting some one to answer my groping questions.

I put my hand in my pocket to count my capital. I had eight cents. By walking to the ferry, five cents had been saved. Three cents was the ferry fare, and that would leave five cents for the stage fare from the ferry to 195 Broadway. But then I would have nothing for luncheon or to pay for the ferry passage on my way home.

XI

I was approaching the ferry-slip when I saw a one-horse truck. I had casually spoken to the driver, who lived not far from me. The ferry fare at that time for a truck included two passenger fares. I ran after the truck, jumped on it, told the driver in detail of my resolution and financial problem and asked if I could ride across the ferry with him, and thus save my three cents.

"Sure," he replied laughingly, "and up Broadway to your building, too. Never you worry: you'll get there." I never knew whether he meant my final goal or my immediate destination.

I have forgotten the name of this man. I wish I knew it, and if he is still living. But from that morning he would whistle and slow up as he passed my house each morning, and take me from my house to the office, and on those evenings when his work was finished he would pick me up at Dey Street and take me home. Blessings be on him if he is still living: he gave me the first "lift" to my determination to reach the goal of American achievement.

FOUR:

MY FRIEND, THE TRUCK DRIVER

"Think naught a trifle, though it small appear;
Small sands the mountain, moments make the year,
And trifles life."

EDWARD YOUNG

———

"Small service is true service while it lasts,
Of humblest friends . . . scorn not one."

WORDSWORTH

MY FRIEND, THE TRUCK DRIVER

I

THIS truck and my friend, the driver, really became important factors in my young life. I lived fully two miles on the Brooklyn side from the ferry, and it was another two miles on the New York side to the office. With the ferry-fare across the river, it meant, therefore, an expenditure of 26 cents a day for car and ferry-fare or $1.56 per week. I was earning $6.25 per week, and on this, with my brother earning the same, we had to support our mother, and pay the rent and all the household expenses. Even in those days, when the dollar bought much more than now, it was not easy to support a household of three on $12.50 per week. So to save 25 per cent by riding free on a truck became a distinct financial factor. I had no occasion to consider the lack of exercise, because of that I got aplenty in my work during the day as office-boy. Besides, the more I walked the faster my shoes wore out—and that was a consideration to be carefully thought of! It cost a dollar to half-sole and heel a pair of shoes—moderate, it is true; but a dollar-bill was an object that I regarded with a wholesome respect in those days when it was saved a nickel at a time. In fact, a dollar-note I handled as reverently as to-day I would a Rembrandt etching. A bank-note may be, as Thomas Jefferson said, only the ghost of money, but it certainly had a very substantial look to me in my youthful days.

47

II

A nickel represented ofttimes days of saving. Every piece of tinfoil on the street I picked up, and after accumulation I would sell it to the junk-dealer,—and a nickel meant a good many sheets of tinfoil! Every newspaper I saved, and sold to the same junk-dealer, and it required a goodly pile of newspapers to bring a nickel out of the pocket of the junk-man. Bottles and rags I carefully saved, too, and those went the way of the other by-products which the more thoughtless and often the equally poor threw away. There was an ingenious Italian junk-dealer who bought the labels that came on the cans of preserved fruit. He pasted them into scrap-books, and sold these to mothers for their children as picture-books. As this odd traffic of his offered a new avenue of earning money, I used to haunt the lots back of the homes of the wealthy where the tidy habit was in vogue of throwing the tin cans over the back fences. I figured out that these wealthy folks partook of luxuries such as canned apricots and green gages which I noticed on the shelves of grocery stores. These were of a rarer kind than the customary pictures of the tomato and the green pea, so that for a liberal assortment of these labels of the fruit indulged in by the rich I would receive a few cents extra. When nickels are earned by such means, a dollar assumes a wholesome aspect.

III

Nor was a nickel saved always a nickel to be put away in my bank. Kindling-wood was in those days sold in small, round bundles at two bundles for five cents. My chief source of supply of kindling-wood was the lots which I would visit at night and pick up what I could. A favorite lumber-yard often yielded a rich supply of discarded chips. But there was far pleasanter employment than picking up wood in this fashion for the next morning's fire, and so when the nickels were coming in particularly well I would take a saved nickel, buy two bundles of kindling-wood at the grocer's and then treat myself to an evening at home, and thus spare myself a nocturnal lot visitation. It is true that such an evening would be spent mainly in sifting ashes, but at least on a bitter cold winter evening that could be done at home where it was warm.

IV

Lunches were a great problem. The practice was, naturally, to take my lunch each day from home. But a healthy growing boy and the same cold lunch day after day did not make an ideal combination. There came days when his soul—or his stomach—cried out for a variation, something warm, for instance, on a cold winter day.

In the solution of this dilemma I found another friend. He was the waiter in the private dining-room on the third floor of the Western Union Telegraph Company's building where the president, the officers, and the directors had their daily lunch. His name was Thomas

ing home, and a very careful polishing on Sundays. The month of May, in my calendar, was shoe month. That was the month of the annual parade of the Sunday-schools of Brooklyn, and a boy might just as well not exist in Brooklyn as to march in that parade minus something new, and it generally was a pair of new shoes. Of course, it was the worst possible occasion to break in a pair of new shoes which, being bought ready-made, never really fitted, were invariably tight, and pinched actively. The day of the parade was always the hottest day in May: that was proverbial, and the boy who was elected to carry the banner of his class, with a charming girl holding the tasselled-cords marching on each side of him, was the hero of the day. I strove always to be that hero! The line of march was long: some five miles! Suffer in those new shoes! It was sweet but untold agony! That mattered not, forsooth, so long as I marched! And carrying that heavy banner! Shall I ever remember anything with such joy as those happy moments when there would occur a congestion, the line of march would halt, the banner could rest on the ground for a spell, and I could shift from one foot to the other to alleviate the sizzling burning of those new shoes? They were always effectively broken in; no doubt of that, and then for an entire year I would have comfort in them. But a year they had to last, with a half-soling and heel-ing over night during the course of the twelve months, so that I could wear them the next morning. It was fortu-nate that shoes in those days were well-made, particu-larly as I could never pay more than three dollars for a pair and more often less!

VII

With such financial problems to solve, it is easy to see what important factors were my friend the waiter and my friend the truck driver. Particularly the latter, for while the former attended to what constitutes so large a part of a boy's anatomy, the latter meant actually to save so many cents each day. Of course, riding on a truck over cobble-stone streets is not the same as gliding along tracks in a street-car, but beggars cannot be choosers, and such differences in transportation never enter into a boy's category—he simple rides! Besides, did not stages on which you had to pay five cents fare ride over the same cobble-stones on Broadway?

VIII

Wonderful days they were—full of seeming strain as now they are looked back upon, but not to the boy who was going through them as an experience. To him they were days of adventure; adventure leading to accomplishment he knew not of. They become but "yesterdays upon which we look back with a smile." How unconsciously large, however, loom my friend, the truck driver, who gave a boy a ride; and my friend, the waiter, who gave a boy a bite!

"Who does the best his circumstance allows,
Does well, acts nobly; angels could no more."

FIVE:

THAT MUFFLER AT DUBERNELL'S

"*When I behold what pleasure is Pursuit,*
What life, what glorious eagerness it is,
Then mark how full Possession falls from this,
How fairer seems the blossom than the fruit,—
I am perplext."

THOMAS BAILEY ALDRICH

THAT MUFFLER AT DUBERNELL'S

I

IN those days of my boyhood, it was the prevailing fashion to wear a silk muffler around the neck under the overcoat, but carefully revealed: not for comfort, but as the last word in good dressing. No wardrobe was complete without one, and there was scarcely one of my chums who did not wear one. Either their parents were well-to-do, and could afford this evidence of wealth on their boys, or, as was as common in those days as it is now, they had mufflers even if they couldn't afford such an extravagance. That I had no muffler was a sore point with me, and I felt that I was constantly at a disadvantage with my boy-friends,—certainly before the girls,—because of this lack of Fashion's hall-mark!

II

The most fashionable haberdashery shop of that day in Brooklyn was on lower Fulton Street. It was called Dubernell's. I always liked the name: it had an aristocratic sound that fitted so well, to my mind, with the contents and repute of the store. To buy one's shirtings, collars, or cravats at Dubernell's was the acme of fashion and wealth. I knew this, and often I would go out of my way and stand transfixed before the windows of this wonderful shop. I couldn't afford to buy anything the windows contained, but at least I could keep myself posted on the latest styles!

One morning there appeared in the window the most wonderful muffler my eyes ever beheld. It fairly spoke the fact that it was of the richest and heaviest white silk, and all over it were the most beautiful of small birds embroidered in old gold. I stood for fully fifteen minutes transfixed, coveting that muffler. What would not be possible to me as a well-dressed youth among the boys and girls if I appeared with that muffler! The picture was radiant, and I fairly glowed over merely thinking of it. But I had only eighteen cents in my pocket! For three successive days I haunted that window, fearful lest the precious muffler should be sold; yet I saw no way by which I could purchase it, although I had made no end of calculations. The fourth day I got far enough to walk into the shop and ask the price of the dazzling muffler!

"Two dollars and seventy-five cents," said the clerk. I thought so! A fortune! He might just as well have said $275.00 so far as my resources were concerned. What a treasure to own, I thought! But what a price! My playmates were paying $1.00 and $1.25 for their mufflers! What would be their reaction if I walked into their midst with this $2.75 muffler, for its very quality and appearance betokened its price! There was no doubt that it was worth all of $2.75,—to the fortunate person who could afford it!

III

That evening my mother said she wanted a barrel of apples, and would I stop in at the grocer's next morning on my way to school and select a good barrel? Where-

upon she handed me $2.75! Now, why, I ask, should that
barrel of apples have happened to be the same price as
that muffler? And what was a barrel of apples compared
with that muffler? The apples would be all eaten within
a given time, and that would be the end of them. But
that muffler! That was a life-time possession! I lay
awake for two or three hours that night cogitating upon
the strange coincidence of similarity in prices. I
thought, too, of how unequal were the tastes of people
in the world! My mother wanted a barrel of apples,
and I wanted a muffler! How the material did ever-
lastingly clash with the æsthetic in this world!

The following morning my mind was made up. I
shrank from the idea of being dishonest with my mother,
yet I felt I must have that muffler. So I repaired to
the grocer's, selected the barrel of apples, and told him
to "charge it." Here was my misstep. It is true I
figured out that I would scrimp and save, and by the
time the grocer would be ready to send his bill I would
have the $2.75. But it was a lie! With my feet hardly
touching the pavement, I made a bee-line for Dubernell's! Suppose the muffler had been sold! I almost
ran into the window, my heart sank, and I stood cold!
The muffler was not there! With a heavy heart I
gazed into that window! After all my dreams, and
that supreme effort! Two new mufflers were there, but
not that one! Somebody had gotten ahead of me.
Some millionaire, of course! Why were there million-
aires, any way?

Then came the thought that perhaps Mr. Dubernell
had two! So into the store I went, described the wonder-

ful work of art, and, with beating heart, asked if he still had it.

"Oh, yes," came back that answer which lifted my heart again. "Took it out of the window just last evening. You mean this one?" And there in the showcase lay the object of beauty!

"That's it," I joyfully answered. "$2.75, isn't it?"

"Yes," was the answer, and in the most matter-of-fact manner, and not as reverently as I felt he might, he wrapped *my* muffler up! It was mine now!

"You want my name, I suppose?" I asked.

"Name?" asked the shopkeeper. "What for?"

Naturally I thought that any one who made so important a purchase would have his name registered, so that Mr. Dubernell might know his purchaser! But, strange as it appeared to me, Mr. Dubernell didn't seem to care who bought his muffler!

IV

If I opened that package once that morning on my way to school, I am sure I must have opened it twenty times. On every corner I stopped, presumably to let some wagon or carriage go by—when none was in sight —but actually just to take a peep at my treasured possession. Of course, the entire day at school was spoiled for me. What were such ordinary things as lessons compared with such a possession as I had in my pocket? I fairly itched to show it to my schoolmates, but I was not ready to share it with any other eyes yet. I wanted to feast upon it all by myself for a period! When I reached home I could not, of course, show my treasure to my mother, because she would naturally want to know where I had obtained the money. That astonishing revelation to her I determined would come after I had saved the necessary sum.

V

In my dealing with the grocer I had left one little item in his system out of my calculations. It was this grocer's custom to render his bills monthly, and as I had ordered the barrel of apples three days prior to the end of a month, I was confronted by my mother on the fourth day with a bill for the apples!

"That's strange!" I said weakly.

"Very strange," said my mother. "I certainly gave you the money."

"You did," I answered. "You let me have that bill, and I will see the grocer to-morrow morning."

Fortunately my mother did not pursue the subject. I presume she decided to await developments. But I was sliding down the hill of deception! Meanwhile I had a night to think over what would be my next step. I had saved 40 cents since the important day of my purchase, but that wouldn't go far with the grocer!

I decided to enter into negotiations with the grocer for an extension of time. But, the next morning, I found that although I was willing, he was not! Bills were payable when they were rendered. He needed the money! (So did I, I thought!) I now bethought myself of one of my boy-friends who was saving up for a goat-cart, and explained to him that if he would lend me $2.35 I would pay him $2.50. But he held out for

$2.65. I couldn't hold out! So that afternoon I paid the grocer, and brought the receipted bill to my mother.

"He apologized," I explained. As a matter of fact, when I had entered and gave him the money he *had* apologized for being "cross in the morning" and not giving me thirty days' extension!

VI

My financial troubles were over temporarily at least, and I could look at my coveted treasure, hidden in my closet, every morning and evening with a lighter heart! But three weeks had scarcely elapsed before my boy-friend asked for his money! His father had given him some; he wanted to buy his goat-cart at once, and he must have his $2.65! I told him I had only 85 cents, which I would give him now and the rest later. But there was "nothing doing" in his phrase: he wanted it all, threatening to go to my mother and get it from her. So to another boy-friend I went, and put to him the proposition that if he would lend me $1.80, I would give him $2.00. He accepted, only to come back within a week to demand the money! I went now to a news-dealer, and made him the offer that instead of paying me 75 cents every Saturday to deliver his paper-route, I would do it three weeks for $2.00, if he would give me the $2.00 in advance. He didn't accept this offer as quickly as I hoped he would, and seeing his hesitation I told him the whole story. This was too much for him, and he let me have the $2.00, and at the end of the third week gave me a quarter. Good friend was he!

VII

The wonderful muffler was now my own, and all paid
for. The only trouble was that spring had come, and
mufflers had been laid aside! Of course, to be out of
style was to be out of life, and for four months that
priceless possession lay hidden from mortal eyes waiting
for October to come! Then came the eventful Sunday
morning when I would tell my mother, which I did, and
when I would burst upon my boy and girl-friends. And
I did! That is, I did the bursting: not they. Showing
as much of the muffler as style permitted, and a little
more, I nonchalantly walked up to a group of my boy-
friends. Not one noticed the muffler. No one even
glanced at it! "Envy," I thought! But I was determined they should not pass over such a treasure! So
under the pretext of getting something out of my trousers pocket, I unbuttoned my overcoat so that the
muffler revealed itself entirely in its full beauty. Still
not a word—except one, and this was it: "Say, Bok,
don't you know that mufflers are out of style this
fall?" At least, all the boys looked! And they also
sniffed!

Just then I saw a group of girls near by; the very
ones, too, I knew would be impressed. The three choic-
est girls of all: Agnes Bowdish, Irene Mackey, and Min-
nie Du Bois. What did I care for the boys? So, with
my overcoat wide open, I sauntered over casually to the
group, and said something about it being a beautiful
morning.

Blessed Aggie came through first with what sounded

like balm to my waiting ears: "Oh, what an adorable
muffler!"

"Rather nice, isn't it?" I said. "Bought it at Dubernell's!" (I didn't intend that this fact should remain
unknown!)

But the conquest of the muffler was not on the whole
what I had expected! It was extremely disappointing
to a boy's soul which had been consumed by the Christian spirit of exciting envy and covetousness!

VIII

The next morning I took the precious muffler to school
with me, and surreptitiously (as I thought) showed it
to my schoolmate under my desk. But unfortunately
the teacher had just come up the aisle behind me, and
I heard a voice at my side:

"Give me that scarf, Bok."

I was petrified! To let any other hand touch that
muffler! To take it away from me. It was unthinkable!
I began to wrap it up.

"That isn't a scarf," I retorted.

"What is it, then?" asked the teacher.

"A muffler! I bought it at Dubernell's," was my
proud rejoinder.

"I don't care where you bought it. Give it to me."

And before I could make up my mind what to do,
she reached out and had it! Of course, I failed in my
lessons, and in the noon-hour I saw my muffler given
to the principal.

After the afternoon session, I went up to the principal.

"I want my muffler," I announced.

"That is not the way to ask for anything," I was told.

"Why not?" I asked. "It belongs to me."

"You will ask for it and say please, and then we will talk the matter over."

I thought a moment, and I presume my Dutch literal sense asserted itself.

"I don't see why I should ask that way," I answered. "Miss Williams didn't say please to me. She said, 'Give it to me,' and then didn't even wait for me to give it to her. She snatched it."

"Never mind what Miss Williams said or did," answered the principal. "You are dealing with me now."

Instinctively, even boy that I was, I sensed that he was avoiding an issue, and I felt the advantage with me, and intended to follow it up.

"I know that," I said, "and I don't think you have a right to my muffler. You have a right to mark me, or punish me, but you have no right to take what belongs to me," and then I added "I want my muffler."

And my muffler I got,—also a punishment!

But I had my muffler, although it was grasped by burning hands!

IX

Two evenings thereafter I had been to a party, and was going home when at the corner of the street where I lived stood a certain Jack Donnelly, dreaded leader of a gang of the toughest boys in the vicinity—which means in the most extreme degree what is implied by the term hard-boiled.

"What's your hurry, Bok?" said the Dreaded One, as he stepped before me.

"Going home," I answered.

"Nice scarf, that," he said, pointing to my muffler. "Let's see it," and he grabbed it.

"Not much," said I, and *not* I was determined it should be. I knew I would never see my muffler again except around his neck.

"We'll see about that," said Jack. But I had a good hold on my muffler with my left hand, and with my right I swung out at him. Fortunately, I caught him under the chin, which made him reel, and he loosened his hold on the muffler, which I immediately jerked off and put into my pocket. He was a tough young brute, and I knew that my only salvation was to land on him first and to keep landing. With an oath, he came back at me, but I was there again first, and pinning him against a picket fence I showed him little mercy. It was nip and tuck for a bit. I knew that if I could get his head in contact with the East River blue-stone of the sidewalk something would have to give, and I knew it wouldn't be the sidewalk! Finally he fell in a heap such as a man falls into when he is about all in, and I concluded there wasn't much more for me to do. I decided to call it an evening. Just then, however, the night policeman came up.

"What's this?" he asked, grabbing hold of me and pointing to the heap on the walk.

"Jack Donnelly, of the Fourth Street gang," I said.

"And you?" turning my face to the light of the street

lamp. Recognizing me, he said, "Well, well, it's you! You two will have to come with me."

"Where?" I asked.

"To the station-house," was the answer.

Fortunately, the policeman was the father of one of my intimate boy-chums. I explained to him that I had simply defended myself: I had on my best clothes, my mother was waiting for me and that I would come to the station-house the next day at any hour he would name if he would let me go home.

"You'll come sure?" he asked.

"You know I will if I say so," I answered. Yes, he knew that.

"Well, I'll take Jack along, give him a bed for the night, and you come to the station-house to-morrow morning at nine o'clock."

I was there at eight. "I have to be at school at nine," I explained to the sergeant at the desk.

"Not a very nice-looking eye you have there," he remarked.

"Well," I answered, "I guess he has one as bad."

"Two," replied the sergeant, and I saw a twinkle in his eye which I felt promised well for me.

"What was the trouble?" he asked, and then to the turnkey: "Bring Donnelly in." And Donnelly came. He was certainly good to look at,—for me.

"I'll fix you for this," he muttered as he passed me. But the sergeant's hearing was acute. "So," he said, "you will, will you? Well, I'll fix you first."

He got ten days, and I got off!

But no sooner was the irate Donnelly released than

it became a daily question with me how to get home, with the still disfigured rowdy and four of his pals hovering about my front door. It grew monotonous to come home from school by way of the back fences, and my mother became impatient with torn trousers. So I sought my friend, the sergeant.

"Why don't you give him a couple more eyes?" he suggested.

"That's all very well," I said, "but it's five to one."

"Quite right," he returned, and thereafter I had police escort!

X

It came home to me now, for the first time, that precious possessions brought corresponding responsibilities. So when a boy-friend offered me one of the first Flexible Flyer sleds on the market and two dollars to boot, I decided to part with that muffler from Dubernell's. It was keeping me altogether too busy!

The muffler had taught me one lesson for good: that the penalty of deception is the agony of an uneasy conscience, and that that is far too high a price for a muffler, —or for anything else.

SIX:

THE TALE OF A TAIL

"Cruel Remorse! where Youth and Pleasure sport,
And thoughtless Folly keeps her court,—
Crouching 'midst rosy bowers thou lurkest unseen
Slumbering the festal hours away,
While Youth disports in that enchanting scene;
Till on some fated day
Thou with a tiger-spring dost leap upon thy prey,
And tear his helpless breast, o'erwhelmed with wild
   dismay!"

BARBAULD

THE TALE OF A TAIL

I

My troubles were, however, not over. In fact, I found very soon that they had just begun. Not only did my speeding sled keep me busier than did the muffler, but it lost nearly all my friends for me. With all the other boys supplied with the old-fashioned high sled, my "Flexible Flyer," built on a low keel, was the champion in speed, and naturally every one of my boy-friends promptly became my enemy. For it must be remembered that in the boy-world, if a boy possesses a personal prowess he will be looked up to, but let him have a superior personal possession, and envy of the greenest hue is born, and with it the idea of destruction. Then I had christened the sled "Lion," and had had the name painted on it so that all who ran might read. I found that my choice of the monarch of the forest as a name was another mistake. It indicated superiority, and while my pals had to concede the superior speed of my sled, they objected to the constant proclamation of that fact by that name. I began to learn that the rôle of leader had its distinct disadvantages, which was the reason, I learned afterward, why the previous owner of the sled had sold it to me. It had kept him too busy, and he was willing I should have a season of it! The boys got together and decided that "Lion" must be crippled, broken, or stolen. Of course, I dissented, and that caused tension. The result was that each time a boy ran into me with his sled, or tried to push me off the coasting hill into a fence, I had a fight on my hands. And while I fought I had to watch my sled. Hence I could never concentrate on my opponent. I could only give him half of my attention, which, in a fight, is a serious disadvantage.

Then one day one of the boys succeeded in running away with "Lion." He had a fairly good start before I discovered him. The ground was covered with ice, and as I looked around for a stone—my mood was for a boulder—I saw the only thing available: an oyster shell. Not a very dangerous missile, one would think at first thought. I threw it after him, and just as the shell reached him the boy turned to see if I was coming. The shell caught him square in the eye. Naturally, he dropped the sled, and while the boys attended to my wounded chum, I took my precious "Lion" home.

An hour afterward the father of the boy appeared at our house with the information that his son's eye would have to be removed. And so it was! Oh, the dire results of the thoughtless pranks of boys, and the agonies of remorse that sometimes result from them. It is no small thing to deprive a fellow-being of an eye. I suffered then the pangs of regret, and I suffer them now whenever I recall the incident.

"Lion" was now sadly put away for the rest of the winter, and for the rest of the sledding season I was a lonely spectator at the sport of other boys with their less speedy but more popular sleds.

II

The following winter I polished up the rusty runners, and once more brought "Lion" out, and with its appearance every evidence of friendship at once left my chums. Still, the unfortunate eye episode remained in the minds of the boys—I naturally kept my feelings of remorse to myself—and there was at least no attempt to steal my speedy sled.

But now Jack Donnelly, he of the muffler episode, with a spirit of vindictiveness true to his kind, decided that the sled was to be his. This would not have mattered so seriously if he had come for it single-handed. But he didn't. He augmented himself with from four to twelve other rowdies, and each afternoon, after school hours, when there was sledding, "the Fourth Street gang" came to call for the sled. The result was that I could not bring it out. Nor was my personal presence, without the sled, very welcome to the pillaging gang, so I had to stay at home with it!

One afternoon, on returning from school, I found "Lion" missing! I went at once to the coasting-hill, but not a boy admitted that he knew anything about it, and I was convinced they didn't. That threw the theft upon Jack Donnelly, but the boys would not go with me into the bully's stronghold to demand the sled, and I realized it would be futile to go alone. In fact, I saw my boy-friends were secretly glad my sled had been stolen. So to my police-sergeant friend I repaired once more, with the result that a policeman was detailed to rescue the sled. In a week's time he did! But that did not make "the Fourth Street gang" less vindictive toward "Lion's" owner. There ensued another season when sled and owner remained closely at home, and my way to and from school lay again over the back fences, which, while good exercise, is apt to grow monotonous, particularly as there were eight fences to negotiate twice each way!

III

Then there came a day when a boy-friend and I took "Lion" and, with our skates, we journeyed to a distant pond. After a period of skating, we coasted with "Lion." My chum was of a venturesome disposition, and despite my own warnings and those of the other skaters, he ventured to coast across a part of the pond where the ice was thin. To prove that his point of view was correct, he coasted across the dangerous surface twice, and I argued that since he had proved his point, why not let well enough alone? But three was his lucky number, he said, and a third coast he would take. I argued that he had weakened the ice by his own weight and that of the sled. But the third coast he *would* have, and then we would go home. We did, but it was to carry his lifeless body home on "Lion." The weakened ice gave, my chum had on his skates and with them he was caught in some "eel-grass" in the bottom of the pond. He failed to come to the surface. No one could go to the rescue, as the thinness of the ice prevented. After ropes had been brought, and a rescuer was let down into the cold water, my chum's

skates were disentangled from the "grass," and his lifeless body was brought up.

As I dragged my sled homeward in grief, I could not
help but look back upon it several times and reach the
boyish conclusion that some "hoodoo" was upon "Lion."
The association now with the accident to one of my closest boy friends made the sled anything but a joyful possession to me. It had been the cause by which one boy
had lost his eye and another, and my friend, his life.
The sight of it now became abhorrent to me, and I put
it once more away.

IV

A certain boy in our group now began to taunt me
with the fact that I had put out the eye of one of my
playmates and was responsible for the life of another.
Though I had put the matter to myself in just these
terms, it was another thing to have it done by some one
else and in that spirit. But as this boy was taller,
stronger, and older, it was not so simple a matter to
argue out his taunts with him. The climax came one
afternoon when I had bought a piece of cocoanut custard pie. I was just about to take the first delicious bite
when this boy came up behind me and, pushing the piece
of pie in my face, rubbed the custard into my ears, my
eyes, my nose—everywhere except into the one opening
in my face where I intended to put it. The group of
boys standing by screamed with delight, and what was
really the wormwood and gall of the occasion, a bevy of
my girl-friends giggled with amusement. After I had
dug the custard out of my eyes and ears and nose, and

washed my face, my tormentor faced me with the taunt:
"Well, what are you going to do about it?"

Of course, there is only one thing that a boy *can* do
under such a condition, and I did it. Rather, he did it.
And after about ten minutes of active combat I left him
victor. I was too mad to fight intelligently, and I sensed
the advantage it would be to wait until I had gotten
control of myself, particularly as the odds were against
me even at the best. The next afternoon my vanquisher
was having laurels placed on his brow in the midst of an
admiring group of the boys and girls when I sauntered up.

"I want to see you," I said tersely.

"Right here," he determined.

"No," I replied. "Same place as yesterday."

Of course, the boys and girls, always keen for a fight,
were in the highest spirits. My father had always
warned me not to start a fight: never to strike the first
blow, but if a first blow came my way to see to it that
the second was so close to the first that you could scarcely
tell the difference, with the third and fourth following
closely upon its heels. In this instance, I felt that the
pie-bath was equivalent to a first blow. I always had a
strong feeling, even as a boy, against starting anything
that I couldn't or didn't finish. I had not finished my
tormentor. He had up to that time finished me. I was
cool now and collected, and knew what I was doing, and
I was determined to do it. So, he had hardly gotten his
coat off before I was at him and on him and, in true
Dutch fashion, I persistently stuck just there. It was
the practice in the fights of those days to get your left
arm around a boy's neck, and then beat a tattoo on his

face with your right fist. This was an advantage which
every boy sought. I got it in this instance, and made
up my mind to keep at it in the most approved style
until the whistle blew!

V

This style of fighting was, of course, very effective,
but if it happened to be bloody, as it usually was, and
certainly in this case, it was apt to leave its marks on
one's clothes. Unfortunately, I wore on this day a pair
of light trousers and a white shirt, and when I let go
of my tormentor, and threw him away from me, the
stains of battle on this light background gained the highest possible emphasis. I went home at once, intending
to avoid my mother until I could change my clothes.
But as I opened the door of the sitting-room, my mother
was there. She gave one look at my clothes, gasped,
and promptly fell into a faint! Now a fainted woman
presents enough of a problem to a grown man, but a
boy stands helpless before such a situation!

Fortunately, my mother had fallen on the sofa, and I
rushed down-stairs to the apartment below, where lived
my mother's most intimate friend. She responded to
my loud knockings and, looking at my clothes, reeled
backward.

"Now, don't you faint!" I cried. "That's just what
my mother has done, and I want to ask you to come
right up-stairs and bring her to."

While we were running up the stairs, she asked me
what I had been doing.

"Oh, Dick Harvey," I answered.

"Is he dead?" asked my mother's frightened friend as she stopped on the stairs and looked back at me.

"I don't know," I answered, but even then, as I thought of the pie incident, I added, "I hope so."

VI

The next day I bartered my sled for a baseball bat and two new balls. I had had my plenty of "Lion." But I was still not to get away from the ill-fortune which any legacy of that muffler, or the deception by which I obtained it, seemed destined to bring me. Try as I might I could not hit with that bat, and I usually found the ball, too. In three successive games, I struck out every time I went to the plate.

I now took a mental count, and decided to cleanse my life of everything related to that muffler. By tracing back I convinced myself that all my troubles had started since I bought that muffler with the money intended for the apples. I had begun wrong, and I had heard or read somewhere that a thing started wrong was certain to end wrong. The next day I presented the bat and the two baseballs to the surprised captain of our club. "To help the club," I said. Had I not been so thoroughly convinced of the "jinx" attached to my muffler transaction, I would have seen a ray of light when, on the following Saturday, the most critical game of the season was pitched and won by the two balls which I had presented to the club, and the only home-run hit made in the game came off the end of my bat! But my mind was not open to any rays of light. It was muffled by that muffler!

VII

It now occurred to me that in the sale of that muffler I had received two dollars, in addition to the sled, and that I had deposited those two dollars in my savings-bank account. I did not want to disturb this modest account, for I was very proud of it, small as it was. But I was determined now to get rid of every possession associated with what I deemed my fateful transaction. I felt sure my ill-fortune would attach itself to the two dollars. I saw the bank suspend payment and all my savings swept away! That would be the next thing to happen, I was sure. So, I drew out the fatal two dollars next day, and as I approached my home I came across a group of my boy-friends—to whom I was now a pugilistic hero! They were forming a club to buy a joint ticket in the next drawing of the Louisiana State Lottery, which was then in full swing, and they asked me to join them.

"Only two dollars," they urged.

I had never gambled; I didn't believe in it. My father had lost his fortune in speculation, and I was fearful lest the love of chance might be inherited. But I had to lose those two dollars, and I could think of no surer way than in a lottery!

"All right," I said, "if I can get a number with a 9 in it!" One of my uncles had told me once that I was born at 9 o'clock in the morning, and as the date of my birth was October 9, 1863, I worked out the fascinating combination that I was born at 9 o'clock in the morning, on the 9th day of the 9th month and that the first two figures and the last two figures of my birth-year each, when added, made two more 9s. 9 became to me, therefore, my lucky number. It was not until years afterward that I found I was born at 10 o'clock in the morning, and that October happened to be the tenth month in the calendar. But I didn't know these little flaws in my magic combination then!

VIII

I had forgotten all about the lottery ticket when three weeks later a group of excited boys rushed to my house, and told me my number had drawn a prize of $3,000! We had only one-tenth of a whole ticket, and so our prize was really $300, and as there were 30 boys in the combination, our individual share was $10.

My "luck" depressed rather than cheered me. Here, instead of having had two dollars to get rid of, I now had ten dollars to dispose of! Would I ever get this pitch off my fingers? On the following Sunday after I had received my lottery winnings I amazed my Sunday-school teacher by handing him the ten dollars, and explaining that it was for the new banner for our class which we were trying to buy for the next Anniversary Day parade.

"Your father and mother give this to the class?" he asked.

"No," I replied. "I give it. It's my money. I made it, or rather I—" but I realized it would be better not to tell him how it *did* come to me.

"Edward," said my teacher with great seriousness, as he shook my hand, "that is very fine of you."

Not, I thought, if you knew how glad I am to get rid of it!

The ill-fortune even entered into that banner! In the middle of that parade, in the following May, a severe rain and wind-storm broke which seemed to centre its force upon our class banner! The rain beat it, the wind tore it into shreds, and as I looked at the remains, after the storm, I thought: "Well, this 'jinx' began with silk, and it has ended with silk. I guess that finishes it." And it did!

IX

But what a long tail had that muffler from Dubernell's! And what a long tale I have spun about it!

SEVEN:

"FROM PAPER, PEN AND INK"

" A little neglect may breed great mischief."
BENJAMIN FRANKLIN

"FROM PAPER, PEN AND INK"

I

My evenings as a boy were generally spent at home. I never contracted the habit of going out evenings for the sake of being out on the street. Besides, there was always something to do to help my mother, or some lesson to be studied, or I would pursue my hobby of collecting postage-stamps. It was in some leisure moments in those evenings that the idea took hold of me to make a collection of the autographs of distinguished persons as a matter of education. I can easily see now that I would have made this hobby the meaningless chase of so many boys,—perfectly natural to a boy,—had not my father given me guidance and made the pursuit mean something distinctly useful, as well as a keener pleasure.

One evening I was steadfastly looking at an autograph I had just received in the mail. (I had only accumulated three at that point.) It read "Henry W. Longfellow." I could not get over a feeling that it was insufficient, and yet I could not crystallize the thought.

My father did. Evidently he had been watching me as I sat there, as I thought, unobserved. "Satisfactory?" he asked.

I looked up and did not answer. I couldn't, for I didn't know what to say. It *was* satisfactory as a signature, of course, and yet——

II

My father then expressed my halting thought for me. He wondered if I would not derive more pleasure from the quest upon which I had started if I were to cease thinking in terms of mere signatures. He explained that he did not think my collection of simple autographs would either satisfy me or lead anywhere. They were practically valueless, he said, and meant nothing. If it were true, he argued, that character could be read from handwriting, even then a mere signature gives little room for such a study. Besides, a man often wrote his signature differently.

"What would you do?" I asked. "Give it up?"

"No," he counselled. "On the contrary, I'd make the hobby something worth while, and make a collection different and better than any other boy ever made one."

"How?" I asked.

He suggested that I should first buy with my savings a work like *Appleton's Encyclopædia,* and then "read up" every man or woman to whom I meant to write. That would give me an intelligent idea to whom I was writing. Then, if some point in his life was not clear to me, I could write to the man about it. This would give to me a knowledge of men and women, for it would show the recipients of my letters that I wrote with some intelligence and it would ensure my receiving letters which would have in them the personality of the writers. Thus was I to think in terms of interesting letters and not mere signatures.

My father also suggested that until I got under way

it might be well if he were to look over each letter I
wrote and thus avoid asking unwise questions. This
method led to the destruction of two or three letters,
from which I was quick to learn that a previous discussion of the man and the question I wanted to ask would
save me time and effort. Naturally, I learned much,
and it was not long before I saw that I was assembling
a collection of really remarkably interesting "personality" letters, as I called them, letters which really said
something, expressed the writers' personality; and, as
in those days the typewriter had not come into use, these
letters were generally in the handwriting of their authors.

III

Another lesson I learned in part, if not in whole, was
the natural confusion of notoriety with reputation in a
boy's mind. My father was careful to point out to me
what constituted a substantial reputation that would
survive after the man or woman had passed on. He
would explain to me, for example, that the mere posting
on the fences, in large letters, of the name of some actor,
the repeated publication of his name and photograph in
the newspapers and on the billboards before the theatres,
did not necessarily constitute reputation of a lasting
nature. That if I wrote to these "popular favorites" I
would be practically wasting my time and money, because I would find that in ten or fifteen years the "favorite" would be forgotten, and the letter in my collection
would be meaningless, and serve, in later life, only as a
reminder of my lack of selective judgment. What food
for thought there is here for those boys and girls who

are now so persistently collecting the autographs of moving-picture actors and actresses, baseball players, pugilists, and the like—few of whom will be remembered a few years hence!

My father would explain to me the difference between the momentary favorites of the stage, and the work of such really great artists as Edwin Booth, Sarah Bernhardt, Joseph Jefferson, Ristori, Salvini, Henry Irving, and others. Then, to drive his lesson home to me, he would take me to see these artists—and also to the performances of the "favorites." It was all very wisely and thoroughly done.

IV

The question of the expense of each letter weighed very heavily with me, too. My father, of course, knew this, and used this advantage with great skill. Letter postage was at that time three cents. My father insisted that each letter I wrote should be accompanied with a stamped, addressed envelope: hence each letter cost me six cents. In fact, each person to whom I wrote represented nine cents, since my father counselled that, in each instance where I received a reply, I should write an acknowledgment of thanks. This point was very difficult for me to grasp: in fact, I do not think I ever fully agreed with him. My feeling was that the transaction was begun with the request and closed with the answer. However, I knew my father had guided me very wisely thus far, and so I followed his lead on this point, although I could not see it. Each answer was carefully acknowledged. Later I was to realize the far-seeing wisdom of my father's counsel. It was the exception, of course, rather than the rule, for an autograph letter collector to write such a note of thanks, and it was not long before I found out that this unusual act had singled me out from the others and made such an impression on the recipients that in later years when I met the men and women to whom I had written the fact was instantly recalled with the mention of my name. It was the courteous thing to do; it was employing thoroughness, but I was to find out that it had been a singularly politic move. It taught me, too, the great lesson of an invariable acknowledgment of a courtesy.

All this guidance at my father's hands was extremely helpful, and I can now the more clearly see and value it. Still, even with all this careful supervision, I find my collection will stand an amazing amount of wise elimination. I remember when, a few years ago, I went over my compilations, it was the easiest task imaginable to select fifty letters from as many persons whose reputations were purely ephemeral and whose names were entirely forgotten. To verify my impression, I determined to make a test on a purely commercial basis, and took these fifty letters to an experienced dealer in autograph letters. The most he would give me for all fifty was five dollars—ten cents each!

V

The solicitor has now become the solicited. The chickens have come home to roost! And it is mainly to save disappointment on the part of our young people, and to avoid their gathering of wrong impressions of our

public men and women, that I write here of my autographic experiences. I know that scores of young people are receiving no answers to what seems to them the
simplest of requests: the asking for an autograph of a
well-known person. The curious part of the situation is
that neither the applicant nor the recipient is to blame. A
young person can hardly be blamed for not knowing that
the rules of the autographic game call for the enclosure,
in such a request, of at least a return postage stamp and
preferably an addressed envelope. Nor can the recipient
of such a request be considered churlish if he concludes
after a while that he cannot be expected to go on indefi-
nitely supplying the omission. Yet the fact remains
that in a hundred applications for autographs, not five
enclose return postage. Nor does a young person understand that the request for a photograph or a copy of
the author's book is not confined to himself, but is mul-
tiplied by the score, and that the granting of these
requests would mean a drain that few could bear.
Naturally, no man, remembering his own boyhood, feels
that he can deliver a rebuke to a well-intentioned boy
or girl, and so the easiest way is sought by many in
not answering the application. But this makes for disappointment on the part of the young applicant; he
conceives a misunderstanding of the situation, and finally
his wonder that he fails to receive answers to his letters
leads him to the immature conclusion that our public
men and women are ungracious and unwilling to be
merely civil.

VI

The fault in the matter lies directly with the parent and the absolute lack of responsibility which he assumes for a child. I cannot conceive a parent permitting his child to write a letter to a stranger without a direct supervision of the act, and yet I know from the letters I receive that not in ten cases out of a hundred has either parent the slightest idea that the child is doing it. What is the result? The child is being humiliated by having his uncensored questions passed upon by strange eyes. Take the child who asks for the present address of Mark Twain, or of Louisa May Alcott, or of Longfellow; or the child who asks for the address of President Coolidge; or the child who makes out a list of a dozen or more well-known persons in a city and asks if you will secure their autographs for him; or the boy who asks you to tell him, exactly, step by step, the road to success in life; or the girl who asks that you will write her graduation essay for her; or the boy who reveals domestic tragedies and asks for advice. We have no right to blame the child. It knows no better. But where are the supervising eye and the restraining hand of the father or the mother? Still more significant is the fact that I have yet to receive a letter from Canada or a foreign country which over-steps the boundary of a simple request, or which fails to enclose return postage. Even from such countries as Serbia, Austria, Hungary, or South Africa, where the difficulty of securing American postage stamps is con-siderable, there is always enclosed return postage or an explanation of the reason for its omission.

Are not, therefore, certain unpleasant inferences concerning American parents justified?

VII

There are few things in a child's life which have such a salutary effect as a well-directed hobby of some sort,— something which every child should have. We all love to collect, and the trait should be encouraged in a child. I remember how much of my knowledge of geography was gotten from my collection of postage-stamps, while the debt I owe to my compilation of the letters of distinguished persons is incalculable. But, like everything else in a child's life, such a hobby should be under the direction of an elder. Lacking my father's guidance, my compilation of mere autographs would have served no end. This does not mean that a child's hobby should be made oppressive: it should be allowed to retain all the element of play and of pleasure. But, skilfully, it should be guided, so that it may be followed intelligently and to some purpose. This is especially true of any hobby that leads a child to express itself on paper. There, particularly, should the eye of the parent follow the child. An education of the most valuable sort lies hidden in an intelligent pursuit of this hobby; on the other hand, nothing but the keenest disappointment and the formation of wrong impressions lies in wait for the child who is allowed its own freedom when it takes the pen in its hand.

VIII

Prior said so wisely:

> "Let him be kept from paper, pen and ink
> So may he cease to write, and learn to think."

It is this truth that the American parent must get into his consciousness. With caution in mind, or under guidance, however, no boy or girl can have a pleasanter or more educative hobby. It *can* lead straight to a goal and a worthy one.

It certainly did with me.

EIGHT:

IN PURSUIT OF THE GREAT

" The great spirits that have gone before us can only survive as disembodied voices."

CARLYLE

———

"Wise sayings are not only for ornaments."

BACON

IN PURSUIT OF THE GREAT

I

I GO so far as to say that I do not think the hobby of collecting mere autographs should be encouraged. As my father well said, a mere autograph is valueless, for it connotes nothing, and it is questionable whether in these days, when the lives of well-known people are so crowded, they should be asked to gratify what is, in nine cases out of ten, a mere compilation of names, unintelligently selected and with no serious end or purpose in view. It is a seemingly ungracious act to turn away a request which is so simple, and yet I believe it is a kindness to the young person in his waste of time in pursuit of an effort that leads nowhere.

I think thy autograph hunt is a remarkable instance persistent of effort for an object hardly worthy of it "What's in a name?"

John G. Whittier

se
di
co

of
pe
me
the
to
be
do
dis
env
chi
ser
der
fro
bro
in a
day
mor
usef

O
first
on
follo
mys
of u
whe
crud

Religion without superstition.
Government without tyranny, and
regulative Freedom to all people.

Henry Ward Beecher

1884

Brooklyn, N.Y.
Plymouth Church.

letters I receive, and which are intended to "blind" me to my own method, it becomes nothing but an imitation and a bad imitation at that. What served one in this respect cannot serve another, for each must find his own

No man has come to true greatness who has not felt in some degree that his life belongs to his race, and that what God gives him He gives him for mankind.

Phillips Brooks

Trinity Church
Boston

way of reaching the same goal. Besides, our busy public men and women would very soon be compelled, and justifiably so, to refuse to answer such letters.

II

When I wrote to Thomas Hardy and asked him if he did not believe that such a collection of the handwritings

As for the good time
that is coming, let us not
forget that there is a
good time going too,
& see that we dwell
on that eternal ridge
between the two which
neither comes nor goes.

Yours truly

Henry S. Thoreau

It is very seldom that I have
an uncomfortable sensa-
tion; it is still more seldom
that I apply for one. When
a man deliberately offends other
folk, he invites sorrow; when he
deliberately offends himself, he
insures it.   Mark Twain

The one and only form
of music is melody, no
music is conceivable
without melody, and
both are absolutely
inseparable. —
Adelina Patti. —

New York — 3rd November
1882

of the great as I was trying to make could be of value
in the sense of showing the characteristics of their re-
spective writers, he answered in the witty vein of the
reproduction of his letter on page 99.

III

In my day there was also a mad desire to ask a famous
man or woman to add a "sentiment" to his or her auto-

graph,—the sentiment which so invariably and stubbornly refuses to come to mind at such a time. I figured out that a double value could result from such an autographic expression: the sentiment, in a sense, would in

I think I may say I have
done my part & ought to leave
the stage to younger actors
I thank you for sending me
the Memorial of my brother.
It is unique — No other man
that ever I knew had such
a confluence of testimony
from so many different sources
With thanks I remain
Yours Ever,
Harriet Beecher Stowe

its purport be self-revealing, and the interest of such a compilation would be manifold. I can now better understand the moments of anguish I must have caused the great of my time, and yet in many an instance the sentiment evoked appealed to me and became part of thought and influenced conduct.

I remember I asked Mr. Beecher what he believed to be the three essentials necessary to successful government, and he wrote as on page 100.

Coincidentally I asked Phillips Brooks his definition of true greatness, and there came from the great Bishop the lines given on page 101.

Can it be doubted for a single moment that such expositions of the fundamentals of living were anything but of the greatest interest and value to a boy? For

"All the world's a stage,
And all the men and women merely players;
They have their exits and their entrances.
And each man in his time plays many parts.
His acts being seven ages."

Shakespeare.

Edwin Booth

April 1882

instance, to be reminded of the life-truth given by Thoreau in the statement on page 102 which I secured through exchange with another collector.

Every one thought of Mark Twain simply and solely as a humorist, and I was anxious to get him on record in a serious mood, and I think I did this as on page 102.

With the first coming of music in which it seemed to me there was a distinct absence of melody, I wrote to Madame Patti, and asked her if she could conceive of music without melody. Her answer, as on page 103, reads even stranger now in these days of Strawinsky and Schoenberg.

I asked Harriet Beecher Stowe during her later life if she intended to continue writing, and she answered

I am really intending to start
before the next new year
my visit like taking advantage
though it seems the
of the times of dearth when we
long whenever even to the
inferior fruit Emerhel.

Yours affectionately,

Walter Emerhel

1894.

Henry Strong

I have reason to believe that an impression
exists that the passage of years has produced
no effect whatever on the great original — that he
has still waving golden hair & wears black
velvet doublets & broad collar of lace. This
is an error. He is sixteen. He plays football
& tennis & battles sternly with Greek. He is
anxious not to 'flunk' in Geometry & his hair
is exceedingly short & brown. He is a pleasant
person with a fine sense of humor and his
relatives consider it rather a good joke
to present him to intimates with these words
— as he appears before them looking particularly
cheerful & robust —

"This is — Little Lord Fauntleroy."
But there are things which do not change
with the darkening of golden hair & the
passage of boyish years. And it is these things
which make it possible for mothers to say
"Perhaps the big world may be better
by little child was born."

Frances Hodgson Burnett

as on page 104. Her reference to "my brother" is to
Henry Ward Beecher.

Of Edwin Booth I asked his favorite lines from
Shakespeare, and he returned the extract given on page
105.

When I could I would exchange with another collector some letter that I had for some letter that he had

from Ben-Hur :
A Tale of the Christ
1880   Lew Wallace. 1892.

Ben-Hur spoke with cold courtesy, and
Iras, after playing with the solitaire of her
necklace of coins, rejoined, "For a Jew, the
Son of Hur is clever. I saw your dreaming
Cæsar make his entry into Jerusalem. You told
us he would that day proclaim himself King
of the Jews from the steps of the Temple. I beheld the procession descend the mountain bringing him. I heard their singing. They were
beautiful with palms in motion. I looked
everywhere among them for a figure with a
promise of royalty — a horseman in purple, a chariot with a driver in shining brass,
a stately warrior behind an orbed shield,
swelling his spear in stature. I looked for
his guard. It would have been pleasant to
have seen a prince of Jerusalem, and a co-
hort of the legions of Galilee."

She flung her listener a glance of pro-
voking disdain, then laughed heartily, as
if the ludicrousness of the picture in her
mind were too strong for contempt.

"Instead of a Sesostris returning in triumph or a Cæsar helmed and sworded —
ha, ha, ha! — I saw a man with a woman's face and hair, riding an ass's colt,
and in tears. The King! the Son of God!
the Redeemer of the World! Ha, ha, ha!"

and I wanted. I craved the letter on page 106 in particular, because I knew that few letters written by Emerson
existed which in the signature dropped his first name.
Besides, the sentiment expressed was interesting as conveying his valuation of his own work.

The fibres of Poland is beyond description. Two hundred towns, 1400 villages, 3500 villages have been utterly destroyed. Millions are starving. Typhus and cholera are threading all over the devastated country. Our cause will, I am sure, appeal to your heart.

Most gratefully yours

I. J. Paderewski.

I asked Henry Irving, too, his favorite Shakespearean lines, feeling almost certain that there would come some quotation from *The Merchant of Venice*. But there came the lines on page 107.

I wrote Mrs. Frances Hodgson Burnett, and asked her what had become of the original of *Little Lord*

The Outlook

287 Fourth Avenue
New York

Office of
Theodore Roosevelt

February 24th, 1912.

> I feel just as you do about the canal. It
> is the greatest contribution I was able to make to
> my country; and while I do not believe my countrymen
> appreciate this at the moment, I am extremely pleased
> to know that the men on the canal do; for they are
> the men who have done and are doing this great job.

Theodore Roosevelt

Fauntleroy (her son Vivian), and if the furore over the character based on him had spoiled him. She answered as on page 108.

I pursued my hobby well into my days of growing manhood. Years later, I asked Lew Wallace if there was one passage in *Ben-Hur* which appealed to him personally more than any other in the book. "This," he answered, and he wrote the extract on page 109.

Jumping to a much later date, here is evidence in the letter on the opposite page from Paderewski of how the intelligent collecting of autograph letters may help to preserve history.

The day has come when America is privileged to spend her blood and her might for the principles that gave her birth and happiness and the peace that she has treasured. God helping her, she can do no other.

Woodrow Wilson

THE WHITE HOUSE,
WASHINGTON.

I had always felt that Theodore Roosevelt's greatest single contribution to his country was his advocacy and completion of the Panama Canal, and when at the Canal I wrote him from there what some of the men said of him and of his visit which had just preceded mine. He answered me as on page 111.

History is certainly writ large in those memorable words, as shown on the opposite page, by which the United States entered into the Great War in 1917.

I think the point will be granted that an autographic compilation along such lines can be made distinctly worth while as a valuable record, as a means of education and inspiration to the collector and a source of the greatest interest to a large circle of friends.

———

My success along these lines, however, was, I found, to lead me into more ambitious paths.

NINE:

THE HANDS THAT WROTE THEM

"Whose lines are mottoes of the heart."

CAMPBELL

THE HANDS THAT WROTE THEM

I

I WAS reading one day, perhaps for the hundredth time, Cardinal Newman's great hymn:

"Lead, kindly light, amid the encircling gloom,
    Lead Thou me on."

No single poem in the language had entered so thoroughly into my life from the first time when, as a boy, I read it in a hymn-book. It became a frequent source of strength and courage. To this day it has remained with me.

The thought occurred to me how much these words would mean to me if I possessed them penned with the hand that wrote them. Eventually, I plucked up courage to ask the great Cardinal if he would give me this precious heritage, and to my joy he wrote out the entire poem and sent it to me. It became to me the closest of all my autographic possessions, and day after day I would hold it in my hand and read it. When, in 1890, the author passed away, I realized even more the treasure I possessed. Perhaps I laid too great value upon it. At all events, one day I missed it, and to this day I have never found it. I had all the rest of my collection, but I had not that which I valued most.

II

Its possession, however, set my autographic thoughts along an entirely new line. No poem would ever mean to me, in an author's handwriting, what "Lead, Kindly Light" meant. I realized that. But there were some precious bits that I loved, and I began to feel the joy there would be in the possession of some of these lines and poems, as familiar to me as my own name, if I could have them written by the hands what wrote them.

There was always something softly beautiful and caressing about Lowell's "And what is so rare as a day in June," and rarely a June came around but I would take my Lowell and read those four exquisite lines. How interesting, I thought, it would be to see and have them in the actual handwriting in which they were originally written. In the belief that others may have this feeling about some favorite verse which has helped or refreshed, I venture to share a few specimens which I succeeded in obtaining from their authors.

III

I give first those exquisite lines by James Russell Lowell, and his transcription of them on the opposite page shows, too, his aptitude in changing defeat to victory in his apt comment on the blot of ink,—and incidentally saving the trouble of a rewriting.

Of course, it was only natural that, as a boy, I should love my Whittier with the result of the valuable transcription on page 120.

I could not quite make up my mind, in the case of Longfellow, whether his *Psalm of Life* or *Hiawatha* was really my favorite. So I didn't, and left it to the author, with the result which was always true of his good nature, that he sent me the two on pages 121 and 122.

THE HANDS THAT WROTE THEM   119

And what is so rare as a day in June?
Then, if ever, come perfect days;
Then Heaven tries the Earth if it be in tune,
And over it softly her warm ear lays.

James Russell Lowell.

*

Deerfoot Farm,
Southborough, Mass., U.S.A.
20th Jan: 1887.

J. R. Lowell

* I am sorry to have
forced, in this way my fine:
=freeing in what Pope calls
" The last & highest art, the art to blot."

(From
  "Barbara Frietchie")

Barbara Frietchie's work is o'er,
And the rebel rides on his raids no more.

Honor to her! and let a tear
Fall for her sake on Stonewall's bier!

Over Barbara Frietchie's grave
Flag of Freedom and Union wave.

Peace and order and beauty draw
Round thy symbol of light and law,

And ever the stars above look down
On thy stars below in Frederick town!

John Greenleaf Whittier

Amesbury
6th mo 4 1882

I had met Louisa May Alcott, and knew of the famous
poem which she wrote at the age of eight, and asked her
whether it was true, whereupon she sent me the copy
on page 123.

Julia Ward Howe's "Battle Hymn of the Republic"
had now captured my imagination, and her contribution on page 124 was my next acquisition.

'All are architects of Fate,
    Working in these walls of Time,
Some, with massive deeds and great,
    Some with ornaments of rhyme

            Henry Wadsworth Longfellow

Cambridge, Mass.
Jan 1. 1882.

I knew I would have difficulty with my favorite
poems by Tennyson, particularly as there were two:
"Enoch Arden" and "The Brook." No author was
more averse to copying his poems, and I was discouraged
on every hand. I learned, however, that it is never
wise to make up another man's mind for him, and that
there are always exceptions to every rule. It proved so,
in this case, for I secured both transcripts. I give one
on page 125.

With my thoughts abroad I included Lord Lytton
in my quest, with the result of the famous lines given
on page 125.

It was on one of those days when Oliver Wendell

From "Hiawatha":

And the Black Robe chief made answer,
Stammered in his speech a little,
Speaking words yet unfamiliar:
"Peace be with you, Hiawatha,
Peace be with you and your people,
Peace of prayer, and peace of pardon,
Peace of Christ's and joy of Mary."

Henry Wadsworth Longfellow

Cambridge, Mass.
November 3, 1880.

For Edward W. Bok.

In the beauty of the lilies Christ was born
across the sea,

With a glory in his bosom that transfigures
you and me;

As he died to make men holy, let us die
to make men free,

While God is marching on..

Julia Ward Howe.

composer in 1860.

Holmes was confined to his house that I found him in
a mood where, physician though he was, he could not

And out again I curse & flow
To join the brimming river,
For men may come & men may go,
But I go on for ever.

A Tennyson
Nov.ᵃ 24ᵀʰ
1882

From 'The Brook'

cure himself. "Well," said the Doctor, genial nevertheless, "I think my favorite poem to-day is 'The Last Leaf,'

Oh for the books that never were written,
And oh, for the words that never were said!
All the fond hearts that never were smitten,
And all the true tears that never were shed!

Lytton. 29 May 1882

and if this sniffling will let me, I'll write it out for you."
And he did, as shown on the following page.

Not long afterward, the wonderful old poet experienced a change of heart,—when his cold passed away:

"I felt dismal when I selected and sent you 'The Last Leaf' as my favorite poem. This is more like it," and he enclosed a beautifully-written copy of "The Chambered Nautilus" in its complete form. I give the last stanza on the opposite page.

It was always a pleasure to look at a piece of manuscript by Eugene Field: microscopic, invariably illumi-

> And if I should live to be
> The Last Leaf upon the tree
>   In the Spring
> Let them smile as I do now
> At the old forsaken bough
>   Where I cling
>
> 1851.
>
> Oliver Wendell Holmes.
> Nov. 26th 1890.

nated, and the perfection of neatness. Barring the illuminated lettering, Field's manuscript looked like the reproduction on page 128.

His letters, like his sentiments, were unique, as witness his playful reference to George W. Cable in the note on page 129.

There were many friends, as there may well be now who shall read this book, who wished to see, in the handwritings which wrote them, the hymns that had meant solace and strength to them. Hence I collected a handful of these.

Of course, "He Leadeth Me" was often asked for, and it seemed to give pleasure to many to see the lines, shown

Build thee more stately mansions, O my soul,
As the swift-seasons roll!
Leave thy low-vaulted past!
Let each new temple, nobler than the last,
Shut thee from heaven with a dome more vast,
Till thou at length art free,
Leaving thine outgrown shell by life's unresting sea!

Oliver Wendell Holmes.
Boston. March 23d 1882.

January 1858.

on page 130, originally written by Doctor Gilmore in 1861, which have meant so much in Life's dark moments. Second only to the above was the desire to see, as on

Jes' fore Christmas.
By Eugene Field.

Father calls me William, sister calls me Will,

Mother calls me Willie - but the fellers call me Bill!

Mighty glad I aint a girl - ruther be a boy,

Without them sashes, curls an' things that's worn by Fauntleroy!

Love to chawnk green apples an' go swimmin' in the lake —

Hate to take the castor-ile they give f'r belly-ache!

Most all the time the hull year roun' there aint no flies on me,

But jes' fore Christmas I'm as good as I kin be!

page 131, Mrs. Hawks's famous hymn, "I Need Thee Every Hour," sung so often and loved by so many.

Doctor Lowry's baptismal hymn "Shall We Gather at the River?" as on page 131, was another often asked for.

There was always an equal demand for Fillmore Bennett's famed lines "The Sweet By-and-By," on page 134.

It always was a matter of surprise that the same hand which wrote "My Country, 'tis of Thee" had written one of the best-known of the hymns of the church, "The Morning Light is Breaking," as on page 135.

It was natural, of course, that, with mention of the

Dear Bok:— I make bold to send you a bit that may seem suited to use in the columns of your able and influential periodical. It is entitled "Shuffle-Shoon and Amber-Locks." Tomorrow I start upon a week's cruise with that frivolous bird, Geo. W. Cable. Pray that I may be spared evil consequences. With much regard, I am, honored sir,

Your obliged,

respectful,

gifted,

but impecunious

friend

and

admirer,

Eugene Field.

Chicago, Jany 28th, 1893.

author of what was then more generally regarded as our national song, there was a desire to see these famous lines in the handwriting of the author, and I will end these autographic contributions by giving "America" in full as on pages 132 and 133.

In these ways I made my autographic collection in-

My faith looks up to Thee,
Thou Lamb of Calvary,
Saviour divine!
Now hear me while I pray,
Take all my guilt away,
Oh, let me from this day
Be wholly thine..

Ray Palmer.

He leadeth me! O, blessed thought!
O, words with heavenly comfort fraught!
Whate'er I do, where'er I be,
Still 'tis God's hand that leadeth me.
He leadeth me! He leadeth me!
By his own hand He leadeth me!
His faithful foll'wer I would be,
For by his hand He leadeth me.

J. H. Gilmore,
" 1861.

I Need Thee Every Hour.

I need Thee every hour,
    Most gracious Lord;
No voice, save Thine alone,
    Can peace afford.

            Annie S. Hawks.

1. Shall we gather at the river
        Where bright angel feet have trod,
    With its crystal tide for ever
        Flowing from the throne of God?

    Chorus.— Yes, we'll gather at the river,
            The beautiful, the beautiful river
        Gather with the saints at the river
            That flows from the throne of God.

                Robert Lowry.
                Plainfield. N.J.

America.

My country, 'tis of thee,
Sweet land of liberty,
    Of thee I sing;
Land where my fathers died,
Land of the pilgrims' pride,
From every mountain side
    Let freedom ring.

My native country,— thee,
Land of the noble, free,—
    Thy name I love;
I love thy rocks and rills,
Thy woods and templed hills,
Thy heart with rapture thrills,
    Like that above.

Coresr

Let music swell the breeze,
And ring from all the trees
   Sweet freedom's song;
Let mortal tongues awake,
Let all that breathe partake,—
Let rocks their silence break,—
   The sound prolong.

Our fathers' God,— to Thee,
Author of liberty,
   To Thee we sing;
Long may our land be bright
With freedom's holy light;
Protect us by Thy might,
   Great God, our King.

              S. F. Smith.

Andover, Mass,
   Feb. 1832.

teresting to my friends and educative to myself. Moreover, it was natural that these varied forms of autographic collecting should lead me to complete manuscripts of books, and then to the autographed book itself and finally to first editions. And it is in this broadening

Sweet By-and-By.

There's a Land that is fairer than day,
And by faith we can see it afar;
For The Father waits over the way,
To prepare us a dwelling place there:
In the Sweet By-and-By,
We shall meet on that Beautiful Shore—
In the Sweet By-and-By,
We shall meet on that Beautiful Shore.

S. Fillmore Bennett.

of the way wherein lies the value of an autographic compilation, provided that each stage has a purpose and is pursued not for the sake of mere acquisition, but for the educative value which one can derive from a hobby, whatever form it may take. Then it deserves the highest praise of a distinct usefulness in one's life, and broadens the mind.

But I repeat, for the benefit of those who are collecting or may be inspired to collect the handwritings of those who have achieved, that no benefit is to be derived from a futile pursuit of the hobby. Like everything else in the world that we attempt to do, it is in the spirit in which we do it, and the work, intelligence, and love that we put into it wherein lies the benefit.

> The morning light is breaking,
>   The darkness disappears;
> The sons of earth are waking
>   To penitential tears;
> Each breeze that sweeps the ocean
>   Brings tidings from afar
> Of nations in commotion,
>   Prepared for Zion's war.

S. F. Smith.

Newton Centre,
Mass.

1832 — Dec. 1882.

TEN:

"AN EXPERIENCE YOU KNOW NOT OF"

"How different from the present man was the youth of earlier days."

OVID

———

"Our youth began with tears and sighs
With seeking what we could not find;
We sought and knew not what we sought;
We marvel, now we look behind:
Life's more amusing than we thought!"

ANDREW LANG

———

"Consent to be poor, and you will always be poor."

MONTAIGNE

"AN EXPERIENCE YOU KNOW NOT OF"

I

I HAVE told in *The Americanization of Edward Bok* much of what happened to me during my boyhood and young manhood. There is no reason to repeat it here. To many a boy, no doubt, my boyhood will seem to have been a struggle,—and it was. No doubt of that. It was hard sledding at times: hard to know at times what was the most advisable course to take.

I remember one evening when my brother fell ill of typhoid fever. I was then working as office-boy, and a nurse was beyond my means. We lived in a boarding-house, and to help my perturbed state of mind all the boarders on the floor on which my brother and I had our room left the house. Typhoid was contagious, they argued. The boarding-house keeper was a woman who could ill-afford the loss which the deserting boarders meant to her. But my brother had grown steadily worse, and there could be no thought of his removal to a hospital. Our doctor was our family friend, and between him and the boarding-house lady a watch was kept over my brother during the day when I was at work, while I officiated as nurse during the night, catching such snatches of sleep as I could. But with a patient afflicted with hallucinations, and determined to throw himself out of the window, an alcohol bath to be given every half-hour, which meant that one bath would begin the moment the previous one ended, there was not much time to sleep. How I ever kept up for those ten weeks it is difficult now to recall, except that youth has a resiliency all its own. But youth has also a craving for sleep!

II

My mother had broken down from the housework to which she was unaccustomed, and to recruit her health we boys had pooled our savings and sent her to the mountains. It was unthinkable that she should know of my brother's illness, since she would naturally come home immediately, and the anxiety and strain might be fatal to her. So cheerful letters went to her every other day, urging her to remain where she was, owing to the torrid heat of the city. But on the mantelpiece, against the clock, stood a telegram, where it had been standing for several days at the doctor's orders. It was to be sent my mother the moment my brother's case seemed hopeless, day or night. When the crisis came, it looked for three days as if his recovery were exceedingly problematical. But the doctor knew my mother, and realized what the shock would mean to her. Twice we debated seriously whether to send the despatch, but each time he decided against it. He was right. The crisis passed, the turn came, the telegram was destroyed, and my brother was well along in his period of convalescence when my mother returned so fully recovered in health that she could assume the helm without fear of unfavorable results to her.

Then her younger son spent almost a continuous week in sleeping!

III

Experiences of illness come, of course, to all families but they rest heaviest upon those who cannot afford the conveniences and assistance which count for so much at such a time. For, after all, there are only three times when money actually counts for much: in illness, to ensure comfort in travelling, and in the possibilities of helping others.

I think always of those days in my own life when I receive those letters which come to so many, and to which if we responded only in part would leave no means for ourselves to live on. Of course, each writer imagines that he or she is the only person asking for help: that his or her own case is pre-eminently the one which deserves help! Little conception have these solicitors of the stream of similar letters which come from every part of the country.

It is a curious fact, too, that these letters invariably assume that one's path in life has ever been that of ease and soft cushions. Such a letter, for example, says: "Has it ever occurred to you, born with the proverbial silver spoon in your mouth, that theoretical writing, such as yours, is pretty cold and futile to those of us who, day by day, and year in and year out, face an actual hand-to-mouth struggle,—an experience you know not of?"

IV

"An experience that you know not of!" Heavens! Don't I, though? If there is a single step on the road of direst poverty or of actual privation that I have not travelled, I should like to know what it is. But where I differ from my correspondents is that I never complained either to myself or to others. My poverty was not a condition to complain of, but a condition to get out of, and I made myself too busy to get out of it to leave any time for self-pity. I made it a positive rule, too, not to borrow money, except in the boyish way I have related a few pages back, for I felt that the only true way out of the distress which surrounded me and mine was not through the help of others, but through my own effort.

Having gone through every thought, every feeling, and every hardship, that comes to those who travel the road of poverty, I say to-day that I rejoice with every boy who is going through the same experiences. Nor am I discounting or forgetting one single pang of the keen self-denials, hardships, and suffering that such a struggle means. I would not to-day exchange my years of keen hardship for any single experience that has since come to me. I learned, as I could have learned in no other way, the earning capacity of a dollar. I realize to-day the value of money as I could have realized it in no other way. Unconsciously I was being trained for my thirty years of editorship, appealing to the home and its manifold problems, and learning them in the school of actual experience. I know what it feels like to look daily at a pile of unwashed dishes. I know what it is to regard with despair a row of buckets of unsifted ashes. I know what it is to be hungry as only a boy can be hungry, and then drink a couple of glasses of water, and let it go at that, turning my head away when I

passed a baker's window and holding my breath so that
I would not smell the odor of the baking bread!

"An experience you know not of!"

V

Yet I repeat with the full recollection of what it means:
I envy every boy who is going through a like condition.
But—and here is the pivot of my strong belief in poverty as an undisguised blessing to a boy—I believe in
poverty as an experience, but, as I said a few lines back,
as a condition to go through and get out of: not as a
condition to stay in. "That's all very well," the poor
have said to me. "Easy enough to say, but how can
you get out of it?" No one can tell another that. No
one told me. I found my own way out, and my way
cannot be adapted to another. Every one must find his
way for himself. The time that others spend in asking
I spent in finding and doing. I had a single goal: the
way out. But I did not pick and choose; I took what
came. Nothing was too lowly. Whatever the job I took
hold of it and did the best I knew how. When I didn't
like what I was doing, I did it in the best way I could
while I was doing it, but all the while determining that
I wouldn't do it any longer than I had to do it. I used
every rung of the ladder upon which I found myself to
climb to the rung above. I did the present, but always
with an eye on the future. It meant work, of course,
unsparing work, tireless and ceaseless, and often work as
distasteful as it was hard as nails. But my job, I felt,
was not to choose, but to do. Out of the effort and the
work and the priceless experience, the constant upbuild-

ing and development, came that capacity, later, to understand the jobs which I was to ask others to do. Nothing can give that capacity to a boy, so that it will burn into him, as the great heritage of poverty and its unforgetable lessons—the greatest blessing in the way of the deepest experience that can come to a boy.

VI

As I grew older, I realized that one of the greatest benefits of those experiences of my youth would be in their value to me when I married and if I had the good fortune to be a father. I had learned lessons of self-dependence which could have come to me in no other way, and I determined that this part of my experience I could and would pass to any son I might have: the tremendous advantage of training the mind to reach one's own decisions.

VII

Then the prospect of marriage became a happy possibility, and my first thought was of a home of my own.

ELEVEN:

"MY OWN FOUR WALLS"

*"My . . . house my castle is,
I have my own four walls."*
                                                    CARLYLE

"MY OWN FOUR WALLS"

I

A few pages back I said that I made it a positive rule not to borrow money. But, as in the case of nearly all rules, there was an exception. I have always believed in borrowing money, if need be, to build a home. I did it, and have never regretted it.

I found that this debt, as I sensed it when I contracted the loan, would stimulate me as would nothing else (save perhaps working for some loved one) to economize and save. It was in my Dutch blood and training to do this any way. Nevertheless, I was young in years and experience and felt it was just as well to have a definite objective as a goal for wise economy.

Besides, I saw many of my friends either renting houses or buying houses built by some one else, and I felt that my home was something to be worked for and to create, step by step. Otherwise it would not be mine. Accepting a ready-made house, built according to another's ideas and tastes, never rang true to me. A home, I felt, should represent one's own choice: it should be expressive of self. This method might call for more time and a great deal of patience, but at the end I would have something of my own which would speak for me.

I had no desire to live in the city, and neither did my bride-to-be. Hence, my quest became suburban, which, in Philadelphia, becomes, of course, the ideal living.

I spent days and weeks looking for a desirable place. My means were decidedly limited and my obligations definite. It was necessary to be near the city for daily commutation, and hence near the railroad station—advantages which do not point to low prices for land.

II

After a long search, I finally hit upon four acres at Merion,—the first suburb outside of Philadelphia on the main line of the Pennsylvania Railroad, assuring good train service, and only fifteen minutes from the heart of the city. But four acres were just two acres more than I wanted, and the price was exactly twice as much as I had calculated upon. However, inquiry revealed the fact that I was buying on a rising market, ground at Merion was not likely to be any lower, and I figured I could, with advantage, sell off two of the acres (which, of course, I never did!).

With the purchase arranged, the seller asked if I was prepared to make a deposit as an evidence of good faith.

I replied that I was, and my bank balance flashed into my mind.

"Say what?" I asked. "$250 until the deed has been searched?"

"Quite satisfactory," fortunately replied the owner, and considering that my bank balance was $400, it was happy for me that it *was* satisfactory!

I had now committed myself to pay a goodly sum (to me) of five figures within thirty days, and my total means counted up into three figures—$150! Of course, a mortgage on the property was the first thought, and as the land fell into the improved property class, I found an investor willing to take a mortgage for one-half of the purchase price. But whence the other half?

III

The next morning I was walking down Chestnut Street when my eye fell upon a partnership sign, one of the partners whom I had met and who had said when I came to Philadelphia: "If, at any time, I can help you in any way, let me know." He could now. I went in, told him my story, explained that I had a conviction against signing notes, but that if he would loan me the amount I needed I would pay him off as I could, and insure my life with him (he was in the insurance business) for the amount. He agreed, and when the time of the transfer of the property came I met the settlement fully. But I was in debt, for which I had an instinctive distaste.

I renewed my efforts in saving and when I married I had paid off a quarter of the loan. After marriage we lived with my wife's parents for a while, and thus with few expenses we were able to pay off the balance of the loan. The mortgage, I felt, could rest for a while.

IV

Meanwhile, we thought of little else than plans of houses. We conceived some beautiful homes on paper, but when we measured the cost per cubic feet, they lost, if not their beauty, certainly their possibility in our eyes. Gradually, of course, we came to plan within our financial means as we could foresee them. A friend offered to draw the plans to scale, and then ensued some more trimmings. In three essentials, we would not economize: plumbing and heating, and our minds were fixed on locating bathrooms not where the plumbing would make them most economical, but where those who were to use them could find them and would want them. And as we had planned seven bathrooms, in a comparatively small house, the plumbing was of course an item. But, we argued, we could economize by plastering these bathrooms first, and tiling them in the future, one by one, as our income would permit. But seven bathrooms we held on to with a grim determination, and seven bathrooms we got, leading one of our friends to call the house, during its construction, "Bok's Bath House." But we had our combined sense of New England cleanliness and the natural Dutch inclinations in that direction.

After we felt reasonably sure that the cost of the house would fall within our possibilities, we concentrated, evening after evening, on distinct features of the house. Several evenings were given over solely to the study of ventilation (and as we knew little or nothing about architecture, this task was not easy of wise accomplishment) and the placing of windows where we felt we wanted them for ventilation, as well as for light. Of course, we provided for too many windows, and thus we went over our plans again and again to curtail the number and yet ensure the results we were after. Then we spent evenings wholly upon placing the heating outlets. Again we spent evenings over the placing of the lighting fixtures. And so, by the concentrative method, we built up the interior of our home as we wanted it in each detail.

Then we called in an architect, and asked him to design the best possible exterior for the interior plans. We realized this called for a skill that we had not.

V

Finally, after what seemed an interminable period of planning, to say nothing of saving, we were ready to begin on the momentous structure. Before I purchased the land I took the precaution to have the ground tested where the house was to be erected. The engineer discovered the four feet thick walls of an old barn which had burnt, from which we figured we would secure enough of the best kind of stone, nearly a half century old, for almost the entire foundations for the house. To offset this pleasant discovery, however, we found a stream running through the place—upon which I had spent evenings picturing a wonderful effect of aquatic plants— to be polluted by uncontrollable sewage. So, at the last moment, the house was again postponed while we spent our carefully-saved money in building a brick culvert and covering up the stream! This put us back a year, and then the house was actually begun, and on Saint Valentine's Day in 1900, February 14, with exactly fourteen workmen in the house, we moved in with not a chair to sit on, and the living-room unhabitable. But we were in, and that we knew would push the workmen out!

VI

The culvert had eaten into our savings to such an extent that we were now forced to put a mortgage on the house to keep company with the mortgage on the land! Ensued another period of saving and deprivation, for the mortgages weighed heavily on our consciences. Where almost all our friends went to Europe or to the seashore, we remained at home every summer. Then on an unforgetable Thanksgiving evening we burned the last mortgage, and our home was ours in fact! We now began the tiling of the bathrooms and the kitchen, and adding those other improvements to the house which we always had in mind.

It was the real building of a home, and naturally that is why every association is so close to us, as, to my mind, a home should be. Had the means been ours to buy the land and pay for it forthwith, and to build the house at once and pay for it without much thought, it is unlikely that "Swastika" would be in our hearts as it is to-day. It would be our home, but not in the same way and to the same extent. It could not possibly have the meaning that it has where every room was self-planned and every window fixed and every fixture placed.

Its meaning was intensely personal to me, because it was my first real home in the United States. For two decades I had lived with my mother and brother in hotels, until my soul used to cry out for a meal without music, and, unknown to my mother, I would occasionally eat all by myself in some quiet restaurant where did not exist the temptation to eat hot soup to a two-step or a steak to a waltz!

VII

The planting of the grounds came into being in much the same way: by stages. As our income began to warrant it, we called in an occasional landscape gardener for guidance, but we found that in the final analysis the actual planting, when done, was of our selective judgment. In this way, a distinct and valuable practical knowledge of trees, shrubs, and flowers became ours, as well as a familiarity with soil conditions.

Of course, the love of the soil inherited by every native of the Netherlands responded to this work in my case, and my happiest hours were spent in planning and planting.

I recall as my birthday was coming one year, my wife asked me what I would like best as a present, and I promptly answered: "Three loads of three-year-old cow manure!" It was the only possession of a neighbor of ours in those planting days which I coveted: a load of thoroughly decayed manure which would pass our place to go into his grounds. I believed in laying a groundwork of cow or horse manure in all my planting, and this called for an unusual amount of the envied fertilizer. I got my birthday present and a load to the good, and I shall never forget my pride and satisfaction as I surveyed that pile of manure! For once I had all the manure I wanted, and the most wonderful time opened before me! My happiness in my possession was such that every true gardener will understand. In those days nurserymen did not use manure as a basis for planting, and consistently counselled me against it. It was not

long, however, before they discovered that success came
to me where similar planting failed with others. Of
course, I was always careful to see that there was a
layer of from two to three feet of soil between root and
manure. But where rains, with other plantings, perco-
lated through the soil and were lost to the planting, the
manure in the case of my plants held the water and, in
addition, acted as a hot-house under the ground. The
same nurserymen who then condemned my method now
employ it, and express the deepest resentment that
there was ever a time when they planted without manure. Such is human nature!

VIII

I speak of this experience because there are those who
have the notion that real homes have some miraculous
way of rising out of the ground of themselves, and the
fact is also frequently lost sight of that a home may
mean a financial struggle to those to whom, later, means
are easy. Our home came to us step by step, and dollar
by dollar, and by deprivation and the strictest economy.
But no experience that we look back upon means so
much to us in actual pleasure, in healthful work, and in
the acquirement of knowledge of a world that is filled
with wonder and interest and beauty. No one knows
the fascination of a nurseryman's catalogue unless he
has created a garden. The most romantic novel is dull
in comparison with it.

TWELVE:

AN EXPERIMENT WITH TWO LIVES

"A well-ordered mind is early trained."

MARCUS AURELIUS

AN EXPERIMENT WITH TWO LIVES

I

WHEN the first of our boys came, his mother and I decided upon two or three rules to which we would adhere, and they have worked out exactly as we planned and hoped they would.

It is always the natural desire of a father to have his name handed down, and so it seemed logical that the first-born should take my name. But I was never in favor of a "Junior." It did not seem to me to give a boy a chance of his own or the individuality to which I felt he was entitled. If the father achieved fame, it gave the son a handicap to carry the same name all through his life and invite constant comparison, generally to his disadvantage. I had seen so much of this in the case of sons who bore the famous names of their fathers, and had heard the sons express themselves and their fathers regret it afterward. If the father, on the other hand, brought discredit to the name, the boy had a handicap for which he was in no wise responsible. Above all, it seemed to me that it robbed a boy of a rightful personality of his own.

II

We decided that we would not prohibit. We would always explain why a certain action was wrong, and why the opposite was right, and then leave it to the boy

to work out the problem for himself. But we never pro-
hibited. When the boy reached the age of understanding we explained that if he would give us his confidence,
and come to either one of us and tell when he had done
something which he felt was wrong or should not have
been done, there would be "only half-punishment," and
his father or mother would at once come to his side and
help to repair the harm or damage done.

A few days thereafter a broken window was discovered, but not reported. The boy was asked: "Why did
you not tell us that you had broken Mr. Granville-
Smith's window?"

"Well," he answered, "you said if I came and told
you of anything naughty I had done, I would only get
half-punishment."

"Yes," I assented.

"Well," he continued, "I didn't care to get the half-
punishment."

Here was a parental lesson in going half-way and not
the whole way to a truth.

"Quite right," I said to the boy. "Now we will make
another agreement. When you do anything wrong, and
you will come and tell either of us about it right away,
you will get no punishment at all."

A week passed by, and the boy came to me and asked:
"Did you say, Father, that if I came and told you when
I did something I shouldn't have done, no matter how
bad it may be, you would forgive it and not punish me
in any way?"

I told him that was exactly what I meant. "Moreover," I added, "you and I will together do what we

can to undo what you have done. We will be partners in crime."

"Well," was the answer, "I just broke one of Mr. Shaw's chairs." And he looked at me to see the effect. "But," he quickly added, "I have enough in my bank to pay to have it fixed."

"Well," I answered, "come on and let us go together and see how much it will cost, and get a man to fix it."

When the chair was fixed, I said he would pay half the cost and I would pay half.

"But," came the answer, "why should you pay anything? You didn't break the chair; I did."

"True," I said, "but don't you remember I said we were partners in crime, and what you do I do, and we fix it up together?"

The following week something else was broken, and the same procedure was gone through. "Well," was his objection, "I don't see the fairness of your paying for things which you don't break." Of course, the result was that very few things were broken, but the bond of confidence always remained.

We simply felt that if we could feel sure we had the fullest confidence of our boys, we were willing to let everything else go—certainly any form of punishment in which we never had much faith, always depending more on explanation and appeal to common sense. Never has there been a moment when we have regretted the experiment.

III

We decided, too, that the boys should not borrow their parents' minds to solve their problems. Each had a mind of his own, and was to be taught to use it. Thus he would become accustomed to make his own decisions. We determined always to present the pro and con of every problem: explain carefully both sides, offer to counsel and guide while they were making up their minds, but at the outset not to decide for them. Thus from early life each boy has decided his own problems, just as he does to-day. They have always come to us before acting, to ask if they were right or wrong, but invariably they decided and used their own minds in reaching a decision.

Thus when the Great War came, and the elder naturally wanted to leave college and go into the service of his country, the question was in which branch he should go: the army or the navy. We both had our decided preference and hope, and told him so. But we also told him that we would not express that preference to him: that he was to give the service, he was to do the fighting and he should determine for himself where he would serve and fight. The matter was talked over, of course, articles were read about both branches, arguments were obtained in favor of one and of the other, and for days and weeks he weighed the question. We had agreed that when he had definitely come to a conclusion, but before he actually took the final step, we would frankly tell him whether he had decided in line with our own preference and hope,—and prayers! Finally, he fixed his preference on the navy, and then, with lightened hearts, we told him of our joy in his decision!

IV

It was the same when, after the war, he went to the
University of Virginia to take a year of law simply as
fundamental knowledge for whatever business he finally
decided to choose. He was surprised at the interest of
the law, and he had not gone far in his course when he
felt he wanted to adopt the law as a life-work. Again,
we kept our hands off. We knew he had come to his
attraction for the law naturally, since so many of his
forbears had been barristers. He pondered wisely and
weighed carefully, and then when he had reached an
actual decision he again found his parents in hearty ac-
cord. The same was true when, upon finishing his studies, he found, from his record, that an association with
more than one law office was possible for him. Here
again the choice was left to him: the desirabilities of
each office were discussed. He talked with those who
held out their hands to him,—and he again decided
exactly as his parents hoped he would. In other words,
with the possession of ordinary common sense, he had
been trained to use his own mind, analyze his own instincts, train his own judgment, and reach his own conclusions. Of course, he doubtless felt the assurance that
his parents would guide him if they felt he was going
wrong. But he didn't go wrong, and therein he made a
success of his parents' experiment.

V

What was true of the elder is now proving true of the
younger. Naturally, he has not faced so many problems
or reached so many turning-points in his life as his

brother seven years his senior. But the same procedure was gone through in his choice of a college. He hesitated between Princeton and Williams. Princeton was closer to his home, and that fact apparently had its attraction. We explained the advantage of being at a college so close by, but we also pointed out the disadvantage to a boy in such a situation, particularly the point that it was much better for a boy learning to stand on his own feet, and beginning to live his own life, not to have his home so near at hand. We pointed out that, Williams having been his brother's college, it might be a pleasant bond in later life to have the same alma mater. On the other hand, we contrasted certain disadvantages of Williams with certain advantages of Princeton. There we left the matter in his mind, and he took the question back to preparatory school with him, and weighed both sides for several weeks. Then he decided for Williams, exactly as we hoped he would, although he acknowledged afterward he had no idea whatever of our preference. He has made other decisions with equal wisdom, showing in his case, as well as in that of his brother, that his mind has been trained to function for itself and can be trusted to reach a wise decision.

Hence, neither of the boys has borrowed his parents' minds.

VI

It is encouraging to see in these days that parents are more and more inclined to follow this method with their children, refusing to let them borrow other minds for the solution of their own problems. Of course, there are instances where the mind of a child must be influenced by its parents. But there is little reason for the method in the case of a healthy child born of intelligent parents. It is not good for the future mental development of a child to realize that it can depend upon its parents to decide what is good and what is not good for it. Nothing weakens a child more than an absolute dependence upon its parents for its decisions. Every day we see deplorable instances of children, grown men and women in many instances, whose mental capacities have not been developed and who find themselves weakened and helpless when the parents are taken away. Except for a wiser guidance born of experience, it was never intended that parenthood should mean a deprivation of the right and necessity of childhood to make its own decisions.

The fundamental life of a child is largely formed in the first seven years. Then the principles for good or for evil are laid down and inculcated in the life: the character is largely fashioned, and the greatest part of a parent's work is finished. After that, it is merely a question of repetition, reiteration, and amplification. Weaken a child during its first seven years by having everything done for it, every whim granted, every service rendered, every mental test avoided, and the strengthening of that child after seven becomes a proposition very difficult of accomplishment.

VII

God gave to our children minds for their use: not to become rusty, but to be trained and exercised for future use when, alone, they face the world and its problems.

"WHICH GRAIN WILL GROW"

I

ONE of our boys, when he was thirteen years of age, said to me: "You were thirteen when you started to work. Why shouldn't I leave school and begin?" Now that he is older, I dare say he sees the wisdom of his parents' decision that what was right for me would have been wrong for him. Had his parents encouraged him to go to work we should have created an unnatural condition, and that never gets anywhere. The point always to be borne in mind is to get our relations right; to create, so far as one can, a natural condition.

II

I had to go to work at thirteen. There was no choice. My father, a stranger to American ways, could not re-adjust himself at his age to the new conditions of a strange country. My mother had not the health to endure house-work; she had not been brought up to it. There was nothing for us boys to do but to get out and help to make the domestic machinery run a bit easier. It was a natural thing to do; it was right. But it was regretful in the sense that the necessity broke into our boyhood days. A boy has a right to a good time, a care-free period in his life; the problems of Life come soon enough. I know that I missed that precious time by having to

take up responsibilities so early, and being made so soon
to realize that there was more than baseball in life.
It wasn't easy.   One's duty is never easy, but it is particularly hard to a boy who in every fibre of his being
cries out for that movement and expression which finds
itself in play.   There were times in my boyhood when
I felt so pent-up that I just wanted to go out into the
street and yell, just yell for the sake of yelling,—to let
off steam, as it were.   That sort of repression is not good
for a boy.   But I could not bear to see my mother bend
under the housework for which she had no training, and
was determined to ease it up for her where possible.   It
took all the love I had for my mother when at times I
had to keep washing and drying dishes before a window
from which I could see my boy friends playing baseball.
Finally, I hung a towel over that window.

III

Not that I was entirely deprived of all boyish pleasures.
I was too much of a boy for that.   I had some fun.   It
was intermittent, but I enjoyed what I got all the more
because of that fact.   I had my innings at baseball,
went to the games as they were in those days, and became so proficient in the "box" that I could, on Saturday afternoons, not only satisfy my boyish longing for
the game, but earn five dollars as "substitute pitcher."
I rowed enough to win cups in both the single and double
sculls classes.   I was just as much a factor as any of the
boys in the barrel bonfires that were then the custom on
the evenings of election day, and always in the front in
the deadly stone fights that invariably ensued from those

fires when the boys from the other streets tried to take
our barrels. Coasting was one of my favorite sports,
and snow-balling was an art in which I learned to excel.
The Simon-pure snow did not suit us boys, so we made
it more "interesting" to those whom we fixed upon as
our marks by soaking the snowballs in water until they
became like balls of ice. We were careful to appoint as
our leader in these sports the boy whose father was the
policeman on our beat, and as that official could not
very well arrest us without arresting his own boy, we
felt a great degree of safety in that direction. So I did
not altogether starve from a lack of boyish pranks and
sports. But at the best they were few in number,—
not enough to satisfy the cravings of a vigorous boy.

IV

None of those conditions of necessity was present
with our boys. I would not for the world take those days
out of my life and what they taught me, and yet I would
not for the world have put them into their lives,—simply
because it was unnecessary. Such a boyhood as mine is
a wonderful period to go through in many respects, but
it is not vital to the development of a boy's character.
All that the drudgery of housework may have done for
me found a counterpart in other conditions for my sons,
—conditions that were more natural to their surroundings. It is not altogether that a father hesitates to have
his sons go through his experiences, if they were hard,
although that feeling unquestionably enters into his
thoughts. It is more the fitness of things. My boys
could have a different boyhood, and it was right they

should have their kind, just as it was right that I should have my kind. I was determined that they should have the boyhood which was their right and the opportunity for education which circumstances denied to me. I knew they would do as much with their opportunities as I had done with mine of another kind. It would have been manifestly unwise for either of my boys to have started out in Life at thirteen just because I did. It is for parents to give to their children all the tools they possibly can to enable them to work to the best advantage. My parents gave me all they could. They would undoubtedly have given me all we gave our two sons had circumstances been the same.

V

There is a prevalent and very dangerous notion that only poor boys achieve in life. Of course, this is preposterous. We have a great deal of earned wealth in our country, because we are a new nation and have not yet outlived the generation of pioneers. But we have gone far enough to prove that the children of parents of easy means have the same road ahead of them as the boys born of poverty. It isn't so easy for a boy born to wealth to carve out a success for himself, although to some it may seem easier. The only advantage that he can have is that the start may be made easier for him; the chance may be opened up to him. But this is strongly counterbalanced by the fact that the spur of necessity is not back of him. He has two roads before him to the one of the boy of poverty, and a choice always presents difficulties and minimizes initiative.

A successful father can more often mean a serious handicap rather than an advantage to an ambitious son. After the first advantage in the favorable approach to a position is had by the young man coming from a family of influence, he arrives at exactly the same point with the young man of no influence: he reaches that point where it depends solely on himself. Business is not conducted in such a manner, least of all in these competitive days, that a young man can be allowed to remain in a position which he is unable to fill. Too much is and must be expected of every cog in the wheel of business so that it may attain its fullest velocity and reach its greatest efficiency. So the two young men starting out perhaps differently meet a little further along in the road on precisely an equal footing. Influence may have started the one, but it cannot sustain him.

VI

It is infinitely more to the credit of a young man coming from a home of ease if he succeeds. Our two boys are not from necessity compelled to work and earn their living. They know that. They know their living will be provided for them. It grieves parents to the heart when they are called upon to do it, but they are compelled to feed and clothe the laggard as well as the industrious son. Our boys have elected otherwise. Their parents knew they would from their characters. They show their quality when they ask only a fair field and no favor. Thus what they accomplish will be of their own effort and the result of their own abilities, and they will find a satisfaction in such achievement that nothing

can equal.   Hence their success will be the greatest credit
to them.

They have willed, in other words, and that, in itself,
spells achievement.

VII

Of course, all boys naturally speculate how far a man
may go, and they are apt to think of the distance in
terms of income.

When I resigned my position as editor of *The Ladies'
Home Journal*, and our boys happened to hear that I
had thereby relinquished a salary of $100,000 a year,
they were frankly surprised at the apparent largeness of
the salary.

"Was that a courtesy salary?" one of them asked.

I explained there was not such a salary in the world
of business.

"Can one man really earn $100,000 a year?" was the
next question.

The question is one which many a man much older,
particularly the man who has missed the path of achievement, has asked and generally in a spirit of doubt.

VIII

Of course, there is no practical way of computing, in
dollars and cents, a man's earning capacity. A man
demonstrates a certain value to the corporation by
which he is employed, and that corporation fixes a compensation which it feels it can afford to pay him. More
generally than not, this measurement is below rather
than above his actual worth; that is, it is below the

actual business which his management of his position brings to the corporation. For instance, I know an executive who receives a salary of $100,000 a year. If he were paid so small a commission as one per cent on the volume of business which his particular department produces as a direct result of his vision and judgment, he would receive three times his salary. This man, therefore, most certainly earns his salary, and so it is with scores of other executives in large corporations who earn even larger salaries. There are a number of corporations that pay their president an annual salary of $150,000; there are at least two presidents that I know of who receive more than that sum.

It is true that such salaries were little known a few years ago; entirely unknown twenty-five years ago. But the country has grown, and business has grown with the country. Large businesses must have not only at their head, but in charge of the various departments as well, men of largest calibre and safest judgment. This type of man is not numerous, and when found he can command an appropriate salary: in fact, he does not have to command; it is gladly and willingly paid him. But never is he paid more than he is worth. That much is certain. No business can afford to maintain an executive unless he represents an asset to the corporation.

IX

There is no more profitable asset in a business than a $100,000 salaried man, because he never receives it unless he is capable of producing the equivalent of that salary many times over to his corporation. This is very easily calculated on the basis that just as the profit on a five-cent article, for example, cannot be very large and the profit on a $5,000 article is proportionately greater, so the profit on a $1,500 or a $2,500 clerk cannot be as large as the profit on a $100,000 a year man. The earning capacity of an able executive is beyond the comprehension of the average man. Take the value of one idea conceived by such a man. In one instance, a single idea initiated by the head of a department in a large corporation meant a greater production, totalling over $1,000,000 a year. That was only one idea; an incident in a day's work. Another executive I know conceived a method by which he effected an actual money saving of $1,500,000 a year; not for one year, but the economy goes on year after year. This, too, was but an incident in a day's work. These men certainly earned their $100,000 yearly salaries. The industries in which these men are engaged are as big as they are because the men are big and are capable of thinking in big terms and of judging signs on the horizon long before others see them. These men are paid not for what they actually do, but for what they see ahead and for planning to meet the conditions which their vision reveals. This capacity to foresee and to plan is inconceivable to the average mind which deals only with the task in hand, but it is that quality which makes the great executive.

X

Young men are apt to envy these men of large emolument. But they judge of them when they have arrived; not during the time of their climbing process. A man steps into a $100,000 salaried position only with years of work and preparation behind him.

Take the average young man of to-day, who is apt to question the ability of any man to earn one of these large salaries, and who likes to think that such positions are generally won by influence and held by favor, and say to him:

"Are you ready to give up the next thirty or thirty-five years to working every day, perhaps holidays, too, from twelve to fifteen hours a day, beginning with the most manual work of a laborer, and going without vacations, and having very few pleasures, ready at any hour of the day and night to obey the call of business?" What proportion of the young men of to-day would answer in the affirmative? Very few, I fear. Yet that is exactly what a $100,000 job means.

XI

See where these $100,000 men came from. Here is one who now receives $125,000 a year salary; he began by sorting rags at 35 cents per day for the same corporation of which he is now president. Another, also a $125,000 a year man, drove an oil-tank wagon for years. Another, a $150,000 a year man this time, got out of his bed as a boy every morning, summer and winter, at a quarter to four o'clock and served a newspaper route, never getting a morsel of food until seven and then going to school all day and working after school hours. Another $150,000 a year executive had his choice between Yale College and a $3.00 per week job. He took the latter, and was the butt of all his young friends.

Now he is their envy! A well-known coal president, receiving $125,000 per year salary, drove the mules of the canal coal barge owned by the company which now is glad to pay him his present salary. A boy came into the office of a great corporation to do errands. He never cared how many he ran a day, or how late after five o'clock an errand would make him, or how long he remained after the hour to see if another errand needed to be done. He was there before his employer; he was there after the employer left. To-day he receives $15,000 a month salary from the same corporation. The highest-paid executive to my knowledge receives a salary of $300,000 a year, paid to him so that after he has paid his Federal income-tax he may have a net compensation worthy of his earning capacity. This man began as a peddler of shoe-strings on the streets of New York.

These are not mythical cases; each is an actual instance, and there are others similar to them. There is no mystery to them; there is no sense in asking these men the secret of their success. It is pure mockery to ask them how they got where they are. They never thought of office hours. Their idea was never to get through, but to get on. The whole process is too obvious. Not one of these men has an inspirational theory to advance. But not one ever worked by the clock or surrounded himself with shock-absorbers. They smile when you suggest influence; their own early beginnings come before them. They never asked: "How much am I paid to do?" but "How much can I find to do?" They are examples of only one way to success: the road of hard, honest work and willingness to do. Their seemingly large salaries are the result of long and sterling service and that intensive application which only the few are willing to give to an appointed task.

XII

So the answer to the question in the mind of a young man "Can a man earn $100,000 a year?" is to fit himself to earn it; "to strive, to seek, to find" work. The question will then answer itself.

XIII

We have a present-day danger, however, that we should not fail to remember when we discuss business success. We are, it is true, slowly getting away from the habit, but it is still all too prevalent, of measuring the word success entirely by the salary which a man receives or the fortune which he accumulates. That may be the only yard-stick by which a certain part of the world is capable of measuring a man's achievement, and no one will gainsay that it is a legitimate means of measurement to a certain point. But it is by no means the Alpha and Omega of business achievement, since if that is all that stands to the credit of a man after a lifetime of work it is solely of itself and in itself a hollow record. The respect of that portion of mankind whose esteem is worth anything cannot be won or held upon an achievement which represents only a monetary valuation. The men who have done most for business in the way of lasting contributions have not always been those who have drawn the largest revenue from its conduct. Many have. But there are also the quiet men of whom the world has never heard, who have put more into business than they have ever taken out of it. And eminently successful are they, too. The man who puts a conscience into business; who lifts the art of trading a bit higher than he found it; who introduces standards which end abuses and stop economic waste; who makes it more difficult for the man of dishonest purposes and methods to remain in business; who adds his contribution to putting that particular part of the industrial system with which he is concerned in better order, so as to command the respect of mankind—that man is in every respect a success, although he may not be able to reckon his wealth by the millions.

We have a good deal to say about the multiplicity of laws governing business, and we resent with strident voice the tendency of too much government in business. But we must not forget that these laws would never have been enacted had not the need for them existed. There is a conceivable condition of business on a plane so high in standard and honest in conduct that there shall exist no necessity for the law to step in. The standards of business were erected before the laws which now strive to govern trade. But the standards were not upheld. There have not been enough men successful in the sense of upholding the standards of two thousand years ago to make restraints unnecessary—restraints which should have come out of business and not been imposed upon it by legal enactment.

The real road to success in business lies open to every young man who will keep in mind the great gospel of making it increasingly difficult, if not impossible, for the dishonest man to do business. The harder he can make it for the demagogue, the simpler he makes it for himself and others who believe in the old but ever-sound doctrine of sterling honesty in one man's dealings with another. He need have no anxiety of the emoluments of business; they will follow where the note of honest intent of the homespun variety is struck. This is not visionary. It is the most eminently practical doctrine in business to-day. Not that "honesty is the best policy," but that honesty is the only current coin in business, or in any other avenue in life, that will give to a man that inner satisfaction that gives him that glow of success with his inner self and wins for his achievement and himself the lasting esteem of his fellowmen.

FOURTEEN:

WHEN YOUTH AND GREATNESS MEET

Gentlemen, each:
"Your name is great."

WHEN YOUTH AND GREATNESS MEET

I

It is an interesting study for parents to watch the reaction of their children to the men and women who visit in their home. It has been given to our sons, as it was to me, to meet early in life some of the interesting figures on the national chess-board, to watch the moves they made in the world and then to meet them face to face at the home-table. One of the men, in particular, much seen at the home-table won his way straight to the heart of each boy. It was not because Josef Hofmann was a great pianist that he became "Uncle Josef." The boys just adopted him as soon as each was old enough to adopt any one. He simply was "all right," and that begins and ends the fact in a boy's vocabulary.

A normal-minded boy never accepts a man for the reputation which he may have in the world. Often he is unconscious of it, and even where he is conscious of it in a way, Fame to a boy is a sort of mist through which he walks, and he either accepts or rejects a man regardless of the plaudits of the world. A boy is never at a loss for a direct route to his estimate of a man. He has only one, and about ten minutes' acquaintance settles the question whether "he is all right" or not.

Josef Hofmann came first to us when he was twenty years old. He was brought to our house by a friend, Barton Cheyney, for luncheon, but a new and unintelligent servant told the invited callers that we were not at

merit, three of the compositions, in particular, excelling
much of the modern foreign school. Again, in another
city, Hofmann gave the programme, with the same result. Then the cities which he was about to visit asked
that he would not insist upon playing the American programme, but should give them the standard compositions of foreign authorship.

The pianist now determined to make a test of the
merit of the compositions themselves, and, selecting a
large city which had refused the All-American programme, he sent a supposedly different programme, but
which was the identical American programme, first carefully changing the names of the compositions and sub-
stituting the names of Mendelssohn, Schubert, Rubinstein, Moszkowski, and Tschaikowsky. The success of
the concert was absolute; the audience was delighted.
Comment was made that Hofmann had never played
the Rubinstein selection so wonderfully—when, as a
matter of fact, no one had ever heard it before. It had
never been played before, because there was no such
Rubinstein composition! The critics, the following day,
praised the programme highly; exclaimed over a sonata
written by a Milwaukee composer as "being typically
Russian and in Tschaikowsky's best vein." The name
of Rubinstein had been substituted for that of Reginald
De Koven, and never, said the critic, had Hofmann
"played the marvellous music of his master in such a
wonderful way!"

III

It is curious how we demand American recognition
for our arts, and when it is given we refuse to accept it.

"Encourage the American painter!" cry some patrons
of art, and when they buy pictures for their own collec-
tions they choose from the foreign schools, ancient or
modern. "See America first!" we cry, and the moment
we have the funds we rush pell-mell to the steamship
docks to sail for Europe. I have seen three "All-
American" programmes of excellent symphonic compositions played by the Philadelphia Orchestra, in each
case to the smallest audiences of each season, and yet
the cry goes up that symphonic conductors will not encourage the American composers. We cry loud and long
for opera in English, and when it is given we either do
not like it, if we attend at all, or we do not know it
when it is given. I remember a committee of fifty presumably patriotic women who insisted directly after the
war that a certain Wagnerian opera should be sung in
English and not in German. The English libretto was
given and the opera sung. The committee of fifty attended in a body, was enthusiastic with the result of the
more pleasing effect of the English language as sung in
the opera, and comment was particularly directed to the
more wonderful singing of the three principals in English. They never knew, the dear ladies who were so
completely pleased, that these same three principals, all
Germans, refused at the last moment to sing the music
of their land in anything but the tongue in which it
should be sung, and sang every bar of their part in the
opera in German, the minor singers and the chorus only
singing in the English. So much for the imagination!

I had a lecture course under my supervision in which
three lectures dealt with English literature; three with

Harken, my child: believe in my word,
Surrender thyself to me: I am thy Lord;
Earth's deepest sorrows they last but a day;
Strength will I give you: I am the Way.
Look up and trust! For the sun shines on high,
No shadow lies there: clear blue is the sky.
On guard are the stars, bringing calm to thy sleep;
Learn peace: believe that thy watch I will keep.
Dry now thy tears, make thy heart bright with cheer,
Grief cannot blind thee, thy way I make clear;
Have faith! I am near, at thy side do I stand,
I am thy Guide: put thy trust in my hand.

V

Speaking of things musical reminds me of a ride I had from Boston to New York some years ago. I had some important reading to do, and so, wishing to be undisturbed, I engaged the drawing-room. I had scarcely started on my reading, and the train had not left the station, when a little man with long black hair fairly waltzed into my compartment, unannounced, and, pointing joyfully to some people standing on the platform, and bowing most profusely, said in broken English: "Ees it not wonderful? They have come to see me off. See? Mees Sears, yes, you know not her? Great Boston family? Yes, Sears, Mees Sears. Ah, yes, Mees Eleanor Sears. Is it not beautiful? I go to platform and bow."

I agreed instantly that he should, and proceeded to close the door. But it was not to be. In a moment the wild little man returned.

"A tribute to my genius, yes, yes," he repeated. "So

beautiful!" and bowing profusely to the handful of people. "I bow on platform again," and out danced the little man again, to the delight of his station admirers. The train had now started, and I was hopeful that I had lost my erratic visitor. But only for a moment. In again he literally waltzed, bearing aloft an orange. "I eat orange always before a meal: so fresh, so, so, what shall I say, yes, so soothing. I have knife, and will cut it so," which he proceeded to do, "and you have please half and I will have half. So."

There was no use protesting. We two were alone in the compartment, and I considered it safer to humor and indulge my unknown friend. Between mouthfuls of orange juice, he told me how great was his artistry, how people adored him, and then everything was repeated about his Boston friends and "Mees Sears." Three times I began to venture an inquiry as to the character of his "artistry," but each time there came a perfect torrent of self-praise and his greatness as an artist.

Finally came a moment's pause when he said: "I love meditation! I meditate on railroad cars. So"—and he showed me by a thoughtful attitude how he meditated. I now forced myself into the conversation, and expatiated on the need of meditation, suggesting that perhaps he would like to go to his seat in the car and meditate.

"Ah, yes," he would go and meditate, and forthwith he went, and I sprang the lock on my door. But only for five minutes! Came a casual knock, which I pretended not to hear, and then another and a third. I made up my mind it would be useless to ignore the man's

remember so well my own boy-impressions of men whom
the world calls great, and how smaller they became as
I got closer to them. They did not bear the test of what
is now called the "close-up." The acid test comes so
often in the attitude of men toward the young, particularly when the young are paid to serve them. Then
more truly than at any other time, except perhaps in
play, one differentiates between the sheep and the goats.
I recall how the great men in the world of finance and
business came in and out of the law department of the
Western Union Telegraph Company when I was stenographer to Mr. Clarence Cary, then attorney for the
company. I saw these giants at close range, and at that
particular close range which is so sure a test of men's
character: when they are under fire and resort to the law.

One of the men who often came into the office in those
days was Alexander Graham Bell. It was in the late
'70s when he had just been granted a patent for the
telephone. The Western Union electricians early saw
the possibilities of the invention, and because of my
legible handwriting many of the initial papers of The
Bell Telephone Company were dictated to me. In this
way, I saw much of this kindly man. His manners were
the same for me, as a boy, as for Mr. Cary, my employer.
He did not have, as so many had, two codes of manners
and methods of address. He always had a kindly word
for my handwriting: was considerate in his dictation,
since he found out very quickly that I was not an adept
at the "pot hooks," and was lenient with my mistakes.
It was instinctive with him to put his hand on my head
and compliment me for my handwriting, which he never

failed to admire. "Like a copper plate," he would say. "Don't write too rapidly or you will spoil it." And with a smile would come the hand resting on my head. The physical contact of others was never agreeable to me, but I never resented it from him: I welcomed his touch.

VII

Always welcome was Thomas A. Edison, who was in and out almost daily. He was then in the midst of his great duplex and quadruplex message transmission inventions, and these called for various agreements between him and the Western Union, all of which I transcribed.

"I can write as plainly as you can," he would say. And he would pick up a pen, write something humorous, sign his name, leaving the top off the T of Thomas, and then say: "Watch me put an umbrella over the whole," and then he would make the half-circle over his entire name, like the fanlight over a door, which is so familiar to all who know his signature, and is exactly the same to-day as it was then. "How is that?" and then he would laugh like a boy as he handed me the paper. "Beat that if you can," and I smiled back at him, but did not accept the challenge. It was unnecessary to tell Edison you liked him; he saw and felt it. And everybody did like him.

VIII

"Been discharged, yet?" Edison asked me one day, laughing.

I told him this was my first job.

And that is exactly what they did, and this amazingly poor business arrangement he again insisted upon when he sold his next invention to the company for another hundred thousand dollars. "I'll only spend it if I have it," was his argument.

IX

An English firm cabled Edison and offered him "thirty thousand" for one of his patents.

"Too cheap, Edison," said a friend.

"Too cheap?" repeated Edison. "The thing isn't worth half of that," said Edison.

His friends induced him to cable back: "It is yours." Within a fortnight he received a draft for one hundred and fifty thousand dollars. It had turned out, of course, that the English firm had meant the amount in pounds.

Edison wanted to cable that some mistake had occurred, but his friends intervened.

"Well," he said, "it beats me."

He was telling Mr. Cary a story one day about the way his friends, when they came into his office, would help themselves to his pure Havana cigars. "They just take 'em by the handful," he said.

"Why don't you lock them up?" asked Mr. Cary.

"Never could remember to do it," returned Edison. "Then," he added, "Johnson, my secretary, you know, did a clever trick. He had a friend in the cigar business and promised to get him to make me some entirely of cabbage leaves and brown paper. I thought that was a fine scheme. But the cigars didn't come, so I asked him one day about it when I noticed my Havanas disappearing again.

"Why, I sent them to you," he said. "I left them with your manager."

I called the manager in and asked him where those cigars were. "Why," he said, "I put them in your valise when you went to California last month. I didn't know what they were."

"Do you know, Cary," continued Edison, "I smoked every one of those damned cigars myself."

X

One day, after a long dictation of an important paper, he looked at me quizzically and asked: "Have you the Lord's Prayer in a handy form so that you can carry it around with you and read it, as you should, every day?"

I shook my head in the negative.

"All right," he answered, "I'll give you one. Got a dime? No? Neither have I. Both alike," he laughed. "You know I never have money. Will have to get married some day, and then get my wife to look after my money. Never had much, but now have a little more. But it's just the same: I never have any. Don't know where it goes. And I hate bills, don't you? Don't like to pay them, don't like even to see them. They sort of insult me. I don't know why people should send bills anyhow, do you? They ought to be glad enough when you take and use what they have, let alone paying for it. Well, let me see where were we? Oh, yes, you haven't a dime, and neither have I. See here, Cary," turning to my employer, "let's have a dime. That's the ticket," as one was produced.

Then, taking out his pocketbook, he held it out to me so that I could look into it. "Nothing in it, hey? That's right. That is, no money. But in here there is," and he opened a middle compartment. "I carry some pens in there: I make them. Very sharp point, see?"

"Well, now," he said, "we take this dime so," and he placed it on a piece of paper, "and then we draw a circle around the edge, close, see, so that the circle is just as large as the outside of the dime. There. Now, then, what do you think I am going to do? I suppose you have asked yourself 'What's all that got to do with the Lord's Prayer?' Well, I don't blame you. I'm getting old, son, do you know it? Getting talkative. Sure sign."

"Now, then," he continued, his fine, thoughtful face wreathed in smiles, "I'm going to write the Lord's Prayer in that circle for you. Sure. You think I can't do it, hey? Well, you watch!"

And he did as I watched him as only a boy could watch and see an unbelievable miracle wrought in his presence. When he had finished, he said: "Now of course you can't read it with the naked eye, but it's all there, every word and comma and dot. Just see if it isn't," and he fished out of his pocket a small magnifying glass which was his inseparable companion, and handed it to me. With breathless interest I looked through the glass, and every word in the Lord's Prayer came before me.

"Now," he added, as he reached for his hat, "you have no more excuse for not reading the Lord's Prayer

every day of your life. You can carry it with you, and
it won't take up much room," and laughing heartily
he went out of the office.

Is it a wonder that a boy loved Thomas A. Edison?

XI

The courtesies which a boy remembers and which
make an indelible impression upon the formative mind
are unconsciously rendered. I recall one day Mr. Cary
sent me over to the general Post Office Building with a
letter to Thomas L. James. He was then postmaster of
New York City: later he became Postmaster-General in
President Garfield's administration.

"Come right in, my boy," said the postmaster in a
genial voice, as I walked into his large office full of
windows looking down busy Broadway. "Have you a
letter for me?"

"Now, what's your name?" he asked.

I told him.

"How old are you, Edward?" came next.

I gave my age.

"And where do you live?" I gave him my address.

"What are you going to be? The Western Union's
attorney, or its president?" was his next question.

"Neither? Why not? Well, how would you like to
be postmaster of New York? That a big enough job
for you? Suppose you see how a postmaster works.
Now I'll tell you. I'll read this letter, and write an
answer, for I know what it is about without opening it.
Isn't that wonderful? Then while I'm doing that, you
sit right here at that window. Here, let me get you this

big easy chair. That's it. Now you'll see Broadway as you can't see it from your building. And when you get tired of looking out there, you can see how I do my job as postmaster so that you will be able to do it when you get here. Unless, of course, you insist on becoming President of the United States!"

I remember it all so well—the geniality of it all, the warm interest of the man in the boy, and when many years later I had grown to man's estate and crossed on the steamer with Mr. James coming home from Europe, he was astonished that I should have so long remembered "so slight a happening," as he called it.

No kindness is slight to a boy!

XII

What Clarence Cary meant to me as a struggling boy when my father passed away I have told elsewhere. He took the place of a father, and was all that a father could be. That is why one of my sons bears his name, and it pleases me to recall that when I took the boy to see him when he lay stricken in bed, the confidence of the youngster went right out to him, and the boy lay in the man's arm with his great blue eyes open to their fullest while he told of his days on the sea when he was a sailor before the mast. And when we left, the boy voluntarily kissed him. It was left to me to see what the boy in his sixth year could not see, that the tears came unbidden to the eyes which for so many years had followed me, and with a warm pressure of the hand, without the word which he could not speak, I departed, never to see him again. Shortly afterward he left this world, in which he had done so much good, and it must have been a very short step which he took from this world into the next.

XIII

It was as a personal friend of Mr. Cary that I met Mr. Edward L. Burlingame. He was then associated with the *New York Tribune*, and would call for Mr. Cary to walk up-town at the close of an office day. Later I became his stenographer when he was editor of *Scribner's Magazine*, in conjunction with my work for Mr. Charles Scribner when I entered the Scribner house. If ever a boy received courtesy and consideration I received them at the hands of Mr. Burlingame, even to the extent that each morning when I entered his room to take his dictation he would not only greet me with a cordial "Good morning," but would rise from his chair. The most gracious manners were instinctive with Mr. Burlingame: he knew nothing else, and my association of many years with him was a continuous season of lessons in the most exquisite consideration of man for boy. When he saw my desire to read and learn, he helped me: sometimes going to the utmost trouble to find some particular book, even sending, in one case, to England for a book he felt I should read. He, too, has gone, quite recently. One of my treasured recollections was the last hour I ever spent with him in his office, when we talked of the day "when I was twenty-one," and I tried to tell him all that his kindness had meant to me in the most impressionable time of my life and how I had tried to "carry on" with those who served me, in the same spirit as he showed me when I served him.

Confucius was once asked, "What must a man do in order to be considered distinguished?"

"What do you mean by the term distinguished?" inquired Confucius.

"One whose fame fills his own private circle and the state at large," was the reply.

"That," said Confucius, "is notoriety, not distinction. The man of true distinction is simple, honest, and a lover of justice and duty."

XIV

Such were these gentlemen of my boyhood days. It is a wonderful thing to be a gentleman, and then to bear the name so that a boy may feel it.

FIFTEEN:

THE TWENTY-SIXTH PRESIDENT OF
THE UNITED STATES

" A man he was to all the country dear."

OLIVER GOLDSMITH

THE TWENTY–SIXTH PRESIDENT OF THE UNITED STATES

I

IT is safe to say, I think, that no man in the recent public life of America was more quickly and universally accepted by boys than was Theodore Roosevelt. I remember the experience with him, which I have told in my other book, when our elder son selected a personal meeting with him at the White House as the most desired of all Christmas gifts. The instantaneous finding of each on the part of the other was remarkable. Equally at home with the most brilliant savant and the most bashful tongue-tied boy, he was more his real self with the latter than with the former. Not that the boy in this case was tongue-tied; quite the contrary. The boy instantly found him as quickly as he found the boy, for Theodore Roosevelt always knew where and how to find a boy. He had a wonderful grasp of the boy-nature which made a boy feel instantly at home with him. Tongue-tied boys were an unknown quantity to him.

II

It was the same when we brought Colonel Roosevelt up to the Hill School, where the elder boy was a student at that time, and how quickly he won his way into the heart of every boy present! As one of the boys said afterward: "After he had spoken five minutes, there was nothing to it. We were his, and he was ours."

It was on that return trip to Philadelphia that we were chatting in the "saloon" of the private car when the conductor came in and said: "Colonel, we were going to express this train, but word comes from down the line that a lot of people are at the stations waiting for you.   What shall we do?"

"Slow up where you like," was the instant answer, "and I'll wave my hat at 'em from the platform here. But don't let me miss my four o'clock train for New York, for I have an appointment with Mrs. Roosevelt in New York at six-thirty, and if you're a married man you'll agree with me that I have *got* to keep that date."   And the Rooseveltian smile was reflected in the beaming face of the conductor.

After we had stopped at three or four stations, at which the Colonel had gone out on the platform, beamed at the crowd and waved his famous sombrero hat, I said "Colonel, you're tired.   Hadn't we better call the rest of the stations off?"

"I am tired, yes," he agreed.   He had talked for over an hour in the open air at the school.   "But I'm never too tired to say 'Hello' to the American people.   They refresh me."

And so it went on at each station.   At one stop, a loud yelling of "Hello, Teddy," greeted him, and when he returned to the saloon I said: "How do you interpret that term of 'Teddy'?   Do you mind it?"

"Not in the least," he answered.   It isn't a term of familiarity, as some think of it.   It's a term of good-will, of camaraderie.   Sometimes, though, there's a note of affection in it, and then, by Jove, I get afraid."

"Why afraid?" I asked.

"A public capable of loving is just as capable of proportionately hating, and hate isn't so far from love sometimes," he answered.

"I don't think you would ever elicit the spirit of hate
from the American public," I argued. "It might disa-
gree with you, might dislike you, but not hate."

"Don't fool yourself, old fellow," he answered.
"There was a large public that hated Lincoln, all right."

III

The Colonel brought this talk back to me one day
shortly after he had returned from his last African trip.
He had ridden up Broadway with immense crowds filling
the sidewalks and roofs and windows and throwing
confetti and paper tape all over him. And there were
two welcoming arches.

"Wonderful reception, Colonel," I remarked at the
end of that day.

"Wonderful, wonderful," he agreed. "But I'll make
a prophecy about those arches. I've got to plunge into
this New York political fight that's on here. Got to do
it, you know," he snapped. "The issue is too big to
side-step, and I'm going into it. Now, mark you, the
same people who hurrahed me to-day will, within ten
days, want to tear down those arches and throw hunks
of that plaster at me. Watch, and see if I'm not right."

He was. Within ten days he was in the midst of the
political fight: the storm-centre of abuse and vilifica-
tion.

"Remember our talk on the car from Pottstown about

the love and hate of a public?" he asked me. "There you are."

But within a year all had been forgotten, and the same public was shouting for "Teddy" and giving him as true an affection as the mob of a public is capable of giving any of its favorites.

IV

Colonel Roosevelt and I had never agreed on the question of woman-suffrage. He became an ardent supporter of the belief, and I remained unconvinced,— "Dutchly stubborn," as he called it. But he never lost an opportunity to say the word which he believed would bring me about to his new way of thinking. But he had also never brought Mrs. Roosevelt around! One day at a luncheon the Colonel introduced the subject, and, having Mrs. Roosevelt and myself as auditors, he held forth on the "stubbornness" of those who had "the intelligence but not the courage to see the light." I glanced over at Mrs. Roosevelt, as the Colonel went on, and she gave me that remarkable smile of kindly indulgence so familiar to her friends. The Colonel caught the interchange of glances, and, stopping abruptly in his tirade, he jerked out: "Now look at that—just look at that! There's that woman (pointing to Mrs. Roosevelt) and that Dutchman over there signalling to each other. I suppose that means 'Let him talk on; he's harming no one.' By Jove, I'm going to keep on talking." And he did.

Finally, turning to me, he asked: "What do you know about this subject, anyhow? How much have you read about it?" And then he answered his own question. "Precious little, I'll wager." Then he continued: "Have you read the enlightened pamphlets that have come out on this subject in Sweden and New Zealand?"

I confessed I had not.

"Well, I have, and you will," he answered. "I'll send them to you."

A few days later a porter announced that a box was outside my office. Should they open it and bring in its contents? It was marked as from Oyster Bay. In a few moments two porters and my office messenger came in with their arms laden with books and pamphlets. I looked at them. The Colonel had sent the promised literature! Literally stacks of them. I stepped outside, and there was an express crate with as many pamphlets and books in it as the three had brought in! Colonel Roosevelt had read them all, and intended that I should!

And yet there were those who said that the Colonel was in the habit of forming snap judgments on great public questions.

V

Speaking of Mrs. Roosevelt, it was wonderfully interesting to see the confidence which the Colonel felt in her judgment, and how he would depend upon her word.

One day I was at the White House talking with the President when Mrs. Roosevelt passed through the office, merely sending a pleasant smile and nod at the President as she was passing through. But the President halted her.

"Very busy this afternoon?" he asked.

"No, indeed," she answered, with just the slightest twinkle in her eyes. "Anything I can do?"

"Sure you haven't something important on?" insisted the President.

"Quite," was the answer.

"Well, then, would you mind taking those papers," picking up what looked like a package of legal papers, "give them a glance, and later tell me what you think?"

"Surely," answered Mrs. Roosevelt, as she went out.

The President looked after her and then, turning to me, said: "You know we *think* we know, but that woman *really* knows. Wonderful mind!"

VI

One day we were at luncheon, and the Colonel was particularly "het up" on a pending political issue. His listeners no more realized the passing time than he. Suddenly the Colonel stopped, looked at his watch, jumped up and said: "Now I'm in for it, all right. Promised to meet Mrs. Roosevelt at the dentist's at three, and it's nearly four. My welcome awaits me," he ended.

"Handles you rough, does she?" I asked.

"My boy, that's just it. She doesn't," he replied. "If she did, there would be something to it. But she never says a word. I do all the talking when I explain. She just looks at me with that indulgent smile that she has. The most maddening instrument I know of, because it really says nothing and yet is the most eloquent thing I have ever seen. Well, so long: I'm off for what's coming to me."

And with the grin of a school-boy, the Colonel bolted into a taxi to receive "the indulgent smile!"

VII

The family was at luncheon at Sagamore Hill, but Mrs. Roosevelt was in New York for the day. The Colonel spoke of a certain picture, and, turning to one of his children at the table: "Run up into your mother's room, will you," he asked, "and bring me that picture?"

"I can't. Mother's room is locked, you know," came the answer.

"That's right, too," he answered, and, turning to my wife, he said: "Clever woman, that! Do you know what she does? Locks her room when she goes out, and takes the key with her. Why? We used to go up and get things that we wanted while she was away, and about everything you want in a home, you know, like that picture, is in mother's room. She said she never knew her room when she came back, and never could find anything, because somebody had carried it off and forgotten to bring it back. So now she never goes out but she turns the key in the door; says it's the only way she can be sure to recognize her room when she comes back!" And the Colonel's face fairly beamed! "Clever woman, that," he repeated.

VIII

Not only had the Colonel the highest respect for his wife's judgment, but he was also quick to respond to her slightest wish. It was, in every sense, a case of her

And later, as we were talking about the matter which had called me to him, I saw him jot down on a pad the title and author of the book.

I had to return the next day to get his answer to the matter under consideration, and carried the book with me, explaining that I had finished it and could leave it with him.

"Oh, I've read it," he said, with a smile. "Sent out for it after you left yesterday, and finished it last evening. It's interesting, but here is where I think he's wrong," and instantly he was off into an analysis of the book showing the most careful reading and thought!

X

On another occasion I happened to be at luncheon when Guglielmo Marconi was present. After luncheon we went into the large room filled with the Colonel's hunting trophies, and the talk turned on Italian literature, the Colonel talking with Senator Marconi. For over an hour the talk went on, until the Colonel was told that his tennis partners were waiting for him.

As the Italian senator left the room to go out on the porch, he took a handkerchief, wiped his forehead, took a deep sigh, and said to me: "That's the most amazing experience I've had for a long time. I thought I knew my Italian literature and history. But that man actually cited book after book that I've never heard of, much less read. He's going to keep me busy for some time just following him in his Italian reading."

XI

It was this marvellously wide reading that made Theodore Roosevelt undoubtedly the most interesting man in American life. He had the added gift of remembering everything that he read,—and on the instant, no matter how quickly he shifted the drift of talk.

I was returning to Philadelphia from New York one afternoon when I was attracted to a large crowd in the waiting-room. Going over to ascertain the cause, I reached the fringe of the crowd just as a lane parted with myself standing in the very centre and with Colonel Roosevelt at the other end, coming toward me. Instantly he saw me, and when he got near enough there came his greeting: "Hello! Going to Philadelphia? So am I. Rather to Scranton. Let's go together. Making this train now."

"What was the trouble in there?" I asked.

"Oh, the usual thing," he answered. "A lot of reporters got after me, so I took them in there, and we talked politics."

"By the way," I said, "if you're going to Philadelphia, why isn't this the chance for you to jump in my car, go down to the office and see those antique Chinese rugs?" Some weeks before I had told him of some precious Chinese rugs I had gotten out of an old temple.

"Can't, my dear fellow," he returned. "Have just ten minutes to make my connection for Scranton. But I remember what you told me about those rugs, and I want to see them. They were the blue and white variety, weren't they, with the butterfly motif? Which dynasty did you say they belonged to?"

And all the way to Philadelphia, holding me even for five minutes on the platform before he bolted for his train to Scranton, I got the most varied and illuminating information about ancient rugs I have ever listened to. Not only did he have the different motifs of the Chinese rugs mentally catalogued by dynasties, but he widened the topic until it embraced Persian rugs, the Bokhara variety and the relation of the old Japanese rug-makers to the original Chinese workers.

And thus did his mind shift from politics to antique rugs and find relief in the change! For, as he said as he left me: "By Jove, this has been refreshing—this talk about rugs. I'll come and look over yours. Just keen to see 'em. Must be beauties. Then we'll talk some more."

And then came the astonishing and parting word: "Do you know, I must read up on rugs!" I wondered what was left for him to read.

XII

Theodore Roosevelt had a wonderful way of giving new courage and leading you back into the right path.

When the Pure Food Bill was before Congress, I wanted to find out the position which the Speaker of the House would take. So I sought him, and it did not take me long to ascertain that the measure would receive scant encouragement at his hands. "No one wants it," said the Speaker to me, "except a few cranks. It will never pass the House—not if I can help it," he ended.

I went to the White House and told the President of my interview with Speaker Cannon. He laughed.

"The trouble with you," he said, "is that you're barking up the wrong tree. Joe Cannon can't see this measure, not until he is made to see it, and only the pressure of public sentiment will make him see it. You go back home, work up and crystallize public sentiment, and let that make itself felt upon Congress and the Speaker. You're wasting your time here in Washington. Joe Cannon is all right—when he sees. But you want to take men for what they are. If I wanted an expert opinion on a Persian rug, I wouldn't send for Joe Cannon, you know. So don't you bother with him on this question *now*. He is sincere when he says there's no public sentiment on this question. He can't feel a thing when it's in the air. You've got to visualize a thing for him. Go ahead and do it."

XIII

A man wrote to me not long ago and asked if I did not think that Theodore Roosevelt's egotism was the chief blemish in his character. I do not think that Theodore Roosevelt was an egotist. Many thought so, but none who knew and understood him. He had a true measure of his capacities: an absolute belief in that what he did was right, and a confidence in his convictions. But that is not egotism. It is a long cry from confidence in one's self and one's actions to egotism. Theodore Roosevelt, too, had all the qualities of leadership, and that fact always put him in the centre of the picture. He was not stubborn; he could follow as well as lead.

I have seen him, in conference, change an opinion in which he had firm faith when he entered the room. "By Jove," he would say, "I think there's something in what you say. I must think that over," and a note would follow in a day or two: "You're right about that. I was wrong." That is not the quality of the egotist.

"I am going to keep your letter," he wrote me once, "for my children and grandchildren. They will hear me knocked often enough after I'm gone, and it won't hurt them to find here and there a rose among the many eggs!"

When he wrote his monthly department of "Men" for me, I had occasion, early in my association, to edit his work and omit some portions in order that his article might fit into the space allowed for it.

"Do you mind?" I wrote him.

"Not at all," came his quick answer. "You're the doctor. Cut out what you think can best be dropped. Of course, you'll pick on my pet argument and drop that, I know. But that's inevitable. Cut or drop— only don't change a phrase or alter my meaning. When a fellow does that, I explode."

At another time he said: "I know I have a wretched style in writing, jerky and unpleasant, sometimes hard to read. But that's me, and you'll have to stand for it."

These are not the opinions of an egotist!

"Do you know," I heard him say once, "I missed it when I didn't study vocal placement. I wonder how I ever get a speech across. I have everything against me that a man can have. Ever think of that? My appear-

ance, my manner, my voice, my delivery, my enuncia-
tion,—everything!"

These are not the mental processes of the egotist!

XIV

An egotist always digs his own grave. Theodore
Roosevelt reared a monument.

SIXTEEN:

THE JOYS OF THE ROAD AND THE ROSTRUM

"Oh, that men would learn that the true speaker is he who speaks only when he has something to say."

PLUTARCH

Respectfully dedicated to those who have experienced these annals and many more, and to whose hardy bravery in persisting in the rôle of the lecturer I pay obeisance.

"Think all you speak; but speak not all you think; Thoughts are your own: your words are so no more."

DELAUNE

THE JOYS OF THE ROAD AND THE ROSTRUM

I

THE point now came in my working life when offers came to appear on the lecture-platform. I was foolish enough to be attracted. I say foolish because I can conceive of no more dismal existence than to go from city to city and lecture. But I did not think so then, and the nearest approach I ever had to a feeling of fear came to me at my first public lecture. It was really acute nervousness. But it came close to the line of fearsomeness. The reason that fear actually did not possess me came from a confidence I felt that I had inherited the gift of my lawyer-forbears and I believed that once I had been plunged into the sea of public-speaking I would be able to find myself. It so came out, but I shall never forget the plunge. I had spoken little in public: practically not at all, and I wanted to "try it on the dogs" in some small place before a small audience. This latter chance was promised me by my lecture manager. But I did not know the wiles of lecture managers then. My first distinct feeling of nervousness was when I reached the theatre where I was to speak and saw more people going in than I thought would comprise the entire audience; I wondered how many had already entered.

"Isn't this rather a large theatre?" I cautiously asked my manager, as we rode past the theatre to go down the alley to the stage door.

"Oh, no," he confidently assured me, "quite medium-sized, in fact. Very easy to speak in, too. The audience won't trouble you."

But the audience did trouble me a good deal!

II

My first shock came when I was being conducted over the stage by the presiding officer. The stage was so filled that only a narrow lane had been left for us to walk through, and when I sat down, those nearest to me were but a few feet away! There was a cramped space for the reading desk and a place for the speaker!

I looked out into the auditorium, and faced a sea of twenty-three hundred faces! An icy cold perspiration came out all over me. The presiding officer turned to me and said for my delectation: "Certainly a flattering audience."

"Yes," I said weakly, and to myself I wished that either the audience or I were at home!

Then my inquiring mind came to my rescue, and I began to wonder why so many persons had come. What did they expect? Wonder began to turn into surprise and then to amazement.

At that point it might have gone into fear when I heard the presiding officer speak my name and I saw him, as if in a blur, retreat from the desk. It meant that my moment had come! Mechanically I arose and received the first salvo of applause that had ever come to me. It was a curious feeling. They were applauding *me!* The moment consumed in the applause was my saving grace: it gave me a chance to find myself.

Then silence,—and that first fearful moment in a lecture that every lecturer knows when he speaks the first word was upon me! It is a situation such as a man might wish for his worst enemy!

This supreme moment was disconcerting enough to a novice, but——

Just then my attention was attracted to a couple sitting in the second row who gave me one wild, terrified look and, reaching under their chairs, got their hats and marathoned up the aisle and out! Then, another couple in another part of the house followed suit. Three others went out, and then the same thing happened in the balcony. I had not spoken a word. It could not be my voice. What was it? What was the matter with my appearance? One look was enough for those folks: they never stopped for even one word.

But I had to begin,—and so begin I did!

Then, it seemed to me as if at least one hundred persons walked out of that theatre in the next few moments. What with my mind on my lecture and on the retreating mass, as it seemed to me, the beginning of that lecture was not what you might call auspicious. Not until after the lecture was the mystery of the marathonites explained: not one hundred, as I thought I saw, but fourteen persons had left the theatre. That gave me the first sense of relief! Their leaving was due to the fact that my lecture had sold out so quickly that the theatre management had removed from the "boards" outside the building the posters announcing me, and had substituted a liberal display of the posters of a theatrical attraction which needed "boosting" and was to appear the following evening. The disappearing fourteen had seen the theatrical billboards and had not noticed the date. They had come to see "a show" and not to hear a man talk! Hence their quick exodus to the box-office to get their money refunded.

III

I have always felt that this first lecture, although as a whole it went off successfully, really cured me of any further desire to lecture. Still, we had to go on. My wife was with me and, considering it an injustice upon her to be compelled to listen to the same lecture over and over again, I determined to put this test of wifely devotion on a business basis, and promised to give her a liberal share of each fee for each lecture she attended (all the time knowing, of course, that she would in the final settlement receive all the fees anyway). She attended them all, and, although she never complained, it must have been a deadly monotonous experience for her. But to such lengths will a devoted wife go!

IV

Being a New Englander, her indelible association with Thanksgiving Day was, of course, the turkey. We were in Saint Louis on Thanksgiving eve, and on Thanksgiving night I was to lecture at Sedalia, Missouri. We were on the cars all of Thanksgiving Day and such a dish as turkey was missing on the menu of a Western buffet car. All that cold, gray day we travelled in high hopes of a hot Thanksgiving dinner at Sedalia, only to find upon arrival at the hotel that the Thanksgiving meal had been served at noon and the only part of the turkey that was left were some turkey wings! At the close of the lecture, we were told that because of the holiday the treasurer had gone out of town, forgetting to sign a check for my fee, and would I object to receiving it in cash? I would not, and, to my amazement, I received it in silver dollars! Nothing was given us in which to carry the silver load. So we brought our handkerchiefs into requisition, filled our pockets and, overweighted with our treasure, we sought our hotel! A cheerless Thanksgiving was it for one New England born!

Kansas City was our next stopping-place, and there I lectured to the accompaniment of a gathering abscess in a tooth, with which I suffered for the next seventy-two hours before it could be lanced. The only single reaction I could see that I got from my lecture, delivered in acute suffering, was the published opinion of a newspaper reporter that I wore the highest collar ever seen in Kansas City, and that I seemed uneasy!

I was uneasy all right!

V

I now sent word to my manager that I was pretty well tired of lecturing and to cancel as many of the remaining engagements as he could. But the lecture at Saint Joseph had already been postponed to suit the convenience of my gathering abscess, and there we journeyed only to find that I was so weak from the pain of three days that when I arose it was to find that I could hardly stand. Worse still, when I was ready to begin I found my memory playing me a trick, and I could not remember a word of the address. I shot an appealing look to the stage-box where the constant and faithful listener was seated. She quickly divined my plight and pointed to the inside pocket of my coat in which she had thoughtfully placed my manuscript. But the torture of that standing posture for an hour and a half was ample warrant for the newspapers' the next day commenting on my "nervous habit" of continually shifting from one foot to another, and of putting my "hands first in one pocket and then in another," although I never could quite make out how the reporter saw me put both of my hands in any one of my pockets!

VI

There was an engagement at Nashville which could not be broken, owing to the lateness of the desired cancellation, so thence we went next, only to lecture in a vast circular auditorium, like a skating-rink, in which the platform was in the centre of the hall, and the speaker had, like an acrobat, to spin around and talk first to one section and then to another. The evening there was enlivened by three accommodating women who, undoubtedly made dizzy with my gyrations, successively fainted, and had to be carried out. There was certainly nothing in my lecture to cause fainting spells, because by this time I was so thoroughly tired of delivering the same lecture over and over again that I delivered it perfunctorily, my one thought being to deliver it for the last time, which I did a few evenings thereafter with such a zest and gusto that the newspapers said that I was "in my happiest mood." I was!

The cruelest blow, however, was still to come when, upon arriving home, we found that our son, then sixteen months old, had forgotten his mother and refused to go to her when she reached out her arms, and it was fully two days before the acquaintance could be renewed!

That was the straw that broke the back of the lecture idea, and we decided then and there to keep off the road.

VII

The only interesting echo of the tour was when, from that inner confine of her blouse in which a woman can deposit so many mysterious articles, my wife drew out a wad of bank-notes,—the loot of the tour! This wad was so large and pretentious that the idea occurred to us to try the test we had so often heard about of placing a Bible in one hand and money in the other and the choice by a child indicated its future character!

Carefully taking her Bible in her right hand and the wad of "the root of all evil" in her left hand, the mother proudly held out both to her young hopeful,—who lost not a single moment in choosing the evil root! But I always contended that the test was not fair, since the Bible had a very much worn cover and the bank-notes were new and of a vivid green. It is the artistic nature which, with new eyes looking out upon a world, seizes upon the colorful note and declares thereby a soul attuned to beauty!

VIII

Speaking of nervousness at a first lecture, the story has never reached print, I think, of the first lecture delivered by Artemus Ward. I have it from one of a com-

pany of five young newspaper men, one of whom was
Ward, whose habitual custom it was to dine together
each evening at an up-town restaurant in New York.
These young men were all making their way in journalism, and their favorite topic was, naturally, their future
careers. Ward, whose real name was Charles Farrar
Browne, soon began to outstrip his companions in reputation by his inimitable humor. One evening the "table"
suggested to Browne that since he was so rapidly achieving a reputation, there was capital in it and he should
enter the lecture field. Browne was very timid, and became alarmed even at the thought.

"Impossible," he said. "Couldn't possibly face an
audience. I would have a mouth full of teeth and nothing else."

His friends kept at him, however, evening after evening. Weeks passed by, when one evening Browne surprised the "table" by saying he had written part of a
lecture, and would they listen to it? He called it "The
Babes in the Wood." Browne read, and his friends encouraged and suggested. There was more to encourage
than to criticize, and so the would-be lecturer was stimu-
lated to go on. It was not long thereafter that Browne
announced that he had finished the lecture, had entered
his name with a lecture-bureau, and he would read the
manuscript to the "table" verbatim. The following
week Browne announced he had received his first "date":
he was to speak before the Mercantile Library of Brooklyn. But while he laughed, it was evident that he was
anything but happy over the prospect. As the date
drew near, his unhappiness became marked.

"My hands will shake too much if I read my manuscript," he announced, "and if I commit the thing to memory I'll forget it when I face the audience. How else can I do it?"

It was finally agreed that he was to commit the lecture, and if his memory failed him he would have the manuscript in his pocket, and could lay it on the desk and read without holding it.

"But I would never remember I had it in my pocket, and couldn't get it out before that audience even if I remembered it," he said in despair.

This seemed to stamp the experiment with every prospect of failure.

"Why not do this?" finally suggested one of the company. "Commit the lecture to memory: if you forget it, let it go: have a lot of your stories ready in your mind and tell them instead of the lecture. You can tell stories all right."

This plan seemed to give Browne courage. "Yes," he agreed, "I think I could tell stories where I couldn't think of a connected lecture. It's a good anchor to the windward in any event."

IX

The fateful evening came, and the five journeyed to Brooklyn together, where they found a packed house,— a fact which added materially to Browne's discomfort. When he appeared on the platform it was plainly evident that he was nervous, and he was not a bit calmer when he rose to begin. He looked at his four friends seated in a box with a look of despair. Failure seemed to be stamped on every line of his face.

What Browne predicted was exactly what happened. He announced the title of his lecture, and then forgot how it began. He made an attempt to lift his hand to the inside pocket of his coat, but that hand acted as if it had received a stroke. It never got farther than the reading desk. This he valiantly clutched, and then told a story. With a wan smile, he said he felt just like the story of the dismal railway station at New Haven, a place then known to every traveller as almost infernal in darkness, with scarcely a gaslight in it. On a beautiful autumn morning, with the air as clear as crystal, said Browne, a very bright little girl with her mother was riding on a train going to New Haven. The mother and child kept up a running talk, the little girl pointing out various objects in the wonderfully beautiful and brilliant landscape which they passed. Suddenly the train entered the cavern-like station at New Haven, the child grew fearful, and the passengers heard the little voice in terror cry out "Mother, is this Hell?"

The story captivated the audience, many of whom apparently knew the station. They broke into such laughter and applause that it visibly encouraged Browne. His face lighted up, he looked toward the box with his friends, with a look of triumph on his face, and for an hour and a quarter kept his audience in a gale of laughter with his stories. He never again referred to his lecture except at the close when, after one of his stories, he explained "that was what I would have said if I had not intended to lecture on 'The Babes in the Wood'."

The idea of a lecturer announcing the subject of a lecture and then never referring to it was heralded by the newspapers the following morning as one of Artemus Ward's best jokes! Ward never said a word, nor did his four friends. He destroyed the manuscript of his lecture, and his talk on "The Babes in the Wood," with no babes or woods in it, became his most famous and successful lecture.

X

Thus from an accident came a success. How frequently this is so! A success so often begins by being something else.

SEVENTEEN:

MY MOST UNUSUAL EXPERIENCE

"'Tis strange, but true; for truth is always strange,—
stranger than fiction."

BYRON

MY MOST UNUSUAL EXPERIENCE

I

SPEAKING of experiences, a man is so often asked to tell the greatest single experience in his life. I think it is difficult, if not impossible, for any one, if he has lived an average life as I have, to say that a single experience is the greatest. There are unusual experiences, however, that stand out from others, and of these "the most unusual" experience is one which follows.

In telling of this experience, I mean that it shall not be applied personally, for I merely happened to be the recipient of the confidence, but rather as pointing to a quality in the American man that I, as a foreigner by birth, am quicker to note than the American-born who takes the point invariably for granted. This is the peculiar position of the knight-errant which the American man holds in the estimation of the American woman. Almost never is this fact commented upon in America. It is, as I say, taken for granted. In Europe it is constantly pointed out. The American woman instinctively feels that when she is in doubt or distress she can appeal to an American man, stranger though he may be, and she is certain that his response will come quick and sure. The American woman's confidence is different from that existing in any other nation. It may be said, and perhaps with some justice, that the American man has spoiled his womankind. But in doing so he has certainly won her confidence, as the main incident here told will prove to a remarkable extent.

239

II

It is no reflection upon the honest intent of the man of foreign birth that his women do not show the same confidence in him: in all likelihood, he is equally worthy of it. It is simply that, as the English say, "it isn't done, you know." I remember how often my father and mother spoke of this characteristic of American life, and I would hear it discussed when friends from the other side of the water would be at dinner with us.

My father stoutly defended the condition as against an occasional accusation of unwarranted freedom and dangerous license. I recall his remark on one of these occasions: "It isn't a case of allowing freedom to the American woman; she knows nothing else. She is trained to the idea that she can trust her men, and that they are always ready to serve her if she needs their help."

It is nevertheless a factor in American life that is of constant surprise to foreigners whose women are trained to ask and receive of their husbands or fathers or brothers, but who would never dream of asking a service of a man beyond those relations,—certainly not in public. But so frequently does it happen here that we have ceased to regard it as anything but the usual courtesy which a man can show a woman who needs assistance at his hands.

III

But to the story in point. I am free to confess at the outset that it was in my case, as it would be in that of any man, exceptional; the unusual kind which passes as plausible in a romance. But it was not unusual if we bear in mind, as I say, the confidence of the American woman in the traditional qualities of knight-errantry of the American man. At least it is true, and I tell it here as an instance of the ultimate confidence which the American woman feels sure she can repose in the men of her soil,—a torch which it should be the pride of every American to pass from man to man. It is also told here to show on what a slender thread the difference some- times hangs on "we would and we would not," and how true again was Shakespeare when he wrote "How far that little candle throws his beams."

It happened upon a visit to England. I had been spending the day with Sir Arthur Sullivan, the composer, at his home at Walton-on-Thames when he suggested that I should hear that evening some music he had written to a ballet which was then being given at one of the London music halls.

Sir Arthur had telegraphed the manager of the music hall to "take care" of me, and when I arrived he con- ducted me to a loge in the first balcony. It was the custom in this music hall to maintain a "promenade" at the back of this balcony where girls and women would walk back and forth, and they had the privilege of self- invitation to a loge where a man was alone. When the next "act" was on, and the theatre was dark, I was conscious that some one had entered the loge, and was sitting on the other side of the small table. I could dimly see that it was a woman.

IV

When the lights went on I looked into the face of a very pretty girl in the twenties, who regarded me with a demureness that was unexpected in such a place, and, to add to my surprise, whose face became suffused with blushes, as she said in a low voice in answer to my "Good evening":

"You do not mind my sitting here?"

"Not at all," I answered. "That is your privilege,—here, you know."

"Yes," she answered, "I know, but—. You are an American, are you not?"

I assured her, and then she said she had been sitting in another loge across the theatre (where I had noticed her before the act began).

"Yes, I saw you," I encouraged her.

"I was *so* keen to talk with some one from the States, as they say here, and somehow I felt as if I could come over and you would understand when I told you I was from the States, too."

She then told me the Western town where she had lived.

"And you have been in London long?" I asked.

"Three months," she replied, as a cloud swept over her face.

"Not happy ones?" I ventured.

"Anything but." She was barely audible now.

"How did you come to London, and why?" I asked encouragingly.

"May I tell you my story?" she brightly asked. "I

would dearly love to do so if it wouldn't bore you," she queried. I could see that she was actually suffering from repression.

I assured her I would be interested rather than bored and then she told how her mother had passed away: her father had married again, and it was the old story of the daughter finding no place in the home of the step-mother. Finally, she took her savings and came to England where, in a new country, she felt she might get a new start.

"At what?" I asked.

"I learned to sew with that care and thoroughness with which they teach girls in a convent, and I never dreamed I would find difficulty in putting this knowledge to some use," she answered.

But she had fallen upon a period of economic depression in London; the shops were laying off hands. She had advertised, but households were economizing, and were not taking on seamstresses. "And so it has gone," she continued, "week after week, until a few days ago I realized I had come to the end of my money. I tried with a renewed effort to find some place, but try as I might I met only with disappointment."

V

"And now here?" I asked.

"Yes," and the face again became suffused. "There was nothing left me but my appearance," and she looked out with an appeal that was dumb-like in its absolute sincerity. "It is perhaps hard for a man to realize that a girl can come to a point where nothing else remains.

But it is the experience of hundreds. No girl takes up this life from choice. It isn't the feminine nature. We are driven to it as a last resort. So I came here this evening."

"Your first evening?" I asked in surprise.

"Yes," she answered. "With the exception of the man with whom I sat over there in the box, you are the first one I have spoken to here. I felt somehow that I could come to you as an American."

"You certainly can," I said, and I purposely put a conviction in my voice so as to invite her confidence. It brought me the most grateful look that I have ever seen on a human face. "Perhaps it will put you at your ease," I added, "if I tell you that I am a friend of Sir Arthur Sullivan and that I came here to hear his music and for no other purpose."

With a smile that I shall never forget she leaned across the table and said, "I believe that. Oh," she said, clutching her hands, "I am *so* glad I came over here."

VI

At that moment there appeared in the curtained doorway the man whom the girl had left in the other loge. He was the type of Frenchman that every man knows,— and despises. In broken English, and with that low bow of servility that is so commonly mistaken for politeness, he turned to me and said: "This young lady was my guest. She excused herself for a moment from my loge. I come to escort her back. I am a gentleman from Paris," and then reaching out a hand to the girl he said "Come." The girl shrank back and looked at me.

"Do you wish to return?" I asked.

"No, no, *please*," with a pitiful emphasis.

The "gentleman from Paris" was just about to go off into that accustomed paroxysm of gesticulation so common to his race. "One moment," I said; "there is no cause for excitement." Just then the manager of the music hall passed the loge, and I beckoned to him. "This man," I said, "does not seem to understand that this young lady is in my loge as my guest. He is about to become excited. Will you kindly take him with you, and make it clear to him?" Two strong English hands summarily closed the curtains, and we saw no more of "the gentleman from Paris": he never even returned to his loge!

"He will not annoy you," I assured her, as words of gratitude poured forth. "Now, may I ask you a question or two?"

She nodded. "Any number."

"Would you like to return to America?" I asked.

"Oh, so much," she replied eagerly. "Not to my home, but if I could only get back to familiar ways and people, I am sure I could get along so much better. But——"

"I know" I assented.

VII

Then I explained that I was sailing for New York the day after the morrow: that I would gladly secure for her a comfortable second-class cabin on the same boat and that I knew of a friend living near New York in a beautiful home who had exactly the position of seamstress which she could fill: that to give her assurance I would cable my friend at once, and bring the answer to her the following evening if she would take dinner with me. Meanwhile I would secure her passage.

As I left the girl at the door of her lodging, the look she gave me and the grasp of her hand assured me I had not made a mistake. It was a genuine case met on the very edge of the precipice.

The following evening I brought her the cable: "Just what I want. Place waiting." I never had dinner with a happier person.

During the ocean passage we greeted each other daily over the railings between the first and second cabins. Upon arriving at New York the finishing touch was given the strange adventure by my friend and her husband meeting us at the dock. I went home with the party, and that evening we rehearsed the wonderful experience.

"Just *at* the precipice," added the girl of her own volition as I finished. When I left her that evening she held my hand for a moment and, with a face radiant with happiness, showed she had read the books I had given her for the ocean trip by the simple, but oh! so apt quotation: "I were but little happy, if I could say how much."

VIII

There she remained for months "with every day a joy," as she wrote, and my friend assuring me "we have taken Eleanor right into the family. She is no longer the seamstress, but one of us."

Until a day when there came to me a clear-eyed up-standing young lawyer out of the West: the type that you know the moment you look at is destined to go far. Handing me a note, he briefly said "I have been asked by Eleanor to bring you this note," and in the note I read:

"I am sending Henry H—— to you. He has asked me to be his wife. I love him dearly. But before I give him my answer I have told him he must see you and hear the chapter in my life which you know so well. I want him to know this, and then he can again ask me if he chooses. But I thought it better that it should be told him from man to man. After he leaves you, will you wire me your impression? I am *so* happy; my cup runneth over."

It was easy to tell him, and I ended with "Make any difference?"

"Why, of course not," was his positive reply. "Why should it?"

We shook hands, and as he was going out he asked with a laughing face: "You will wire your impression?"

"Immediately," I returned, "and I think it will recommend you for the job."

IX

A beautiful wedding they gave her, and then came a period when she reared her family: years of such happiness, she would write "that it sometimes makes me afraid, and I wonder if it isn't all a dream."

There came a lapse of years when I heard only intermittently. Then, two years ago, a card was brought in to me, and in a moment her eldest son stood before me, giving me his eyes in that direct manner that speaks such volumes to a father.

"I am on my way to New York," he explained, "and mother asked me to stop off to tell you that I have just been elected on the Independent ticket to our State Legislature as its youngest member. You know how mothers are about such things," he added.

I knew how one mother must be!

"And your father and the others?" I asked.

He gave the family news. The father had become the leading lawyer of his city and was twice elected Mayor. The eldest son had gone into his father's office, and now he was off to the Legislature. Father was beginning to pick and choose in his practice and "play around with mother." The next boy had now just gone into the office. "Bob" was at Yale, and the youngest at "prep" school. "Mother had this taken for you," he finished, and I looked at the photograph of one of those splendidly typical American families which form the bulwark of this land and keep it steady and true.

"And all making good," I commented.

"Because of mother," he assented. "She is back of all of us: made father what he is, and now is making us." And then, as a wonderful light came into his eyes: "She is the finest woman in the world."

X

I looked after him as he went out of the door of my office, and the wonderful tribute to the mother came back to me: "She is the finest woman in the world." Five men there were who believed that!

What a crown for a woman!

EIGHTEEN:

A GENTLEMAN AMONG THE NATIONS OF THE WORLD

I am grateful for the opportunity afforded me here, as an American in heart and deepest feeling, of giving to those who may read after me, what follows in the next few pages. It is one way in which I may help to discharge, even in a small way, the debt which I owe to both of my countries; the one which I honor as the land of my birth; the other for which I feel such a deep allegiance as the land of my adoption.

> *"Breathes there the man with soul so dead*
> *Who never to himself hath said,*
> *This is my own, my native land!*
> *Whose heart has ne'er within him burn'd*
> *As home his footsteps he hath turn'd*
> *From wandering on a foreign strand?"*
>
> SCOTT

A GENTLEMAN AMONG THE NATIONS OF THE WORLD

I

I was much interested when one of my sons put this question to me: "You were born in the Netherlands, and yet you are an American citizen. Suppose a war should occur between the two countries, on which side would you fight?" I recall the intent look which both gave me as they waited for my answer.

Naturally I replied that such a contingency was rather remote, that I would be fairly old for service of any kind, but if such a contingency did arise I would cross that bridge when I came to it. Of course, they expected me to say, without hesitation, "Why, America, of course," and I felt that they were disappointed when I did not. They felt as if I had side-stepped the question. It was quite right that, being American-born, they should wish their father to give such a direct answer, which, of course, in his heart he did.

II

The point which American boys born of foreign parents cannot understand, however, and it is natural they should not, is that when a man is born in one country and adopts another, he always is and remains a man of two countries. I have heard my boys express themselves in no uncertain terms with regard to those Ameri-

cans who, although born here, leave America and reside
permanently abroad, forgetting they were ever Americans. "Poor specimens" they have called them. They
are. There is something fundamentally wrong with a
man who ceases to hold the land of his birth in affectionate remembrance, or who fails to feel a pride in it
and gets no thrill when he returns to his native shores.
I never want to lose the thrill which I feel when I enter
the Hook of Holland on the steamship from the United
States,—that tugging at the heart-strings and that swelling up within me when I catch the first glimpse of my
native shores. I consider myself no less a good American
because of those emotions. For, by the same token, one
of the few sights that can make of me an early riser is
the first view of American shores upon my return.

I know my boys have been puzzled when, in signing
after the word "Nationality" in some document requir-
ing that declaration I invariably write "Netherlands."
What else could I write? Nationality connotes nativity,
—the land of birth! Not the land of adoption or of
citizenship. English declaration papers are far more
careful in this respect than are similar papers with us.
One almost invariably finds on all such papers in Great
Britain and Canada the distinction between "nationality" and "citizenship." Some friends keenly resent
my proclaiming myself a Dutchman and say "No, you're
not: you're an American." They think they are teaching me a lesson in patriotism. But that is unintelligent
patriotism, for it has neither the basis of truth nor of
force. A man always remains what he was born! Not
in feeling or in spirit, perhaps, but in fact. Some of the

more radically-inclined call this a species of "hyphenated-Americanism." We heard a great deal of this during the Great War, and it became a synonym for disgrace.

III

I remember very well Colonel Roosevelt's vehement denunciation of "the hyphenated American." Of course, we know the type he had in mind. But as he warmed up to his subject he became more and more all-inclusive and less and less discriminative, forgetting the excellent maxim that "all generalizations are false, including this one."

I was talking one day with Colonel Roosevelt when, for the moment forgetting his visitor, he launched forth into a tirade on "the hyphenated American." When he got through, I asked him first whom he meant by the phrase, and whether he intended it to be all-inclusive.

"I do," he snapped out. "I am for the 100 per cent American—the man who is American all through, warp and woof."

"Birth, too?" I put in.

"Birth, too," he returned.

"Then, Colonel," I asked, "where do I come in, where does your forebear come in?"

"Oh, I don't mean you, you know that. But what do you mean by my forebears?" he jerked out.

"Your Dutch forebear who, born in the Netherlands as I was, came over here and became an American? You are here, are you not, because of him? Suppose he had not come; suppose he had chosen to remain in the Netherlands, wouldn't America be minus a few Roosevelts,—in fact, all of them, including yourself? He was a 'hyphenated American'; a pretty fine one from what you have told me. His prototype is everywhere in the United States to-day; you eliminate him with one sweep; you eliminate some of the finest men in America to-day who are giving yeoman service to American arms. The trenches are full of them: so are the ranks of the officers on land and on sea. How can you be, as you say, all-inclusive, and say that an American is an American only if he is 100 per cent American all through—'birth, too'? Can a man only be an American if he is born here? Where do you go back to with that sort of argument? Back to one race: the American Indian, who is of course the only true American. All the rest of us had somewhere a hyphenated forebear, as you had. You put yourself under your own ban."

It was not always possible to say as much as this in an argument with the redoubtable Colonel, but he listened intently as I spoke, and I managed to get it in. He saw that I keenly felt his all-inclusiveness and resented it; in fact, it had been made apparent to him that others resented it deeply, as he afterward acknowledged to me. "You don't get me," he said, "and neither do they." But before I left he said to me with his wonderful smile, "Of course, you are right, that's the irritating part of a Dutchman,—he is nearly always right."

IV

We cannot be too careful of our use of the phrase "100 per cent American." It is obvious enough, perhaps, what we mean, but we are apt to give offense to thousands of our citizens who are, in every respect, as loyal and as good Americans as any of those who were born here,— sometimes even a shade better, as their lives and achievements have demonstrated. The history of the people of the United States would read vastly different if those of foreign birth but of American adoption had not written some of their deeds on its pages. Nor is it lacking in true Americanism to point out this salient fact. It may be well within the nature of a distinct service to those who are apt to forget it.

As a matter of fact, very few of us correctly understand what we mean by this "Americanism" and "Americanization" that we become so wrought up about. We think of Americanism as something that we can imbibe, understand and practice in our lives only if we are born in the United States of America. We interpret America as a place, a locality, and think that only those who are born within its borders can be true Americans in their lives and follow the spirit of Americanism in their achievements.

But America in the truest aspect, in the real sense, is not a place on the map only: to be an American is possible to others besides the man born within certain geographical boundaries. Americanism is not alone a matter of birth or ancestry.

The real America is an ideal—a vision yet to be fulfilled.

The real American is he who feels that ideal, makes it a part of himself—and does his share and makes his contribution to the attainment of the goal and the clear realization of the ideal, whether he be born in the United States or thousands of miles from its borders.

Americanism is of one's inner self: a God-given responsibility: a faith: a trust: a devotion to an ideal: a belief in one's fellow-men stronger than a belief in one's self: a tenacious, unswerving confidence in service.

V

Again, how many of us, born here or elsewhere, could qualify as a "hundred per cent American?" Scarcely one, because, in truth, there is no such American. Listen to the words of a typical western American editor, that vigorous type of the American who reads in the quiet seclusion of a small town, who thinks and reaches his conclusions with a careful perspective,—much truer than that of the man in a large city. That is the real American. I am quoting now the editor of the Rockville (Indiana) *Tribune,*—a small Main Street paper, if you will, but with an editor wielding a trenchant pen and seeing things with crystallike clearness.

"There is no such thing as a 'hundred per cent American'," says this American of the true type. "Most of us are doing right well if we can qualify as one-half per cent Americans. What is a hundred per cent American? Let us name a few things that none will deny as being among the attributes that define a hundred per cent American. He must first of all, before considering his own rights, have a higher regard for the rights of others; he must obey the laws—not the laws he chooses himself to obey and demands enforcement on others, but ALL the laws. He must never swear falsely to a tax return; he must never run his automobile on the public highway faster than the speed laws declare; he must observe whatever laws are made to preserve the sacredness of the Sabbath; his daily life, and particularly his nightly life, must be such as to cause his fellow citizens to respect him as a man of high morality. And above all, when it comes to casting stones, he must himself be without sin.

"To be 'one hundred per cent American' a man must be one hundred per cent Christian. He must always and everywhere observe the Golden Rule. He must put in practice the precepts of the Sermon on the Mount. In all sacred and profane history there never lived but one Man who could qualify as a hundred per cent American; and men who deny or abridge the rights of others for religion or race should remember that that Man was a Jew!"

VI

I would indeed be a poor offspring of my native land were I lacking in a feeling of the highest pride in that amazing people back of the dykes of the North Sea. It is not for nothing that so many Americans have pride in their Dutch ancestry and make such careful tracings in order to substantiate their claims, although in so many cases they have to go many generations back in order to verify the fact. Have you ever met an American who does not pride himself on a Dutch ancestry? A weak nation does not inculcate such feelings; it must have a historical background of remarkable achievement to engender such deep pride in the American who never loses an opportunity to show and express that satisfaction when he has even the slightest trace of Dutch blood in his veins. Such a land is not to be forgotten by one who was born in it and of its people. It is a wonderful quality of blood to have in one's veins.

VII

A friend asked Theodore Roosevelt if he knew a certain man with whom he was to be associated in large business transactions.

"Very well," answered Colonel Roosevelt.

"Can I depend upon him?" asked the friend.

"Depend upon him?" echoed the Colonel. "You certainly can. He's a Hollander. Do you know what that means?"

Colonel Roosevelt's remark will recur to many who have had occasion to visit the Netherlands.

VIII

I remember asking a Scheveningen hotel *portier* to change a bank-note of large dimensions. "Certainly," he replied: he would send the change to my room. Shortly a boy appeared bearing a tray heaped with bills and silver, the boy having his palm on the pile to prevent the bills from being blown away. The money must have felt good to the touch of a poor boy!

"Is that not rather a risky manner of sending money to guests?" I asked the *portier* afterward.

"Why do you think so, sir? What could happen to it?" he asked in complete astonishment. I took the veil of silence.

IX

"I owe you for six hours, I think," said an American to the Dutch driver of a victoria.

"Less one-half hour spent in harnessing, sir," was the quick response.

X

On the station at Basle, upon entering Switzerland, a party of tourists assembled some ten pieces of luggage and wondered what to do with it while the members went into the station for breakfast.

"Shall I look after these for you?" asked a station porter as he approached the party. The tourist conductor with the party looked the man over and asked: "You are a Hollander?"

"I am, sir," answered the man in Dutch.

"You will not leave this baggage?" he was asked.

"No, sir; I will be here with the baggage when you return," was his answer.

The conductor was reminded of the value of the contents of the luggage.

"I know," he replied; "but this man is a Hollander," and then, curiously enough, he asked the question of Colonel Roosevelt: "Do you know what that means? It means absolute honesty. He will do exactly as he says."

"I have travelled now for over thirty years," said the conductor later at the breakfast table. "I have been in every country in the world except the United States, and not only once, but twenty, thirty, forty times. I know the peoples of Egypt, of Asia, of Arabia, as I know those of every European country. And I say this to you: I would trust the native of no other country in the world as I would a Hollander."

"That is a high tribute," remarked a member of the party.

"The absolute truth," was his answer, "and every experienced traveller will tell you the same."

XI

One of the leading educational authorities in the Netherlands was asked to what extent and how the trait of honesty is taught in the public schools.

"Not at all—directly," was his answer. "Honesty is a national trait with the Hollander. It is deep-rooted, it is inherited. We do not have to teach it in the schools. We do not think the schools are the place for such teaching. That is for the home, and we can always rely upon the parents to implant those ethical ideas in the minds of their children.

"Of course," he continued, "I would not for a moment say there is no dishonesty in our land. That would be preposterous. But the Hollander is instinctively honest, and thousands live their lives and deal with their fellow men never thinking of two methods. To them there is only one. And, when you come to think of it, it simplifies life very much, doesn't it?"

XII

We hear a great deal nowadays about the need of nations' resting their international differences upon justice and international law. Let us not forget that in the Netherlands there is a nation which has invariably rested her case upon international law. With other nations at war, and reaching out for each other's territory, here is a nation which has retained every inch of her own soil and of her vast colonies, which are practically unknown to the average American, and she has kept inviolate her neutrality. It was a difficult and perilous thing to do during the last war, but she did it, and she met every question during that time and afterward upon the tenets of that international law which was first laid down by one of the greatest of her sons. Things move quietly among the sedate people of the Netherlands, but they move exceedingly sane and sure. There is a quiet manner, with a smile, in her people which is sometimes misunderstood as phlegmatic. But there is an alert mentality, with a quiet force underneath, which awakens when it is needed. The former Kaiser got a glimpse of this when on a visit to the Queen of the Netherlands, and in expounding the wonderful quality of certain picked troops, he said significantly: "Do you realize that my Prussian guards stand seven feet in their stockings?"

"Not quite tall enough," quietly answered Wilhelmina.

"How do you mean?" asked the Kaiser in surprise.

"When we open our dykes," cryptically answered the clear-thinking Queen, "the water is ten feet deep."

They think, do these people of the land back of the dykes. They must think, for thinking with them is what doing is with more powerful nations. Had the people of the Netherlands been without the capacity to think, there would be no Netherlands to-day. Some one has said that "the Dutch mind is too full for foam or sound." It is because of the mental capacity of her people to think, and think straight, that the nation stands where for decades she has stood,—quietly, but with complete confidence, looking the world in the face. Her colonies and her methods of administering those colonies are the envy of every nation on the earth; her coast line is coveted by all. Through diplomatic storms have both of these precious possessions gone, but always have these storms been weathered by a type of diplomacy which has the respect of every diplomat in the world. She has not protected her possessions with battleships, because she has practically none. But always has she rested her case with the tribunal of the law,—that desired goal to which all the nations of the world are now so surely tending.

XIII

My sons are fond of having their joke over their father's pride in the achievements of his people, and at the marvellous influence which their institutions have had upon the fundamental institutions of the United States. But as the history of America becomes more and more honestly written and given to boys, so larger and larger will loom the debt which this land owes to the Netherlands. The people of the Netherlands are proud of the fact that they were the source of so many of the institutions of this greatest of all countries on the earth to-day, but they are prouder of what the United States has done with them to bring them to their fullest

accomplishment. They have been quiet about it, and
have sought to set up no claims. It is not in the Dutch
to boast of their achievements. They invariably leave
that as they have left their past for history to record
and tell.

XIV

A national characteristic may well come in here for
record. It was told not long ago by Dr. A. J. Barnouw,
of Columbia University. In nearly every nation to-day
there is a book equivalent to the American volume of
Who's Who. The accuracy of this book depends upon
each person cited therein either to write his or her biography in brief or to contribute the facts. In the
Netherlands, a few years ago, a publisher decided that
his country should follow the lead of other nations and
have a Dutch *Who's Who*. Immediately he encountered
the national feeling that publicity is a state of exposure
that the Hollander shuns rather than seeks. The men
and women approached for the contemplated book found
something positively indecent in the inquisitive request
of a publisher that one should write his own life-story.
Finally sufficient co-operation was secured to publish
such a book, but it was obviously incomplete as a record. Then, the Dutch public would not buy it, and the
experiment was dropped. This national aversion in the
Dutch character to writing even a miniature account of
one's self explains the few books of memoirs or autobiographies which are found in Dutch literature. Even
where an autobiography is written and put away for
posthumous publication, there still comes the aversion

of the family and heirs to overcome, with the result that the work seldom reaches the public. And even were such a book published, it would be accepted with misgivings by the public and in all probability left on the shelves of the bookseller. Yet the Hollander will read, with avidity, the memoirs or autobiographies of the men and women of other nations: in fact, even of a Hollander, but only if he has left his native heath. The people of the Netherlands accepted *The Americanization of Edward Bok* as the most convincing proof of the thoroughness of the author's Americanization!

The American may regard such a national characteristic with surprise, and yet one cannot but view it with admiration.

XV

Let one read aright the history of these people behind the dykes, from authoritative sources, and surprise always grows as the realization comes home how little, in all her years of turmoil and conquest, she has asked of the world and how much she has given to it. No nation has asked so little; few nations have given more. Some one has given a very fine description of a gentleman as one who always gives more than he asks and takes. If we accept that definition, then it follows that the Kingdom of the Netherlands comes pretty close to being, by right of history, a gentleman among the nations of the world!

NINETEEN:

"WELL, I DIDN'T KNOW THAT!"

"Ah, yes," said the American, "possessions! Are they considerable?"

"Well," came the answer, "you Americans think in rather large terms, and I don't know whether you would consider large what we think of in that way. For instance, you are very fond of citing Texas as one of your states into which you could put several of the European countries, and not 'find them,' as you say."

"One of our pleasant little methods of comparison," said the American.

"Yes," said the Netherlander. "Well, suppose I use the same illustration: we could put Texas into one of our possessions and *you* couldn't 'find it.'"

"Really?" asked the American.

"Or, to carry the simile a little further," said the delegate, as he saw that the surprise extended to the entire group, "our possessions equal, in area, New York State, New England, the Middle Atlantic States, and nearly all the Middle West. We have a coast-line of three thousand, five hundred miles."

"Great Scott, man!" said the American, "how much population have you?"

"Almost one-half of the entire population of the United States: about forty-nine millions, and nearly seven millions in the Netherlands proper. You understand now why we are here?"

"I surely do"; and then, almost in a chorus came: "Well, I didn't know that!" And until midnight the delegate held the group in his description of the Dutch East and West Indies, in their area equal to over one-fifth of the entire area of Europe.

III

"I see you were born in Holland?" said a man to me recently.

"In the province of North Holland, yes," I answered.

"I meant the country of Holland."

"No, I couldn't have been born there," I replied; "there is no such country."

"No such country as Holland?"

"Not unless you are willing to have me call the United States by the name of Carolina, simply because there are two states in the Union of that name: North Carolina and South Carolina. The simile is, to a great extent, identical, except that the Carolinas never held the dominant position in the United States that the two Holland provinces in the Netherlands have held. There are two provinces: North Holland and South Holland; but there are also nine other provinces, just as the United States has forty-six other states. The President of the United States doesn't send a minister to Holland to be presented to the Queen of Holland."

"Where does he send him, then?"

"To be Minister to the Netherlands, for presentation to the Queen of the Netherlands. Take this atlas, and show me Holland," I answered.

Of course, he couldn't.

"Well, well," was the final answer, and then: "I certainly didn't know that. Then," with a ray of hope, "why the Holland-America Line of steamships?"

"Just a compromise to lack of American knowledge. Look at the flag on the ship, the towels, the cutlery, the bathmats, everywhere you will see the initials 'N. A. S. M.,' which, translated, mean 'Netherlands-America Steamship Company,' which is the actual title of the line."

IV

"Then how did the world 'Holland' come to be?" asked one of the party.

And the answer is interesting.

The time was—the world was a great deal younger, then—when the soil of the northwestern part of the Continent of Europe was still a wilderness. The three rivers—the Rhine, the Maas, and the Scheldt,—poured their waters into that part of the Atlantic Ocean now called the North Sea. The coast of what now are the southern and eastern parts of the Netherlands was already formed, but the northwestern part did not exist. On their way to the ocean, the rivers took with them clay and soil from the mainland, and deposited a great deal of this soil on their banks. For ages this went on, until the alluvial deposit built up, slowly but surely, a large piece of mainland, just as did the Nile in the Mediterranean. Along the coast beat the turbulent ocean, which, in turn, lashed the new mainland with sand, and built up great dunes and sand-banks. These protected the forming mainland, which consisted of nothing but the slime and muck of the rivers. And so, in time, there came to be a great morass. Here and there a bit of the slime showed above the surface, like an island; and, as time went on, these bits of mainland became larger, vegetation came out of the rich soil, and the rivers took different courses. The morass was beneath the level of the sea, and it seemed useless for any purpose.

Then there came along, one day, a man of Roman foresight and sturdiness, who concluded that the land could be drained by waterways, the sand dunes strengthened and used as protections from the sea. What the sea had in part created, he argued, it could be made to protect. In those days, as in these times, success came in "cans" and failures in "can'ts," as has been well said; and the sturdy new adventurer began to drain the land and strengthen the sand dunes. And others of the same type and vision followed his lead, and there began to arise a settlement of farms, the soil of which naturally had no superior in the world. Owing to the lowness of the land below the sea, the land came naturally to be known as land that lay in a hollow: hollow-land, in other words.

It is difficult, if not impossible, now, to trace accurately the derivation of the word Holland. Some historians contend that the word Hol originated in the word Holtland or Houtland, meaning Woodland, from the trees which rapidly sprang from the rich soil and wooded the land. Another derivation, and one accepted by many, is that the word Hol, meaning Hollow, came from the fact of the hollow lands. Be the exact derivation what it may, the Romans toiled, and brought a state into being; and, whatever its derivation, it was called Holland. All this land was in the most northerly part of the new mainland; and as the adventurers drained the soil next to the sea, the land back of them came into view, and there states sprang up. The next was more to the south, and this was the southerly part of the holland; one became known as North Holland and the other as South Holland, although the official differentiation did not take place until the nineteenth century.

This tract became the most powerful and the richest tract saved from the sea. Other communities, seventeen in number finally, came into being, and were given other names, until the entire vast tract, including what is now the Kingdom of Belgium, for the larger part being lowlands, became known to the French as *Les Pays Bas*, and to the Anglo-Saxon mind as the Nether [low] lands. But the definition of Holland for the originally reclaimed tract persisted; and slowly but surely the word Holland came down the ages as applying to the country, and not to a section, despite the fact that, after the Eighty Years' War, the seven northern states (including Holland) were welded into a republic called the United Netherlands. But custom is strong: the word Holland was shorter than Netherlands; Holland it erroneously became, and remained.

V

There is also a singular confusion in the mind of the average American in his indiscriminate use of the word Dutch as applied to the people of both Germany and the Netherlands. When the Low Countries were one, naturally only a single language was spoken—Dutch; that is, *Duitsch*, which is the Netherlander's word for German, since to him Germany is *Duitschland*. But when the independent Netherlands came into being, and their people developed a civilization peculiarly their own, the need naturally arose for a separate language, and the tongue now spoken in the Netherlands came into being. The World War has made the differentiation in the American mind between a German and a Hollander much clearer and the confusion less. But it is curious how the confusion still persists. Even in representative newspapers, in fact, in novels and books of reference, we find the term "Pennsylvania Dutch": an absolute error, since the Pennsylvania Dutch are Germans—descendants of the German colonizers of Pennsylvania under Pastorius, who, in 1683, settled Germantown; and likewise, in part, descendants of the Hessian soldiers who fought against the United States in the Revolutionary War, and were left stranded there because the Grand Duke of Hesse refused to pay homeward fare. But they are not Netherlanders.

It is never agreeable to a native of the Netherlands to have his people confused with those of Germany, when you analyze history and find that the Netherlands has always been the friend and champion of the United States, whereas the soldiers of Germany twice have taken up arms against the people of the United States. As a matter of simple fairness, is it not time that the American people should get this distinction clearly fixed in their minds?

VI

I was watching a brick road being laid in Pennsylvania, when the contractor said to me: "Best kind of a road, this. We have brick roads in Pennsylvania, Ohio, and Missouri, that are from twenty-nine to thirty-two years old, with the roads still in excellent condition. We Americans beat the world in road-building."

"I thought the Romans laid a road or two abroad which have stood up pretty well," I ventured.

"Yes, but not of brick. No country has ever tried brick roads. We lead the world," returned the contractor; and then he added, "Do you doubt that?"

"No," I answered, "I don't doubt it; I know America never led the world in brick road-building."

"Where have they ever tried it and got away with it as we have?" he asked, with a delicious contempt in his voice.

"Well," I replied, "England, for one country, has a few brick roads that have done their bit. There are brick roads in the Netherlands, where they are over one hundred years old, laid in Napoleon's time, and just as good as when they were laid, if not better."

"Of brick?" he asked.

"Of brick: vitrified brick; in fact, the vitrification of brick was brought to practical perfection by the Dutch."

And then came the inevitable, "Well, I didn't know that!"

VII

We were golfing one day, when one of the foursome remarked: "We certainly owe a debt to the Scotch for golf."

"Why to the Scotch?" I queried.

"Because they discovered it, invented it, so to speak. Didn't you know that?" I was asked, in astonishment.

"No, I didn't know it," I replied. And when I reached

home, bringing my friends with me, I said to them, after dinner: "Now, let me show you fellows something apropos of the Scotch 'discovering' golf. Read the beginning of this article on 'Golf' in the *Encyclopædia Britannica:* an English publication, which would most likely have credited the game to the British Isles if history permitted, wouldn't it?"

"First played by the Dutch," read my friend. "Well, what do you know about that?" And then, from another article, "Brought to Scotland from the Netherlands by two Scotchmen." And then, of course, there followed: "Golf, a Dutch game! Well, I didn't know that!"

VIII

I was watching the erection of a great building in New York one day, when one of the most noted engineers engaged in the work said to me: "We are erecting this building entirely on piles; do you realize what that means? No other nation in the world would dare do such a thing, and yet the method is perfectly feasible and safe. It shows how far the United States has gone ahead of the world in engineering skill."

I pondered for a moment, for the man was very pleasantly suffused with his achievement; I hated to spoil an illusion, and yet——

Very meekly I asked: "And how do you think they built Amsterdam?"

"Amsterdam?" he echoed. "You mean Amsterdam, New York?"

"Not exactly," I answered; "Amsterdam in the Netherlands."

"Oh," he corrected, "you mean the Dutch city, in Holland. Oh, I don't know. Never been there. America's good enough for me. An American engineer can't learn anything over there."

"No?" I wondered.

"Not for a minute," was the positive answer. "Do you think so?"

"I was just wondering," I answered, "as I remembered that the entire city of Amsterdam, in the Netherlands, with thousands of houses, the largest Bourse in the world, one of the largest railroad depots in Europe, is entirely built on piles, and was so constructed some few hundred years ago. You mention that the piles you are driving here are, some of them, twenty-four feet long; "the largest in the world ever used for building purposes," you say. I happened to see piles thirty feet long driven as foundations in Amsterdam. And speaking of foundations," I continued, "do you realize that there is one dyke in the Netherlands, protecting the land from the sea, where the dyke itself is forty feet in height above the water; while underneath the water there is a wall two hundred feet deep, all made of solid Norway granite? And that there is a province in the Netherlands, called Friesland, where the foundations of every village and town are of artificial construction? I am saying all this," I concluded, "wondering whether we are so very far ahead of the Old World in our ideas as we sometimes think."

"Well, this is all news to me," was his comment.

And when, a year later, this same engineer was appointed one of a committee to visit the Netherlands and study the plans of the most astounding piece of engineering skill ever conceived in the history of the world,—the reclamation of the land under the Zuyder Zee,—he sent me upon his return the laconic message: "My dear fellow, we are pikers compared to those fellows in the Netherlands. You must have thought me a fool that afternoon in New York."

And then followed the inevitable phrase, "I simply didn't know."

IX

"What does Mengelberg do when he is at home?" a man, supposedly of musical knowledge, asked me not long ago.

"Conducts the Amsterdam Symphony Orchestra," I replied.

"Oh," he replied nonchalantly, "I didn't know the Dutch had orchestras like ours." And then this delicious bit: "It must seem strange for him to conduct an orchestra like the New York Philharmonic."

"Why?" I asked.

"So large and so fine," he ventured.

"It isn't as large as his own in Amsterdam." I remarked.

"Not as large?" he echoed. And then another titbit: "Does it play often?"

"About one hundred and forty times each season," I answered. "And then it visits the great capitals of Europe, because it is now recognized as the finest symphonic orchestra on the Continent."

And then it came, as I knew it would and always does: "Well, well, I didn't know that!"

XI

Now, of course, this phrase, "Well, I didn't know that!" takes on a humorous aspect after constant repetition. But there is a more serious side to the matter, which takes the form of the question, "Should not the average American know whence his great institutions emanated?" For it is little short of pathetic to note the amazing lack of knowledge among the people of the United States of the great debt which they owe the people and institutions of the Netherlands. I am not speaking now of the historic help which the Dutch gave to America in the way of financial aid in the War of the Revolution, when no other nation would extend it credit; or of the fact that it was the first nation in the world to salute the American flag after the signing of the Declaration of Independence. Creditable as these are to the people of the Netherlands, and showing how far back extends their loyal friendship for the people of the United States, they were, after all, merely evidences of good-will. When I speak of the American people's being indebted to the Netherlands, I mean something more fundamental.

Take, as an example, four of the institutions enumerated a moment ago: the four vital institutions upon which the United States rests, and, more than that, which have caused it to be regarded as the most distinctive nation in the world. I mean our public-school system of free education; our freedom of religious worship; our freedom of the press; and our betterment tax of property benefited by adjacent improvements. It is popularly supposed that these came to the United States from England.

But how could they, since scarcely one existed in England when they were introduced into the life of the United States by the Pilgrim Fathers, who had lived for eleven years in the Netherlands? Each and all of these four institutions were flourishing for years in the Netherlands; the Pilgrims absorbed them there and brought them to the United States.

Take the two documents upon which the whole fabric of the establishment and maintenance of the United States rests—the Declaration of Independence and the Federal Constitution of the United States: one, the Declaration, is based partly upon the Declaration of Independence of the Republic of the United Netherlands; while all through the Constitution its salient points are based upon, and some literally copied from, the Netherlands Constitution. So strong is this Netherlands influence upon our American form of government that the Senate of the United States, as a body, derives most of the peculiarities of its organization from the Netherlands States-General, a similar body, and its predecessor by nearly two centuries.

XII

New Yorkers do not begin to realize the extent to which they are indebted to the people of the Netherlands for their very existence: that there might be no such city as New York to-day but for the sturdy Netherlanders.

There is not one New Yorker in a thousand, I believe, who knows—or cares—that his city was originally founded by the Netherlander; that it was named New

Amsterdam; that for forty years, from 1625 to 1664, it
was governed entirely under the flag of the Netherlands;
that its first Mayor (then called Governor) was a New
Netherlands colonist; that its present official flag is
the Dutch emblem of William of Orange; that its
motto, "Eendracht maakt macht" ("In union there is
strength"), is in the Netherlands tongue.

He may know that he owes the name of his beautiful
Hudson River to Henry Hudson; but does he know that
Hudson came over in a Dutch ship, the *Half-Moon*,
and that he was an employee of the Amsterdam Chamber
of the East India Company; that his cruise not only was
financed by Dutch capital, but was due to Dutch initiative?

Does he know that the names of his suburbs—Brooklyn, Flatlands, Harlem, Flatbush, New Utrecht—are all
Dutch; that the name of Wall Street came from a wall
built by the Dutch as the end of the city at that time;
that his foremost families of to-day, such as the Van
Rensselaers, the Stuyvesants, the Beekmans, the de
Peysters, the Cowenhovens, the Lefferts, he owes to the
people of the Netherlands?

"Little does he care," you say. No doubt. But there
are the facts, nevertheless.

XIII

The surprise naturally occasioned by the extent of
Netherlands influence upon American institutions is
lessened when it is borne in mind that the early influences
which fashioned American life were largely brought di-

rect from the Netherlands in the lives of the early settlers.
The men who founded New York were, chiefly, from the
Netherlands. The Pilgrims who settled Plymouth had
lived eleven years in the Netherlands. The Puritans
who settled elsewhere in Massachusetts had all their
lives been exposed to Dutch influence. New Jersey, as
well as New York, was settled by the Dutch West
India Company. Connecticut was given life by Thomas
Hooker, who came from a long residence in the Netherlands. Roger Williams, who founded Rhode Island, was
a Dutch scholar. William Penn, the founder of Pennsylvania, came of a Dutch mother, whose teachings were
a potent influence in his life. These men introduced one
Netherlands institution after another into America.

Take the common modern practice of the state's allowing a prisoner the free services of a lawyer for his defense,
and the office of a district attorney for each county.
These are so familiar to us that we regard them as American institutions; or they have been credited to England;
whereas, as a matter of fact, it is impossible to find them
in English history. Both of these institutions existed
in the Netherlands three centuries before they were
brought to America.

The custom of equal distribution of property among
the children of a person dying intestate was brought from
the Netherlands by the Pilgrims.

The recording of all deeds and mortgages in a public
office, a custom which affects everyone who owns or
buys property, came direct from the Netherlands.

The township system, by which each town has local
self-government, with its natural sequence of local self-

government in county and state, came from the Netherlands.

The practice of making prisoners work, and turning prisons into workhouses, was brought from the Netherlands to America by William Penn.

XIV

What we are apt to forget, unless our histories lie very close to us, is that the Netherlands was an influential nation in commerce, art, education, statesmanship, when the United States still lay undeveloped. With its three millions of people in 1555, for example, it was the most prosperous and most highly intelligent nation in the world: the centre in Europe of all things that stood for progress and culture. A reading of the history of those times reveals the tremendous part that the Netherlands played in the institutions of the world. Ranking as one of the first states of the world, her people added to the intellectual and moral resources of mankind in nearly every art which heightens and adorns human life, and in nearly every aspect of human endeavor.

It was the Netherlands that gave to the world some of the towering figures of solid and abiding culture. It was the Netherlands that produced William the Silent in statesmanship; Rembrandt, Hals, and Vermeer in art; Erasmus in philology and theology; Boerhaave in medicine; Spinoza in philosophy; Grotius in international law; De Ruyter in naval strategy; and Vondel, the poet, traces of whose influence have been so manifestly found in Milton's *Paradise Lost*.

In education it contributed a tremendous impetus to

the world by the founding of the great University of Leyden in 1575, making the Netherlands the centre of learning for all Europe.

In finance, it led the world by the establishment of the Bank of Amsterdam, pointing the way to the establishment of the Bank of England one hundred years later.

In medicine, Boerhaave so greatly influenced medical science that the medical schools of the Netherlands became great seats of authority.

The founding of international law by Grotius attracted the attention of the entire world to the Netherlands as a seat for the learning of jurisprudence.

From the Netherlands also came the great lesson of the publishing of books, under the famous Elzevirs.

Its great step of placing the reader and the spelling-book in the hands of every child, irrespective of means or station, marked an epoch in the annals of the world's educational system.

It is conservative to say that Erasmus led the world in education by his epoch-making editions of the New Testament in Greek, and of classical authors, and by his teaching of pure Latin.

The Netherlands introduced to the world the manufacture of woollen cloth, which marked an epoch in history; and followed this up by developing the manufacture of silk, linen, tapestry, and lace, until it made Flanders the manufacturing centre of the world.

Then came the invention of wood-engraving by a Dutchman, followed quickly by the printing of books from blocks; the substitution of movable type for the solid block of wood, and we have the printing-press—the

invention of which Germany may never concede to the
Netherlands, and yet the germ of which was in the
block books to which the Dutch lay unquestioned claim.

XV

Practical as well as artistic, the Netherlands not only
contributed to, but actually led the world in, those forces
which add materially to the fabric of civilization.

It was the first nation to master the soil, and teach the
possibilities of wresting a land from the water.

It taught the world the art of gardening as has no other
nation.

The skill of its engineers became acknowledged in
every part of the globe, as it is to-day.

It taught the art of commerce to the entire world when
it ranked as the great commercial nation of the globe.

It has given a demonstration in successful colonization,
which has outstripped all other nations.

Take its five great innovations and inventions, and
stop to consider just what this quintette from the brain
of man have done for the enlightenment of the world:

First: the inauguration of a system of equal education
for girls and boys, making no distinction of sex in its
common-school attendance.

Second: the invention of the telescope.

Third: the pendulum clock, to which can be ascribed
the beginning of what may be called accuracy in time.

Fourth: the microscope.

Fifth: the method of measuring degrees of latitude
and longitude.

It seems almost incredible that so many momentous

contributions to the enlightenment of mankind should have emanated from a single people. Is it too much to say, then, that the people of no other nation make so bold and strong an impression on the mind as one after another of their achievements passes before it; and especially when it is considered that all these contributions to humankind were done coincidently with the supreme effort of saving every foot of land from the rushing waters? But the people of the Netherlands always remained cool, balanced, and solid. It was that same patient, but deep, perfervid spirit which built the dykes and saved the land at one period, and opened those same dykes, built by the very life-blood of the people, at another, and flooded the land against encroaching enemies. It was that same spirit which built up a nation unrivalled in history as a financial, commercial, maritime, artistic, literary, medical, and political centre, from which have radiated the strongest influences for the upbuilding of great empires, not only in the new Western world of America, but also in the Far East, where to-day exists an empire of such unknown and untold wealth as to stagger the imagination by its potentialities.

XVI

Nor is this glory of the people of the Netherlands of the past alone. One has only to visit this amazing country to-day to be convinced of the peculiar solidity of its life and its institutions. Nearly every American traveller, with seeing eyes and receptive mind, sees, as he meets the people of the Netherlands, that there is less intellectual veneer among them than in any other country in Europe;

that there is more solid and abiding culture of the very highest kind; and that the modern Dutch family represents a repose of mind, a simplicity of living, and a content with life in general that any nation might envy.

Few know of the enterprise and the business acumen of the people of the Netherlands of to-day: its annual export trade of from 2,000,000,000 to 3,100,000,000 gulden (the gulden is about 39 cents in American money); its port of Rotterdam, now leading Antwerp and Hamburg in tonnage; its steamship combine, with a capital of 200,000,000 gulden; its Royal Dutch Oil Company, capitalized at 370,000,000 gulden, with its annual output of over 30,000,000 barrels of oil; the marvellous development of the air, by a daily aeroplane service to London, Paris, Hamburg, Prague, Warsaw, and other European capitals; its 30,000,000 gulden invested in model workingmen's houses.

Nor has the nation ever taken a backward step in its leadership in the education of its people. The principal item in the national budget is still for education, until to-day the nation occupies the enviable position of being foremost in the enlightenment of its people, with an illiteracy of one tenth of one per cent! Can any figure speak louder for the vision of its people?

XVII

And yet always, with their material progress, have the people retained that idealism which has ever distinguished them. One recent illustration will suffice. A wealthy resident of Amsterdam found himself hard put to it to meet the heavy taxation caused by the war, and decided that he would have to dispose of one of his priceless works of art. He chose Vermeer's Straatje (The Little Street) for the sacrifice. This painting is one of the Delft master's greatest works, and its probable sale to some one outside the Netherlands hung over the people like a pall for weeks. Foreign dealers vied with each other for the treasured painting, held for nearly half a million of dollars; and every report of its reputed sale caused a chill to run down the backs of the people.

Then came the report of its actual sale. The General Director of the Royal Dutch Oil Company, Sir Henri W. A. Deterding, was to celebrate an anniversary: he had purchased the picture and presented it to the Netherlands Government in perpetuity.

XVIII

Is it to be wondered at, then, that there is so much pride among the people of the United States in their Dutch ancestry? But there is much room for a greater enlightenment as to the facts upon which that pride rests. Fortunately, there has recently been noticeable among the American people a distinct national awakening in everything pertaining to the Netherlands and its people; and that this rests on the solid foundation of an inherent influence and blood-kinship, none who know the facts, as they have been only sketched here, will deny.

TWENTY:

DO WE REALLY DO THINGS?

"The power of spiritual forces in the Universe—how active it is everywhere! Invisible to the eyes and impalpable to the senses, it is inherent in all things, and nothing can escape its operation. Like the rush of mighty waters, the presence of unseen Powers is felt, sometimes above us, sometimes around us."

CONFUCIUS

DO WE REALLY DO THINGS?

I

As I progressed with my work and began to "do things" as the public labelled them, I began to get deeply interested in the processes by which achievements are accomplished.

We say, or it is said of us, that we do things. But, in reality, do we? As the world progresses, and man's mind becomes more attuned to phenomena hitherto beyond human penetration, it is being clearly revealed to us that there are powerful forces working outside and around us which influence and control our lives and yet which we are utterly unable to control. Those who have thought at all and probed into the more subtle sense of things, know that we are surrounded by a spiritual atmosphere as distinct and definite as is the accepted fact that we are surrounded by a physical atmosphere. Thoughts and perceptions, finite or Infinite we know not, float unseen all about us.

No man lives fully and deeply in the right spirit who has failed of experiences which have left him in a state of perplexity at these unseen forces outside of him. Nor does the scientific exposition of a Sir Oliver Lodge or the more popular explanation of a Sir Conan Doyle seem to make clearer their character. Experience convinces us more than exposition, but beyond the assurance that these unseen forces are present, we cannot, in our finite knowledge, seem to progress. Lecky is clearly insistent that a large proportion of the external forces of a man's life lies wholly or mainly beyond his control.

II

What are these forces? We cannot explain them. Then, how do we sense them? How do we know that they exist for us?

My mother passed away on April 13, 1907, at three-twenty o'clock in the afternoon. Each year on this day, exactly at the twentieth minute past three o'clock, my hand instinctively reaches for my watch and I note the passing of the moment. In this there is nothing unusual. I know, when the day begins, that it is the date of her passing, and the mind does the rest at the exact moment. But an experience such as what follows is not so easily explained. On one of these anniversaries, recently, a friend of mine, who had known my mother, had a business appointment with me which extended over the particular time. Exactly at the minute I looked at my watch. He had no idea of the significance of the act or that the day marked the passing of my mother. My friend was in the midst of an explanation of his business proposition when I looked at my watch. Suddenly he halted.

"That is most remarkable," he said as I glanced up from my watch and saw a puzzled expression on his face.

"What's that?" I asked.

"Why just that moment when you looked at your watch, it was amazing how much you looked like your mother," he explained.

"And now, too?" I asked.

"No, not now," he answered. "It was just for an instant when you looked at your watch. A look spread over your face that was identically the familiar look of your mother that I know so well. Curious," he ended.

It seemed all the more curious to him when I explained why I had looked at my watch. My friend is not telepathic: he was absolutely in ignorance of the day; it was years since we had spoken of my mother.

III

I was at a large luncheon of publishers and editors at my father-in-law's house. An editor sitting at my right leaned over to a publisher sitting at my left and suggested that the latter explain to me a question of editorial ethics which they had discussed previous to the luncheon and upon which they had failed to agree.

The publisher began his story, when suddenly there appeared before me as plainly as if she were in the flesh my wife's mother, who had passed away two years before. It was just such a gathering as she would have enjoyed and, radiant in smiles, she began a series of questions to which I gave answer, and began describing her state of wonderful happiness. The next thing I knew I felt a hand on my shoulders, and I heard "Well, how about it?" and I discovered editor and publisher looking at me.

I experienced the severest mental reaction as I readjusted myself to my surroundings, and I could only stammer "How about it? How about what?" I recalled then that I had been supposed to have listened to the question under argument. I felt sensibly dazed at the sudden transmigration of self that had occurred, and need hardly add that my friends were equally so with what they called my "preoccupation."

I apologized and pleaded a period of abstraction.

"You just didn't seem to be here," said the editor.

That was true. I had not been there. But where had I been? I learned afterward that the publisher's explanation lasted fully five minutes!

IV

If such unseen spiritual forces are at work outside of us—and these experiences are only two of several which have come to me—is it so difficult to believe that our impulses which we think are of ourselves come to us from similar forces?

I was talking one day to Herbert Hoover just after he had embarked on one of his great undertakings when he said "I don't know why I am in this thing."

"How did you get into it?" I asked.

"I don't know, sort of forced into it," was the answer.

Every man who has achieved, has experienced this similar feeling of uncertainty. An undertaking is proposed or brought to his notice; he receives it in a sort of quiescent mood; he cannot quite understand why it should be brought to him; it does not seem to be in line with his past endeavor and yet, for some reason or other which he cannot understand, he accepts. Many a man has said to me of some position in which he has found himself: "I don't know for the life of me why I accepted."

But invariably he ended by doing a distinct piece of worth-while work.

V

The idea becomes pregnant with the most interesting thought if we follow it through. May it not well be that, with the cultivation of the right spirit, our lives are more constantly directed than we have any idea of? Are we not in reality mere agents in a Divine scheme of things selected to do certain acts of service for which we have unconsciously perhaps been given the ability? What other means are there through which God's spirit can work for the accomplishment of His purposes than men? As Henry Drummond says, the only fluid thing in the world is man. If this be not so, then why is it that we find ourselves so often in positions in no wise of our selection and carrying through certain work for which we are surprised ourselves that we have the requisite talents? We say of a man who suddenly achieves "I never thought he had it in him." Nine cases out of ten neither did the man. It has been a common experience to have men acknowledge this and express surprise at their own achievement. But if we are, by these outer forces, called and deputed to do certain work in this world, it follows that we are given the ability and the resourcefulness to do it and the way to a successful termination is made clear to us as we go along.

VI

This explanation, which for my own part is the one I have accepted, would account for a man set to do a cer-

tain task and going through the utmost difficulties without any thought of final failure. I have carefully watched
men function in service to others, and have never joined
in the chorus of discouragement or advice for anything
but a clean carrying on and carrying through. I have
heard such men called "willful," "stubborn," "unwilling to listen to reason," "aggressive" and what not.
But if we believe, as we must if we think our experiences
over at all, that our work is given to us by those Divine
forces, or by whatever name we may choose to call them,
which select our ways of service for us, then we must
also believe that the work is not given us to do without
the strength and acumen necessary for us to carry it
through to achievement.

VII

We find a verification of this belief in the fact so familiar to many that after we have achieved a certain
end we are absolutely unable to explain ourselves how
we did it and why the methods we employed were successful. The same procedure had been tried by others
to bring about the same end, and these had failed. Our
finite explanation is that "the time was not right."
But is that the true explanation? We say, too, "he
builded better than he knew." The truth is, he often
doesn't know at all. The building, while of his effort,
may not have been of his inspiration. I have had men
tell me in complete surprise that they had no idea of
the magnitude of what they had attempted, or of the
importance of the result they had created. Very often
such a man, while conscious of his effort, remains totally

unconscious of the fact that he has successfully created what he set out to do. It is there before his own astonished eyes before he is actually aware of it, and he is often the least aware of the importance or potentiality of his own creation. "It beats me," said a man to me who had accomplished what the world acclaimed as a great piece of work. "I don't get it at all. It was done before I knew it was done: everybody else knew it before I did. And now I can't see it as others can. It all seems very simple."

"Do you feel as if you did do it?" I asked.

"That's the strange part of it all," he answered. "I don't. I was sort of unconsciously pushed into it, didn't feel I could do it, but was doing it all the same before I knew it. And here it is done! Strangest feeling in the world."

"Just as if the forces which pushed you into it were outside of you?" I ventured.

"Exactly," he returned quickly, "exactly that."

And that is precisely as far as, very likely, we will ever get to really understand the forces which are the propelling power in most of our lives.

VIII

And——

What would we really gain if we knew more?

TWENTY-ONE:

THE WORST BIRTHDAY IN A MAN'S LIFE

*"We are the ancients of the earth
And in the morning of the times."*

TENNYSON

---

*"We do not count a man's years until he has nothing else
to count."*

EMERSON

THE WORST BIRTHDAY IN A MAN'S LIFE

I

I HAVE been quoted as saying that a man's retirement from business should occur when he reaches the age of fifty. Of course, I never said anything of the sort, since no definite time can be set for such a decision. What I did say was that I had intended myself to retire at fifty, but that the War had interfered with my plan at that time, and it was six years later that I could carry out my determination.

Speaking of a man reaching the half-century age reminds me of a talk I had one day with Colonel Roosevelt apropos of my approaching fiftieth birthday.

"The worst birthday of your life," was his instant comment.

"Why?" I asked.

"Because you can't help translating it into the fact that it is half a century and because it isn't likely that you will live as long as you have lived. In other words, the realization is brought home that you have lived the larger part of your life."

"But you have no fear of the end of life?" I asked.

"Not a bit," came the quick answer. "Not an iota. I've had a wonderful time. But so much to do. The world is so interesting."

When I did reach my fiftieth year I confess I had the same feeling as did Colonel Roosevelt, and, as I fancy, has every man.

II

It is really funny to watch the average man when the calendar one day tells him the day has come to change the first figure of his age from four to five. There is something psychological about the half-century mark that he doesn't like. Whether it is the realization, as Colonel Roosevelt said, that the span he has lived is longer than the span he will live, or that his vanity is touched by the fact that he can no longer be rated in the young-man class, a man simply does not like his fiftieth birthday. Inevitably he begins to take stock of himself; he convinces himself, so far as a touch of lumbago, or a slight murmur of the heart, or a letting out of his belt will permit him, that he feels just as fit as he did at thirty. Then he goes out and proclaims it to all his friends. "Keener than I ever was." "Wonderful how I can sleep." "Eat? Eat more than I ever did," and all the familiar mental caperings which come with fifty. And the friend to whom he proclaims it wonders why John is stressing all these things when never before was he compelled to give an inventory of his health to every one he met. Probably the friend begins to suspect that John has reached and passed the fiftieth milestone. He may listen politely to John's protestations, but he smiles and chuckles as he walks away.

III

Meanwhile, John is busy with another problem that comes with fifty. He sees the young men of thirty with whom he compares himself coming along, and, worse still, he sees, almost feels the young man of forty at his heels. He does not like the pace of either of them: particularly the forty-year-old who seems to be crowding him a bit. He looks ahead and sees the sixty-year-old man secure in the contentment of his age of wisdom, and he doesn't like that picture either. He gets the feeling of being between two walls. He feels sure he is at the very top of his stride, and yet—! He is not so sure of it as he wishes he might be. He must exercise, he decides. Golf, and, when the weather does not permit, then "twelve daily lessons to music." He has heard, too, that it is very good for the girth to be able to bend over and touch the tip of your feet with the tip of your fingers. Then his dress. His shirts may be just a little gayer of design, perhaps; he has noticed that there are some specially beautiful shades of red in cravats this season. The cut of his clothes could be a bit snappier. Of course, he must see "old Doc" about that little twinge: that foolish little stiffness which seems to come and go: there's a hump that shouldn't be there. "They're nothing, of course; a man can't be one hundred per cent," he argues. Still, one might see what "Doc" has to say. The teeth, too, might stand a bit of looking over, and, when he comes to think of it, he hasn't had his glasses corrected for three or four years.

IV

To himself—of course only to himself—the half-century man reads what I have written here and thinks "That chap has my number." Well, you see, I have been there. I know, and, let me add, I know the foolishness of it all. What we need at fifty is a little more common sense,—a realization of the facts; then no excuses and self-deception but an honest admission and a readjustment. Why this pretense of being a thirty-year-old when we cannot meet the specifications? Why offer this excuse, create that alibi, or try to fool ourselves with futile explanations, when in reality we fool no one—not even ourselves? Why be ashamed of being fifty? What is there to be afraid of? The span of life is lengthening, and it is very largely within our own hands to determine how long we shall live and enjoy life!

V

It gets us nowhere, however, to proclaim ourselves to our friends as what we are not. We did not do this before fifty; why call attention to the fact now by assuring everybody that we are as keen as a razor and as bright as a new penny? Our friends know a fifty-year-old penny when they see one, although they may be too considerate to say so. All we have to do is to take a reasonable care of our health, confessing first to ourselves, and convincing ourselves of it, that we cannot endure at fifty what we did at forty, nor can we eat the same things, nor as much. Of course, a man will immediately say, "How can you prevent yourself from catching the diseases that are all around you?" We can, in a measure, but the chief truth to get lodged in our minds is that the diseases which really lay us low are not those that we catch from others, but which we present to ourselves. We cannot "catch" a valve in the heart or the fatty degeneration of that organ. Nor is it any one's fault if we strain our heart to the point where it puts us out of the running. Our arteries are not hardened by others: we accomplish that process ourselves. No one gives us Bright's Disease, or diabetes, or a case of strained nerves; we present those to ourselves, and we do it by excesses,—not of the other fellow's making, but of our own. The contagious diseases to which we are exposed by others' carelessness are bad enough, but why make the battle harder by personal and self-imposed contributions? If it be true that a man can give the organic diseases *to* himself, is it not also then true that he can keep them *from* himself?

VI

It is a very satisfying statement for some to make, in theory, that a man can, at fifty, play thirty-six holes of golf a day, and feel just as fresh as he did at thirty. Some men can, but they are exceptional, and the chances are against your being the exceptional man. Besides, golf is determined not so much by the number of holes played a day as it is by the manner in which you play them. "I can walk ten miles a day and not feel it," is a proud boast. But, unless one is a letter-carrier, why walk ten miles a day? The body does not require that amount of walking a day to keep in trim. Let common-sense rule, and it can be easily demonstrated that two miles a day are infinitely better at fifty, just as satisfying and certainly wiser, and that eighteen holes of golf are just as efficacious as thirty-six if not more so. The extremes are never wise, because unnecessary.

VII

It is astonishing, too, how susceptible the average man becomes at fifty to the faddists and the charlatans who have as many notions of how to keep well as there are days in the calendar. The general start is with "only five minutes of this exercise every morning just after you wake up." If the exercise is one that has to be taken while you are in bed, before rising, then some one comes along and gives another "five minute exercise" for the bathroom. The third acknowledges that while these may be good, they are not sufficient for an all-round exercise, and he prescribes a full dozen, some with music and others without. Of course, the musical exercises always depend upon whether the bathroom can accommodate a victrola, in addition to the bath-tub and other accessories, while you are exercising. If the size of your bathroom does not permit such demonstrations, the booklet of instruction advises doing the exercises in your bedroom; which raises the point whether others may not want to sleep just at the time when the music thrills you to kick in various directions or to fan the air wildly with your arms.

The advertisements, of course, do not present these obstacles, but the experience does, and that is perhaps why so many exercises with music are put away in closets to exercise the housewife's patience in finding room for them "when no one uses them"! I confess I had at one time some six or seven of these early morning diversions prescribed by doctors, dentists, aurists, and oculists, until I found myself taking from an hour to an hour and a half to dress, with each diversion deemed more "important" than any other by the prescriber! I never tried the twelve daily lessons set to music, because, while I may be peculiar, I prefer my music without exercising at the same time. But I did try to raise myself from the floor by lifting the abdominal muscles only: to touch the toes with the legs erect; to stand on my head and wave my feet rhythmically in the air; to shape the inside of my hands like a cup over my ears twenty times and pull the hands away quickly; to take twenty-five deep breaths standing before an open window. In addition to this, I learned to eat two raw eggs before breakfast; and to drink eight glasses of water while dressing. As a result of these exercises and activities I found a day's work, if I were nimble, beginning at eleven o'clock in the morning! And I was pretty tired when I began!

VIII

Where the half-century man most often errs is in the comfortable belief that he can eat everything he could at thirty and digest it just as well. "I can eat nails," he says, and he does everything short of trying to prove that he can. Phrases and so-called truisms are perhaps the most misleading things we have: we forget in the acceptance of a truism that it was, after all, but the utterance or opinion of one man who was just as likely to be wrong as to be right. There is one truism that has the basis of a hard truth to it, and this is that we "dig our graves with our teeth." Very few men, however, like to have their diet disturbed, particularly the man who has always eaten what he chose. He is a slave to his palate, and so the road which leads to an acid stomach, flatulence, an unpleasant breath, palpitation, and dizziness beckons easily to him, and soon he begins to travel on it, wondering all the while what is the matter with him. That it is his diet is the very last point he will concede. As a physician of forty years' experience with stomach troubles said to me recently: "There are two things a man doesn't like to be told: to eat less and to smoke less. The moment I tell him those two I generally find I have lost another patient. And yet," he added, "that is just what the average man should be told when he passes fifty." Another stomach specialist said: "If only the average man would give food to his stomach with the same care as he gives gasoline to his automobile, we stomach specialists would have to seek some other profession."

IX

The average man seems unable to attain a reasonable mean between eating too much and what he calls a starvation diet. Suggest taking anything away from him, and he immediately sets up the cry either that they are "springing new-fangled notions" on him, that the doctor "is a nut," or that his "wife is starving him." He will recognize no middle-ground. He will assure you that he needs what he eats: he can't keep going unless he does eat just so much. He must have a hearty breakfast (meat, generally!) to start the day; his luncheon must "have something to it" after "an exhausting morning"; and, of course, in the evening, he "simply must have a complete dinner!" Then he goes to "fix the car for to-morrow" or to "fix the furnace for the night," absolutely oblivious of the fact that if either of those inanimate objects had been fed as he has fed himself all day, the car wouldn't run and the furnace would be clogged with fuel. Make this comparison clear and he waves it aside with the all-sufficient (to him) argument that you can-not compare an automobile or a furnace to a human being. But make the comparison to fit his ideas of eating, and he will at once agree with you. "Sure," he will say, "that's what I always say. A man must be stoked just like a furnace,—fill it up." And the gases which fill his house during the night from the over-stoked furnace seem to tell him nothing of the danger of overstoking himself.

X

Man, with few exceptions, is a glutton, and he will not have his eating interfered with. You can argue all you like with him about speedier fermentation of food after fifty, less perfect elimination, digestive processes that do not work with the same creamy-like smoothness with which they did at thirty, the less need for the same amount of food, and he listens with patience or irrita-tion, according to his nature, and then goes on and does exactly as he did. Or even if he slows up, it is only for a short time, and then, feeling the healthful reaction from a more moderate diet, falls again into the old rut of overeating. If it were true that organically a man is the same at fifty as at thirty or forty, all this would be correct. But the organs are not the same, and will not perform at fifty as they did with the fresher, more youthful and freer flow of blood at thirty. A food specialist has said that a man at fifty should eat thirty per cent less food than at forty, and that for every five years thereafter he should take off ten per cent until he reaches fifty or sixty per cent reduction. Of course, no table of percentages is applicable to each and all, but in the main it is conceded by stomach specialists that this moderation is by no means too drastic; if anything, too conservative. Then, of course, the quality of the food comes in, and there must be taken into consideration the question of well-balanced meals.

XI

The point of the whole matter, however, is the realization of a reduction in food when a man reaches the half-century point in his age: the amount of that reduction must be decided by him. Drinking (water) he can increase, and wisely, but to eating he cannot hold as in the past, and the sooner he gets the truth of that idea securely fixed in his mind the better. It is truly amazing when one tries the experiment, how little food is needed not only to keep a man feeling fit, but also enable him to do a prodigious amount of work. Gradually I have cut down my eating until sometimes I seem to my household to belong to the family of orchids. But invariably with such reductions my health has been bettered, my mentality became more alert, and there was no diminution in the quality or quantity of work accomplished. "Enough is equal to a feast."

The physiologists tell us that the life of a man is

divided into cycles of seven: that during each of these cycles his organisms undergo changes, and that the time between the seventh and eighth cycles,—that is, between the forty-ninth and fifty-sixth years in the male,— is a period that should receive the particular attention of every man. Of course, this is but another way of saying that at this time of a man's life there should come a readjustment of his habits of eating, a moderation in his exercise, in the speed of his activities, and in his general watchfulness of himself, if he would reach his sixtieth year with any degree of vitality and with the blood flowing freely in his arteries. The particularly watchful point of observation is the appetite, which has a way of taking on an avariciousness during this cycle out of all proportion to the needs of the body. It is then either by gratifying or curbing his appetite, that the man determines his future health and longevity. If because he simply has the craving for food he satisfies the appetite, he will find the organism weakening under the pressure, and trouble begins. If, on the other hand, he curbs his appetite, and trains it according to the needs of the body, a healthy vigor takes the place of a torpid condition. A man can wisely eat only what he can easily digest after it is eaten, and this truth simply means that his digestive organs will not take care of the same quantity of food between the seventh and eighth cycles of his life as during the sixth and seventh periods. Because the palate craves food it does not by any means follow that the digestive organs can take care of it.

After all, there are only three points to which a man at fifty should pay attention: less food, with a more generous drinking of water; a rational amount of exercise and eight hours sleep. These, with a contented mind which casts off worry, are very likely to lead to a ripe old age.

XII

The wise Marcus Aurelius was right when he wrote, "Remember this: that very little is needed to make a happy life."

TWENTY-TWO:

WHEN TOM WENT TO FRANCE

*" Better to die ten thousand deaths
Than wound thy honor."*
ADDISON

WHEN TOM WENT TO FRANCE

I

THERE is also something vital, when a man reaches the half-century mark, in how he has spent the period approaching his fiftieth year. A man can hardly expect to reach his fiftieth anniversary if he has led a life which makes his previous birthdays resemble tombstones rather than milestones. This is not the place for a preachment as to what kind of life a man, previous to his fiftieth year, should lead. The ground will be covered, I think, for young men in a "letter" which I once wrote and published, and which I reproduce here. Its content, in a general way, is quite as applicable to a time of peace as to a time of war.

II

It came out of one of the most satisfying experiences of the Great War. I was appointed Chairman of the Young Men's Christian Association Commission in Philadelphia to recruit men for civilian duty in France and England, and was fortunate in securing the co-operation of the finest committee of men with which I have ever worked. For more than a twelve-month we met once or twice each week, and had men appear before us who desired to work in the ranks of the Y in the war zone. We had the satisfaction of sending over some three hundred men who gave service of a quality as high as ever men rendered.

It was during the accompanying service of visiting the near-by camps in connection with the civilian recruiting, so that I might be the better informed as to the type of men that the boys wanted to serve them, that I came into contact with hundreds of boys who were being trained for service in France. I got to know the boys in this way, and to enter somewhat into their needs and feelings. One day a boy from Arizona said to me: "I wish some one who really understands us would write something that we could put into our pocket-book that would give us heart, and show us the way to the right thing when we get over there, and which we could take out and read when we felt in need of a bit of a bucking-up." I thought much of what the boy said, and finally wrote and published the following article in the form of a letter. It was not, as some have said, addressed to the elder of my sons, when he went into the service of his country. It was addressed to no boy in particular, but to every boy in general who went to France.

The "letter" happened to win the approval of a large number of boys, and the National War Work Council of the Young Men's Christian Association requested authority to reprint it, which was done to the extent of over a million copies. All during the anxious months of the War I received word from officers and boys in the trenches with regard to the helpfulness of this "letter." It is really at their request "to put it in one of your books" that I include it here:

TOM

THE LETTER THAT HIS FATHER SLIPPED HIM WHEN HE LEFT
HIS MOTHER FOR "SOMEWHERE IN FRANCE"

It has been something of a grip to your mother and me, my
dear boy, these last days. But I hope we have kept our feelings in our pockets. We tried to look Right in the face. We
wouldn't have you do otherwise. I would have hung my head
in shame if my son had not wanted to go when his country
called. God knows I would go with you, shoulder to shoulder,
if I could.

It's going to be very hard on your mother. She has been
very fine so far, don't you think? But mothers have a way
that children don't know about: of lying awake in the darkness and talking to the God of their boys at such times. She
has. And she will. She is giving all.

But you have a wonderful chance to repay her. You are
going into a big thing: a big war: a big army: standing for a
big idea. But don't forget that the biggest thing about a
principle or a battle or an army is a man! And the biggest
thing that a war can do is to bring out that man. That's
really what you and the other chaps have gone over for: to
demonstrate the right kind of manhood, for it is that which
weighs in a fight and wins it. The measure of any successful
result is the men who make that success.

You neither want nor need maxims. I think you inherit my
distaste for them. There is only one thing that counts in
this life, and it beats all the maxims ever penned—that is,
for a man's spirit to be all right. If that is what it should be
all the details of his life will fall into their proper places. I
think your spirit is all right, my boy. It should be, for it
came to you from your mother. Live that spirit.

And as that spirit came to you from a woman, do you play
the game and show that you have it to other women. It is the
finest thing you can do with it, and you can't very well do

less, because it is why your mother gave it to you: that you should stand four-square before men. And men, in this case, means women. For when you get "Somewhere in France" you will meet women: all kinds. Some of one kind in particular. Many of them will have their men-folks at the Front. They will be alone—alone for other men to respect and honor and show the right consideration.

These women will make much of you, for an American in khaki in France is very welcome, and will be made so. But don't let that welcome for your coming to save their homes and honor mean an approach or opening for you for anything but the highest consideration. Don't forget that when you are invited somewhere to hang up your hat it doesn't mean to hang up your conduct also. You will hear that in France they have "let the bars down." But there is no such thing anywhere as letting the bars down to a man's conduct toward a woman. To be a gentleman in a French home is no different from being a gentleman in your mother's home. Think of every woman you meet as a member of your mother's sex, and treat her accordingly. Think of every girl you meet as you would of Nell, and treat her as you hope every chap in the camp near us will treat her. It is a tremendously big "bit" that every chap who goes to France now does, who upholds his own honor at the same time that he upholds the honor of the United States, when it comes to his considerate treatment of the women of France. It will be the finest tribute in the world to our great country if, when our boys leave France, it can be said of them that they were Spartans of personal honor. Nothing—no results in battles—will count for so much as that one record. These French women have suffered much: let us, as men from America, not ask them to suffer more.

When you are called to get into the game, get into it good and strong. There's no fun in going through life spoon-fed: in finding the soft seat. That makes a man soft, and a soft man is an abomination before God and men. Find your place and hold it: find your work and do it. And put everything you've got into it. Take hold and carry the biggest load your shoulders can carry, and then carry it right. Set the pace for others; don't let them set it for you.

Then when the hour comes for fun and recreation, have it also "full up"; only get clean fun. You have the good manners that your mother taught you. Be true to your teacher, for as a son acts so does he reflect upon his mother and father. And in no relation in life can you so truly know a man as in his play. See how a man plays and you can tell every time whether he is a quitter or a standpatter. It is in his playtime that a man meets with the things that test him.

I would be mighty wary, in those play hours, of the wines of France. A man never needs alcohol in his being, and he never needs it so little as when he is up against the "trick" that you and your fellows are going to "put over" in France. You will need every bit of real vitality, of strength, of clear-eyed vision that you can muster, and not one of these comes from alcohol, which, after all has been said of it, for and against, is the chief mantrap in the world. You will want and have your convivial intervals. They will be welcome from the tension of camp and trench life. But convivial times can be had without playing mischief with your head and your body.

Let me say this to you, too: attend service: "if not invariably, then variably." A lot of the fellows won't, and you won't have to if you don't want to. But, take it from an older man who has been over all the way, you can't afford not to go. Get the true understanding of this one fact: this war will, in its finality, have to be settled on one basis, and only one: the spirit of Christ. Why? Because any civilization that is worth the name is based on that, and only on that can it survive. Christianity may seem to have a black eye just now: it may seem almost not to be in the world. But that is only in the seeming, for when the time comes for men to get together you will see that peace will come out of that Great

Fountain of sanity, tolerance, and political and social wisdom that is the Gateway to all kinds of truth and the only sure basis on which the world can rest. So keep a bit close to it in your fighting days, and learn to know the Greatest Lessons that a man can know and by which every decent man lives and is measured.

So go to it, my boy! Do your duty and do it strong. If it be God's will that you come back to us a silent tribute to your sense of right, so be it. We will bear and live it, as thousands of others will be called upon to do. But I have a strong feeling that you are going to come back to us a bigger, finer man than you are leaving us to-day. I cannot help feeling that this is God's will. And when you come back, more than any honor that may come to you for duty done, I want to feel that, clean-blooded and clear-eyed, you can look your mother straight in the eye and that she will feel that most glorious and satisfying of all exaltations that comes to a mother, that tremendous inner satisfaction, when her mother-heart says within her: "Thank God, my boy has kept the faith." Keep you that faith with your mother. Nothing can count so big.

Until then, dear boy, remember me as thinking of you throughout each of the long days and the nights to come as

Your loving and believing

DAD.

TWENTY-THREE:

YOUR NEIGHBOR AT AN ENGLISH TABLE

"A deep meaning often lies in old customs."

SCHILLER

YOUR NEIGHBOR AT AN ENGLISH TABLE

I

IT is the recollection of the war days revived by the letter given in the chapter before this, that reminds me of the visit which thirteen of us American editors paid to Great Britain and France, and to the front during the days of the Argonne fight as the guests of the British Government.

To an American, unfamiliar with the English custom of not introducing guests to each other, the usage is very apt to lead to embarrassing and amusing results. There was, naturally, much of this confusion during the War, when so many Americans visited England for the first time. It is very likely to happen that a guest's plate card becomes invisible under a menu or some of the accessories of the table, and the guest is left in absolute ignorance of his neighbor's identity.

An American who had attached himself to our "war" party had an experience of this sort. He had been crying aloud for an opportunity to meet H. G. Wells, the author, for whose works he had an ardent admiration. At one of these luncheons, it was arranged that he should sit next to Mr. Wells, and all through the luncheon he had a wonderful time talking to the source of his admiration. After the luncheon a friend said to him: "Well, you had your opportunity at last to meet your patron saint, didn't you?"

"Who is that?" he blandly asked.

which prevailed at the rest of the table. After I had paid my respects to the woman at my right, whose name I knew as I had taken her into breakfast, and exchanged a few pleasantries, I turned to my left to find my neighbor had pushed his chair back from the table about three feet, had buried his chin in his shirt-bosom and was reaching forth for his eatables, and practically eating them from his lap, his cup resting on his knee. I caught a glance from the woman sitting at the man's left which indicated bewilderment. There was something familiar about the features of my neighbor who was eating in the most grotesque fashion I ever saw, and yet I could not place him. I looked for his place-card, but I could see none. So I shoved back my chair, and tried to engage him in conversation. But I was not rewarded by even a glance. When I asked a question I received either no answer at all or a grunt. After a few heroic efforts, I gave up the struggle and saw that the woman at his left had done likewise. Then she handed me her place-card, upon which she had written: "In one of his impossible moods."

"Quite," I said to her across the space which separated us.

At the close of the breakfast, I asked Wilde: "Who in the world was that chap at my left? I tried my best to be decent to him, but he wouldn't have it."

"I know," returned Wilde. "I saw your valiant struggle. He gets that way once in a while, and this morning happened to be once of those whiles. That was Whistler!"

IV

If the awkward situation in which a stranger often finds himself by reason of this custom of the non-introduction of guests were understood by Englishmen, they would be the first to feel deeply chagrined at the realization. For instance, I was at a dinner at a friend's house in Portland Place, and the usual custom was followed of an announcement of the name upon one's entrance—which scarcely any one hears—but no introductions followed. I roamed over the room and among the sixty-odd guests until dinner was announced when I received my sole introduction to the lady I was to take into dinner. At the table I was particularly attracted to the friendly face of a young woman sitting opposite. I caught her eye once or twice, and she smiled a sort of a welcome to me, and after dinner, cutting short my smoke with the men, I sought the drawing-room to find the particular young woman, whom I saw surrounded with a bevy of admirers. As soon as she saw me she held out her hand and, drawing me to a sofa, said: "You are from America, and I am keen to hear what is going on over there. Do tell me." It pleased me to think that an Englishwoman should be so interested in matters "in the States," and I launched forth and not only told her what was going on, but described some of the cities, principally New York.

"Yes, New York," she urged.

Which naturally encouraged me the more, and I plunged in upon those better phases of New York life which counteract so much of the blatant side of the metropolis, and explained them at length, as one would to a stranger who had never been in the city, only to learn from my hostess, at my departure, that I had studiously explained New York to an American duchess born and bred in New York.

V

An English friend of mine had a brother who was at that time the Liberal whip in Parliament, and I was very anxious to meet him and to get his angle on British politics.

"I will give you a dinner at my house, and I will have him there," suggested my friend.

I thanked him, and on the appointed evening I went to his house to find some thirty guests, not one of whom I had ever met. Fortunately for me, I was belated by a slow hansom horse, and when I arrived it was time to go in to dinner. So I was spared the embarrassment of a stranger wandering aimlessly about in a roomful of humans, as I had done on other occasions. During the dinner I asked my hostess: "Which one is your brother-in-law?"

"Just near the end of the table," she answered. But as there were some six or eight men "near the end of the table," this did not help me much.

The dinner was the usual formal affair, and after three hours at the table, the ladies retired and the men were left to their cigars. I started for my host to ask him to present me to his brother, but was waylaid by a guest who was "sailing for the States in a fortnight," and would I "give him a few points?" I did, until it was suggested that we join the ladies. This pleasant diversion lasted until after midnight, when the party broke up.

As I was going home, my host said to me: "Well, did you get my brother to tell you all he knows about British politics?"

"My dear fellow," I answered, "I still have to meet your brother, let alone talk with him."

"You mean to say you didn't meet him?" he asked with the greatest surprise and concern.

"How could I?" I asked. "I wasn't introduced to a soul, and I don't even know what your brother looks like."

The following day I lunched with the two brothers, but not a word was said about the previous evening.

Finally, at the close of the luncheon, I said to the brother whom I had known so well, and who had been several times in the United States and thus knew our customs, "Just what is your idea in not introducing guests? You English always have a good reason for your customs. What is the reason for this?"

"Well," he answered, "you see, it's this way. It—you see—well, it's this way—it just isn't done, is it?"

VI

Gradually, the uncomfortable custom is disappearing in England, especially at public dinners, where introductions, particularly in the case of Americans, are beginning to be made. It is awkwardly done, it is true, but the custom is breaking in. In private houses, however, where the usage can easily be much more embarrassing, the custom rigidly prevails. The awkward part is that the identity of the American guest is, as a rule, known, since the dinner or week-end party is often given for him, but it may be hours before he has any idea of the identity of the person to whom he is speaking.

It must be said, however, that the English usually have an excellent reason for their customs, strange as they may seem to us. I remember how during my earlier visits to England I was invariably surprised that, upon arriving at some small railroad station to spend the week-end, I was never met by my host, although the friendship might be of years' standing, but always by a groom who conducted me to a waiting "fly."

On one of these occasions I asked a close English friend the basis for this custom.

"Well, you see," he answered, "you greet a friend at the portal of your home to which you have invited him. You haven't asked him to the railway station. have you?"

Which, of course, was not only neatly said, but true.

The fact must never be overlooked by the travelling American that his English friend is quite unconscious of any variation from customs with which the Americans are familiar. He is simply following the usage of his people upon which he has been brought up. It is just as natural for him not to introduce two persons to each other as for us instinctively to do the opposite. In such a matter the American should intelligently understand and gracefully accept the familiar behest,—while in Rome do as the Romans do. The basis may have been outlived, and not in touch with modern times. It may go back to far-off days, but I have never yet known an English custom which did not have some plausible reason.

VII

"We have always done that," laughingly said a Briton to me once of an English custom. "Probably it was done when London was the capital of Denmark, and before that. I presume we always shall do it. We are like that, you know."

TWENTY-FOUR:

THE MAN WHO SAW THE SEA

"What was his prayer is all the world's."

RUDYARD KIPLING

THE MAN WHO SAW THE SEA

I

THE recollections of the Great War brought to mind by the two preceding chapters naturally lead to some experiences I had with the great figure who on this side of the water sat with his hand on the American helm.

It was a good many years before that war when a man dropped into the seat beside me as I was riding one day on the "shuttle" from Princeton to "the Junction," and said: "May I sit here and talk with you? My name is Wilson."

"I wanted to tell you how much interested I was in your successful fight against patent-medicines," continued the President of Princeton University.

We talked all the way to Philadelphia, and the next day, at the office, a card "Woodrow Wilson" was brought to me.

"Just to continue our chat of yesterday," said the caller as he followed his card, "and to ask if you will join me at lunch. I want to see if some fillings I have had put in my teeth work all right."

At the luncheon table we sat and talked for nearly three hours, after which the Princeton President went to his train.

"Was that your brother with you yesterday at luncheon?" asked a friend the following day.

"My brother?" I queried.

"Yes," replied the friend. "He looked enough like you."

As the Princeton President did nearly all the talking, I had a wonderful opportunity to study him, and I was particularly impressed with the orderly quality of his mind. He had what a friend once termed "a beautiful thinking machine," and it acted at his will. Even when he grew enthusiastic and spoke fast, which was not often, there were no bumpings evident in the operation of his mental mechanics. I was amused at that time, as I was later when I visited him in the White House, at the extent of his knowledge and use of slang and the street idioms of the day. It was almost ludicrous at times to suddenly hear a well-rounded sentence, in fault-less English, broken into by a slang expression.

I once asked him about his seeming fondness for slang.

"Nothing in the language more expressive," he re-plied, "than some of our slang words and phrases."

"Do you deplore that fact?" I asked.

"No," he answered, "slang is perfectly permissible, to my mind, both in conversation and addresses. I frequently resort to slang in my talks with the students. Makes them feel I am human."

"Which they generally don't?" I asked.

"Which they invariably don't," he corrected, with a smile.

I asked how he had acquired his command of language.

"From my father," was the answer. "He had a rever-ence for words, and he would never allow us to misuse a word. Not only would he point out the misuse, but he would explain its misuse and stress the correct use of the word. And he was always interesting. I do not know a man who could be so absorbingly interesting in the explanation as to the use of a single word."

It was a memorable luncheon talk, for the President was in the midst of his troubles at Princeton, and I asked him about them, saying that I had a son coming out of preparatory school and was considering Princeton for the boy.

"I might unconsciously influence you," said Mr. Wilson. "Better probe into the facts yourself. Then you will get both sides."

"But I got the other side until three o'clock in the morning the other night at Princeton," I persisted.

"That is different," he smilingly returned. "I can't promise you such a long session as that, but if you have the other side, I'll give you mine."

For an hour he did.

Thus began an acquaintance which ripened into a friendship and an admiration, on my part, for the man who, in the future, was to go so far,—farther than almost any man of his generation.

II

It was the human Woodrow Wilson that I met and knew. Our relations never became official. I had sought his friendship and apparently won it long before he entered political life. I had not sought the Governor of New Jersey or the President of the United States. In fact, I met him only once while he was Governor, on a train going to New York, and then as each was wearing the same kind of pepper-and-salt suit and precisely the same style of soft gray felt hat, he laughed and said "Look more like each other than ever, don't we? Well, that's an advantage for me. The people in the car will think you are the Governor, and as the Governor of New Jersey isn't very popular just now, I'll get all the pleasant bows intended for the more acceptable Editor of *The Ladies' Home Journal*. Let's walk down the car and try it out. You were on your way to the smoking compartment, weren't you?"

Then, by one of those strange coincidences which will sometimes happen, a woman in the middle of the car bowed to the Governor and called him by my name: then saw me following behind, and looked non-plussed. Convulsed with laughter, the Governor literally ran to the smoking compartment, and with a "What did I tell you?" threw himself on the seat, in high glee.

III

During the early part of his Presidency, I saw little of Woodrow Wilson. He was busy, and the little I had to offer I wrote him. He felt secure in my readiness to serve him, and on two occasions he called upon me. He knew I had no axe to grind, no interests to serve and no ambitions to gratify. There was no position within his power to give which I would accept, although he did offer me one, and urged my acceptance of it, only later to assure me that he felt I was wise in having declined it. Contrary to a general impression, Woodrow Wilson was not a man who wanted you to go along with him whether you agreed or differed with him. He indicated not the slightest feeling of resentment when I refused the honor he held out to me; all that he asked was an intelligent and convincing reason for my declination. There came several occasions when I differed with him, and each time I found him receptive to argument and more than willing to get my point of view. I remember on one occasion I was diametrically opposed to what seemed his point of view. I told him I could not see his point.

"Why?" was his invariable question.

I explained, and he asked question after question. At the close of an hour, I said: "Well, I think I have said enough without convincing you."

"Why so sure?" he queried. "On the contrary, I think you are entirely right. You have made me see the question from a different angle."

"I thought from your questioning—" I said.

"Just drawing you out and getting what I wanted," he answered with a smile. "What I ask of a man is that he shall not alone be destructive, but constructive. You have been. The trouble with ninety per cent of the people who come in here is that they want to destroy, but have no suggestion for anything in place of what they seek to tear down. I have scant patience with that type. Then they go out and say that I am stubborn, or that my mind is closed, or that I won't take advice."

"Look over that calendar for the past week," he said on another occasion when he had an important public question before him, as he handed me his engagement pad. "They say I am playing a lone hand in this matter, and will not see people who know. How about these?"

I looked over the pad, and confessed I was surprised at the number of influential men he had seen and talked with,—all on the one question before him. "I am going around the clock on this question," he commented.

"But the public doesn't know this," I argued. "I confess I didn't: I was getting the impression you were not seeing enough people."

"Oh, you want me to be like your friend, T. R.: publish a list of all my callers, and give a first-page story to the newspaper boys every day," he said with a hearty laugh.

"No, Mr. President," I returned, "I don't want you to be like Colonel Roosevelt or any one else. You couldn't be, for one thing, and it would do you harm rather than good. Your friends want you to be yourself, but they feel, as I do, that you might have a greater regard for the power of the first-page of the newspaper."

"Publicity," he rejoined: "always publicity. I am expected to work in the public glare. No, it isn't my way. Look at the notes I have made of all these talks after the callers had left."

And he handed me a sheaf of sheets covered with stenographic notes.

"Oh, I forgot," he said as he reached out his hand to take back the sheets. "They are not for you. You know shorthand." And, smilingly, he put the note-sheets in the drawer of his desk.

IV

Only once had I occasion to bring an official matter to his attention. I presented the facts to him.

"Of course, you know," was his comment, "that you should take this to ——," mentioning a member of his

Cabinet. Then seeing the expression on my face, he added, with a smile, "You don't seem overjoyed at the prospect somehow."

"Frankly, Mr. President, I am not," I replied.

"Why not?" he asked. "You don't join in all this push against —— ?"

"I don't have to join in any push," I answered. "It is what I have personally experienced at his hands. I don't believe in him, and you must admit it is hard to deal with a man in whom you have no confidence."

"Very," he returned. "But what are your grounds?"

"These," I answered, handing him two letters, one absolutely contradictory of the statements in the other.

The President read and handed them back to me. "Not quite according to Hoyle, I admit," he said. "However, you are too old to overlook the fact that all of us lapse from grace sometimes."

"Lapse, yes, perhaps, but not flop," I answered.

"Well, I guess you're hopeless so far as —— is concerned. Let me have your memoranda, I'll see him to-morrow and ask him to write you."

As I left him, he said: "Don't forget, my good fellow, that if one lapse from grace made of us a criminal, we would all be in jail. Nor do I by that remark excuse ——'s flop, as you call it. Life is a game of give and take, you know, and the best of us are none too best," he said. And with a smile he added "Go and parse that sentence."

V

It was late in January, 1917, in those troublous times of the War, that I called at the White House to pay my respects to the President. I was on my way South for the winter, I told him, and I also mentioned that I was turning in my mind my resignation from the editorship of *The Ladies' Home Journal.*

"Not now. Not for one minute," he answered. "You stay where you are. This is no time to consult your own wishes or pleasure,—not in these times."

"I judged from what I read that we might not go into the War after all," I commented.

"No escape from it," he answered. "It is inevitable that we should go in."

"When?" I ventured.

"That I can't answer now. Come back in a month, and I may be able to tell you more. Cut your stay in the South down to that period, and don't resign. You will be wanted where you are. You have the ear of the American woman by the millions, and there will be much for you to tell her. The War, so far as America is concerned, won't be fought in France. It will be fought right here,—in the homes and in the factories. And the women are going to loom large in the picture. So, no resigning. This is no time to think of that."

VI

I explained to him the predicament in which I would find myself if the United States did go into the War. I was editing a magazine which because of its huge circulation had to be prepared and put to press three months before publication. It would hardly be helpful to publish peace issues if the country was at war. How was I to know three months in advance?

"The embarrassment of success, hey?" queried the President. "I should say you have something of a puzzle there."

"But you will be better informed than any other man in the United States," I argued.

"Perhaps," he answered. "What do you think I can do?"

"Just let me come to you once in a while, and guide me as well as you can. That's all."

"Of course," he said. "That's understood. And if you can't get at me, see Colonel House. One of us will tell you what we know. But in modern warfare and in a war of this size, that won't be much. One battle of the magnitude of modern battles will change the entire scheme of things overnight, one way or the other. Remember that. If I were you, with your fearful disadvantage, I would leave the questions of the actual front to the newspapers, and you handle the domestic questions. There will be enough of them, and big enough for you. And they will be more stationary than events in France. In these, some of us can help you, and of course we will."

VII

In a month I was back, as he had suggested.

"Well," said the President. "We are nearer, and I think you had better begin, since you prepare your magazine so far in advance. You said you wanted to be guided so that you can teach your big elephant to dance. Well, tackle the navy first."

"Not the army?" I ventured.

"No, that will come later. The navy first. Get the mothers into a frame of mind to let their boys enlist in the navy. That is first. Then, tackle the Red Cross. Better have a regular monthly department devoted to that, and get the women to go in and get ready. For when the Red Cross is needed it will be needed badly."

And with a vision as clear as crystal, he sketched out for me my work, even to the prophecy of a food department with which all the women of America were to co-operate.

VIII

One day I got word to come to the White House that evening.

"Do you know Herbert Hoover?" the President asked me.

"Only by reputation," I answered.

"Well, he is winding up his Belgian work in London, and sails in a few days to come here and organize a Food Department. Hoover, better than any man in the world, understands the food question in the large sense. He may not see it so easily in the small family unit. There is where you come in. I want you to get back of Hoover, and give him your fullest support, and open up your magazine to him, so that he can reach the women under the most favorable auspices. There will be much to explain to them and ask of them."

"Along conservation lines, I take it?" I asked.

"Yes, and actual sacrifice: a case of conserving until it hurts. So get in line with Hoover when he arrives, and start your campaign of educating the American housewife as quickly as you can. There may be necessity for educating women to know substitute foods if we get enough of an army over there. The boys will have to be given the best, and we must get along with what is left."

Thus, with an instinctive editorial sense, did the President forecast a situation that later confronted the American people in grim earnestness.

IX

Yet, so far as any publicity concerning himself was concerned, he was the poorest kind of a publicist. As a matter of fact, he was resentful of any personal exploitation.

At this same interview, where Mrs. Wilson was present, I cautiously suggested that I would like to get him more into the picture.

"That's an inspiring thought. Had an idea I was very much in the picture,—more than some people like to have me, I should judge. How do you mean?" laughingly asked the President.

"I want to give a double page of photographs depicting your personal side," was my careful approach to a subject which I knew was not to his taste.

"Why?" he asked.

"Well, I think the people should know better the man behind the official," I argued.

"How solicitous you are that I should be correctly understood, as you call it, aren't you?" he smilingly queried. "The trouble is you can't see that you want to put the emphasis on the wrong side of me. That part belongs to my family."

"Not altogether," I persisted. "The trouble with you is, Mr. President, if you will let me paraphrase your statement, you won't let your friends put the emphasis on the side the public wants to know about. Your fine distinction between your private self and that of the President of the United States satisfies you, but not the people."

"I think he is right, dear," interposed Mrs. Wilson, who was sitting by, sewing. He wants a picture like this, for instance, you reading and I sewing. Why not?"

"Two to one," returned the President.

"Well, can you beat the combination?" I asked.

"No," he hopelessly assented, "I don't think I can. What do you want?"

"Pictures of you playing golf, walking out, driving, on horseback——"

"Stop right there," he interjected. "Not on horseback. Ever see me on horseback? No? Well, you have missed something in your young life. I saw myself once. I met a man on the road carrying a large mirror. I stopped him purposely so that I could take a look at myself on a horse. I wanted to find out whether folks I met stared at the President or at the grotesque figure on the horse. One glance was enough. I looked like nothing else so much as a smoke-stack gone wrong. 'Me for golf after this,' I said to myself, and golf it has been. I pride myself on a sense of humor, but it didn't carry me far enough to that stack on a horse."

"Very well," I assured him, "we will leave the horse out of it."

"I'll get you a picture I have," ventured Mrs. Wilson, "and it has never been published."

"Keep it so," interrupted the President.

"It shows Mr. Wilson on donkey-back," went on Mrs. Wilson, "in Egypt, years ago. No one has ever seen it outside the family."

"Nor should any one," added the President. "Well, I see it's no use. I don't expect either of you to use discretion, because I don't think you have any. I suppose all I can expect and ask is mercy! Be sure," he concluded, as he picked up a book, "to add a list of my favorite one hundred books, the poems I love best, my favorite dishes, my favorite chair and how I like to sit when I am reading, how many hours I sleep, and on which side I sleep. These details will add to the unusual quality of the article and give it literary distinction. If you don't know any of these points, come to me, and having nothing important to do in these war-times, I'll take a day off and devote myself to deep thought on all these important points in my life, and, if necessary, I can go to sleep for an hour or two, and you can photograph me and get the exact angle at which I commune with Morpheus. If you two are going to do this thing, you might as well get every detail right and leave nothing to the imagination. You make me tired," was his final thrust, as he yawned to give his parting shot the desired effect. But he couldn't refrain from furtively looking over his shoulder at the photographs which Mrs. Wilson had brought in and began to assort on the table.

"Be sure to put one in when I wore Burnsides," was

his last comment. "That picture ought to make a killing."

After an hour's discussion between Mrs. Wilson and myself, the President, who had gone on reading, finally yawned most expansively and turning to me asked: "Doesn't your hotel close at all at night?"

"Don't mind what he says," returned Mrs. Wilson. "Up-stairs here he is just like any one of us, and we pay no attention to him."

"I move," said the President, "we adjourn to a floor below."

A little later I did!

"Well," said the President, "I hate to say it, but come again!"

X

It used to call forth all my restraint—as it does to-day, for that matter—to listen to men who knew Woodrow Wilson only from what they read of him or what others chose to tell of him to his disadvantage, and listen to their unintelligent and baseless analysis of him. He was afraid, he was cold-blooded, distant, reserved, always playing a lone hand, a poor mixer, and so forth.

I once mentioned this opinion to him.

"Oh, I know," he answered. "I am anaemic, academic, a hard-boiled school-teacher. Of course," he said, "my life has been spent, much of it at least, in my study; among books and papers rather than among men, and perhaps I carry the smell of the study about me. Then to be a college president does put a man apart from his fellow men. The faculty looks upon you as its superior officer, and the students as their enemy. So there you are: perforce pretty well alone. Ridiculous, but true, as every college president knows."

"They say I am always writing, never acting," he said to me one evening at the White House: "they talk about a multiplicity of notes which I am sending. Those who say these things, including your friend, Colonel Roosevelt, forget that they can talk all they like: I can't. I am the only man who can't let off steam when he wants to. Everything I say is official; everything you say is unofficial. I have to sit on the lid and wait with what damned little patience I have for every happening to be checked up officially before I can write or speak or even think out loud. Do this, do that, I am told, in connection with something that has happened and is reported with scare-heads in the newspapers. But how do I know that this something *has* happened, until it is officially reported to me? And sometimes the facts get to me officially checked up after the public has forgotten this particular something, and is off prodding me up on another something that is in the papers. A pretty figure I would cut if I acted officially on unofficial information gathered from the newspapers. The very people who would prod me on would be the first to criticize me for acting on information without official proof. And if you have ever dealt with the foreign offices in Europe and tried to get rapid action,—well, it's easier to teach a fish how to sing."

XI

In another talk he said to me: "Your people in Philadelphia, and the newspapers, are all writing to push me into the War. And what is true of Philadelphia is true of the newspapers and people living in the other cities on the Eastern seaboard. They are very loud in their patriotism. But wait. Into this War we will go, because we can't keep out of it. Then, mark this prophecy, and I'll wager you anything you like on its fulfillment: when war is declared and the quota for volunteer service is given out, each one of those Eastern states will be the last to reach its quota."

This turned out to be the case, exactly as he prophesied.

"And," he continued, "the Western states, whose people are now indifferent and plead with me to keep out of the War, will be the first to raise their quota of men."

This also came true.

"I know that kind of patriotism. You have only to read the corresponding period in the Civil War. What these folks in your town and others forget is that I am not the President of the Eastern half of the United States; I am President of the United States as a whole. I know the lack of war sentiment in the West, and until I can rally that and bring into the War a united country, it would be foolhardy to go in. Nor can you blame the Western people, removed as they are from the European contacts with the Eastern seaports. They are busy with their own affairs, their crops and their manufactures. They see no reason why their young men should be asked to take part in a quarrel five and six thousand miles distant from them.

"A prominent newspaper owner from the Northwest was in to see me to-day, and frankly acknowledged that

he answered, "better see me, and I will give you some-thing you can do." He did, and when I reported to him upon my return he told me he was going to Paris.

"Risky," I commented.

"For whom or what?" he asked.

"For you and your personal prestige," I answered.

"That is not the question," he fairly snapped out. "My personal future or my political fortunes matter not. It is what I can do on the ground better than from this distance. I know I cannot realize the impossible things that the people of Europe feel I can do. I know all that. I know there will be a tumble, and I'll be the one who will do the tumbling act. That is inevitable. No man can make good as a Deity. It's the cause I am after: not what becomes of me. The cause," he repeated, as he wheeled around and looked out through the window. Then as his eye fell on the distance where the Lincoln memorial was to be, he turned to me and said: "I be-lieve Lincoln would have gone."

Those were his last words to me in the White House.

XIII

My next meeting, and I saw to it that it was to be my last after what happened, was in the S Street house. My visit was in response to a note asking Mrs. Wilson if her husband was seeing any one. I received the com-plimentary word: "Hardly any one, but he will be glad to see you." He received me in bed. "I have been at my correspondence all morning," he explained, "and if you don't mind I'll see you here while I rest." I could not help contrasting the circumstances of our first meeting, and said so.

"Yes, I remember distinctly," he agreed. "A good deal of water has gone under the bridge since that time."

We talked of olden days, of his Princeton tenure of office, of his Governorship,—of anything save of those turbulent days in the White House which, by understanding with Mrs. Wilson before I entered the room, were taboo. But he would not have it so. I was conducting in Philadelphia, for Colonel House, the series of talks on "What Really Happened in Paris," and he wanted to know how the talks were progressing. "You have kept me splendidly posted, but I want to get a first-hand impression," he said.

This led, naturally, to the days to be avoided in our talk, and, despite a warning from Mrs. Wilson, he persisted.

"I must talk to some one," he said in a moment when the faithful wife had left the room, "or I'll explode." And he went on, and told me much. It was the day upon which Secretary Lansing's book was published, and the newspapers were full of extracts from it. We touched upon it, and he asked me if I had read the book. "That's one side of the story," he commented. "There's another." And he gave it to me in interesting and convincing detail.

"The public should know this," I said.

"Not from me," was his quick retort. "Nor from you. History will set that all straight,—after I am gone."

"But—" I began.

"That won't be long," he cut in. "Remember the

lines in Kipling's 'If' which you sent me in his auto-graph?"

"Which lines?" I asked.

And with a choke in his voice and tears in his eyes at the close, he recited:

> "If you can stand to hear the truth you've spoken
> Twisted by knaves to make a trap for fools,
> Or watch the work you've given your life to broken,
> And stoop and build it up with worn-out tools."

"They are searching,—those lines," commented the man in bed.

"But you forget those other lines by Kipling," I ventured.

"Which?" he asked as he wiped away the tears and said: "Don't mind those tears; they are always good for us."

"These:

> "'Let us now praise famous men—
> Men of little showing—
> For their work continueth,
> And their work continueth,
> Greater than their knowing'."

"That's the other side of it," I added.

"Perhaps," he partially agreed. Then, with his ac-customed smile: "Let us go on with what you are telling me. A useless man is not a fruitful topic for a talk."

But as we talked—and I arose twice to leave—it was increasingly evident to me that the reversal to the stormy days of the past was not for the best of the invalid.

Try as I might, however, I could not change the drift of the talk into other channels.

Then, suddenly, came the moment which I feared. He gave a deep moan, the face went pallid, he called my name and stretched out his right hand to me, which I clasped, and unconsciousness came. I was all alone. Gently I unclasped his hand which had tightened around mine, rushed out of the room, sought Mrs. Wilson, and telephone calls went out for the doctors. It was a full half-hour before consciousness was restored.

As I left the house, I concluded that I would not again seek another interview. I suggested the past too strongly to him; and the past was not a wise resting-place for the stricken man who had been so great a figure in it.

XIV

It is a remark made and oft repeated that Woodrow Wilson failed in his great vision. But did he? Is it not more likely that time will prove that it was not he, but the American people who failed? They could not go along with him. They could not see the vision which he saw and which will become visible to other eyes and then come to a realization. It may be that he fell short of his destiny. But it has happened before that a present age has been unable to properly understand and appreciate the man in its midst, and has left it for Posterity to make a pathway to his shrine. The man of vision often precedes the doer, and his message is not always understood. Marcus Aurelius fell short of his goal. The vision of Christ had to be tempered to human understanding by Paul. The vision of Washington had to be translated into actuality by Jefferson. It is not at all beyond the pale of likelihood that time will demonstrate that, like many another prophet, Woodrow Wilson ascended the heights too soon, and that it was destined his life was the price he was to pay before the idea in which he so passionately believed was to come into being. Because he did not live to see victory for the cause for which he stood, it does not by any means follow that the echoes of that higher morality among nations which he preached will not come down to us in the years to come, as, in fact, it is already returning to a weary world. It seems strange that a life must be the penalty before we learn to do right. It was always thus, and probably always will be so. But it is also singularly true that the dead have their way.

XV

There is a legend of an Indian chief who was wont to try the strength of his youths by making them run in a single effort as far up the side of a mountain as each could reach by his main strength. On an appointed day, four left at daybreak. The first returned with a branch of spruce, indicating the height to which he had attained. The second bore a twig of pine. The third brought an Alpine shrub. But it was by the light of the moon that the fourth made his way back. Then he came, worn and exhausted, and his feet were torn by the rocks.

"What did you bring, and how high did you ascend?" asked the chief.

"Sire," he replied, "where I went there was neither spruce nor pine to shelter me from the sun, nor flower to cheer my path, but only rocks and snow and barren land. My feet are torn, and I am exhausted, and I have come late, but ——"

And as a wonderful light came into his eyes, the young brave added:

—"I saw the sea."

TWENTY-FIVE:

THE PRESIDENT

"Count me o'er earth's chosen heroes,
They were souls that stood alone."

EMERSON

THE PRESIDENT

I

THE flames of war were rising over the land. The pressure upon the President had been, for months, intense and insistent. Appeals poured in asking that the President take action. The newspapers, particularly along the Eastern seaboard, clamored loudly. Government officials, delegations, and organizations of all kinds joined in the demand. Even the personal friends of the President echoed the insistent cry.

"Have we no self-respect?" wrote one editor.

"Are we to stand before the world afraid?" asked another.

"Have we a coward in the White House?" came from a famous orator.

Silence hung over the White House. To those who called upon him, friend and stranger alike, the President looked grave, shook his head, and merely said, "War is a frightful thing." Then, one day, he went a step further and said "I can only watch and wait."

Derision now broke out in the newspapers. "Watch and wait, forsooth. How long? Until our name is a reproach to courage and a byword for cowardice?"

The business interests of the country insisted that the uncertainty of war was endangering the economic structure of the country. Even the churches began to counsel war "for God and the right."

In volume and violence grew the demand. Stronger words now found their way into the newspaper editorials. "Coward" was frequently met with. "Bungler," cried an orator. "Deaf to reason and unwilling to listen," was the universal opinion.

Not a word came, however, from the man in the White House, whereupon he was told that "silence may at times be golden, but there are also times when it may spell cowardice."

Weeks grew into months, and yet the President sat calm and, to all outer appearances, undisturbed.

He was now adjudged "remote." Friends and officials ceased to counsel. He was "only willing to commune with himself and not with others." If advice was offered "it was met with rebuff." He was told that "he was untrained for the position and unable to grasp the situation." He "had proclaimed himself for an ideal and then had not the courage to fight for it."

So it went on. Patiently sat the President, and when friends told him of the widespread impatience he replied wearily, "Yes, I know. But they don't have to make the decision."

II

Then, one day, came the hour for action.

"At last," was the exultant cry.

The people got ready. Orators orated. Bands played. Registration places opened over night. The "regulars" marched through the streets to their armories. Women began to sew, and girls said good-bye to their sweethearts. Men too old to go into service wrote the President and told him how to conduct the War. All got busy,—for human slaughter!

Then followed another cannonade on the doors of the White House. Matters were not moving fast enough,— particularly to suit those who could not enlist. Now came "the right to know." What plans had the President? Why did he not reveal them to the people? Had he any? When Cabinet members were asked about preparations, they nodded toward the White House. When members of Congress were approached, they answered, "The President." Nobody knew but the President.

Again the President was silent.

"Is this a one-man war?" the editors now asked.

"Are the people to be told nothing?" inquired another.

"Will the President kindly oblige?" sarcastically suggested a third.

"Watching and waiting again," ironically said a fourth.

From no quarter came encouragement to the man holding his lonely vigil in the White House. Gradually it became apparent that all was not harmonious in the Cabinet. There was little or no support of the President in Congress.

III

Then came a victorious battle, and newspapers cried out in exultation, and the people shouted and cheered,— until the tidings of the dead and wounded were learned. Then sober thought reigned.

Again a battle,—and again a long list of boys killed in action.

"Is victory to be bought at such a fearful price?" the people asked.

To which the President replied, "There is only one kind of war."

Soon the question was asked for the first time, "How long will this last?" And it was not long before appeals came to the President to "stop the war."

"But it was only a short time back that you urged me to start the war," was the answer from the White House. "You can't start and stop a war as you can a watch."

The same voices which only a few weeks before had called the President a coward afraid to fight, now began to tell him that he was "regardless of human life." He was "thirsting for blood to realize his ideal!"

"This fearful thing must stop," was the repeated word at the White House as the casualty lists grew by leaps and bounds. Folks began to recall the President's earlier words that war was "a frightful thing."

The President was again "willful, remote, insensible to argument, unwilling to listen to counsel; or, he was "filled with a self-importance. Although with no military training or background of statesmanship, he is attempting to run the war himself. No one is consulted. Advice falls on barren ground."

The President was "playing a lone hand." The American Ambassador to the Court of Saint James's hinted that he could receive no definite information from the White House or Department of State on those questions which involved the nation to which he was accredited. Cabinet members said in confidence that the first information they had of orders which came within the

scope of their departments they learned from the newspapers at their breakfast-tables.

The President was running the war; no one else. He
would listen to no one; he would counsel with no one.
"The lonely man in the White House" became a universal characterization of the President.

So the war went on to the dissatisfaction of every one.

When in a momentous address the President defined
the crisis in human civilization which he was trying as
an honest and high-minded leader to meet and solve,
showing the people most truly and clearly the right way
and the wrong, it was only to be met by the criticism
that he was "a spinner of fine phrases."

IV

Then came the first rumors of peace. But again silence hung heavily over the White House.

"Have not the people the right to know what is going
on?" again became the cry.

"Whose war is this, pray?" came the ironical query.

"No morsel of hope or comfort to those whose boys
are at the front comes from the solitary figure on Pennsylvania Avenue," complained one editor.

"We shall know in time," counselled another editor.
"In a year or two, perhaps. That is, if the President
wills it. Remember, he is watching and waiting."

The closing days of the war thus dragged on, and little
came from the White House. Meanwhile the President
toiled and passed many a sleepless night, perceptibly
aging, physically spent, steadily advancing, step by step,
to that day when, as a bolt from the blue, he fell,—

just as truly a soldier in the war as any one of "his boys," as he used to call them, that fell on the battlefields.

As always happens, there followed an aftermath of sorrow, and it was not long before those who pushed him aside during his life-time began to see that he knew better than they. Calumny ceased. Praise took its place. The man who was President was now standing, as we must all stand, before God for that judgment that faileth not.

"A true picture, very true," commented the Critic when he had read what is written above. "But don't you think that if the President had not been so remote, or seemed so self-centred, so willing to commune only with himself, he would have avoided much of the anxiety which he thus brought upon himself, and which after all was the direct cause of his downfall?"

"Downfall?" I repeated. "Whose downfall?"

"Woodrow Wilson's," answered the Critic.

"But this sketch is not of Woodrow Wilson," I ventured.

"Of whom, pray, is it, then?" was the astonished query.

"Of Abraham Lincoln."

TWENTY-SIX:

TWICE-BORN IN TWICE THIRTY

"Like, but oh! how different!"

WORDSWORTH

———

"Yet I doubt not through the ages one increasing purpose runs,
And the thoughts of men are widened with the process of the suns."

TENNYSON

TWICE–BORN IN TWICE THIRTY

I

IT was five years ago now that I wrote and published *The Americanization of Edward Bok*. In a prefatory word, I explained the reason why I had chosen to write the book in the third person, instead of using the personal pronoun, because, among other reasons, "the Edward Bok, editor and publicist, whom I have tried to describe in this book, has had and has been, in many respects, a personality apart from my private self. I have again and again found myself watching with intense amusement and interest the Edward Bok of this book at work. Not that I ever considered myself bigger and broader than this Edward Bok,—simply that he was different. His tastes, his outlook, his manner of looking at things were totally at variance with my own. In fact, my chief difficulty during Edward Bok's directorship of *The Ladies' Home Journal* was to abstain from breaking through the editor and revealing my real self. Several times I did so, and each time I saw how different was the effect from that when the editorial Edward Bok had been allowed sway. Little by little I learned to subordinate myself and to let him have full rein.

"But no relief of my life was so great to me personally as his decision to retire from his editorship. . . . Since that time my feelings have been an interesting study to myself. There are no longer two personalities. The Edward Bok of whom I have written has passed out of my being as completely as if he had never been there, save for the records and files on my library shelves. It is easy, therefore, for me to write of him as a personality apart: in fact, I could not depict him from any other point of view. To write of him in the first person, as if he were myself, is impossible, for he is not."

II

Folks in numbers have written and asked how this could be true; how two distinct personalities could exist in the same physical person, with one active and the other inactive. "I can imagine this might be so for a short time, but it seems incredible that one personality should dominate continuously for a period of thirty years," wrote one correspondent. But I did not say continuously: on the contrary, I distinctly wrote that I did break through at times, and that whenever I did so I saw how different was the effect from that when the editorial personality was uppermost.

As an instance of what I mean: the writings of Rudyard Kipling were never popular with the readers of *The Ladies' Home Journal*. I was determined, however, that the people should get at least a taste of them and get acquainted at first hand with a writer whom I reckoned as the greatest of his day. So I broke through the editorial personality, and persistently published in succession *William the Conqueror*, the *Just So* stories, the *Puck of Pook's Hill* stories. As each story appeared a stream of letters would come in asking what Mr. Kipling meant and why we published the material. Inquiry grew into irritation, but still I persisted, until after the first six stories in the *Puck of Pook's Hill* series I gave way and, as Mr. Kipling always permitted an editor to preserve his prerogative, it was decided that the second series of these stories should not be published in the magazine. But decided by whom? By myself? Not at all. I should have persisted and published the second series because I believed in the series and knew their merit. The fight simply grew unequal, and the dominant editorial personality became so insistent and strong that I became submerged. It was a mental battle which I distinctly remember as peculiarly exhausting, and resulted in a nervous breakdown.

From the editorial standpoint, and that is the only point of view which Edward Bok could ever assume, the decision to withhold Mr. Kipling's writings from the magazine was entirely correct. So irritated did many readers become that they stopped their subscriptions to the magazine, frankly giving their reason. But my real self recognized the literary quality of the work, and felt the necessity of giving the people the best obtainable,— not only what they thought they liked, but what I thought they should have. With this view the editorial Edward Bok never had the least patience. "Give the people what they want," was his slogan. "Give the people what they ought to have and don't know they want," was mine.

III

One day at Mr. Kipling's home in Sussex he read to me his latest poem, and at its conclusion said "You can never publish that. The Journal sisters would break all your windows with the stones they would fire at you. You wouldn't have a whole pane left." I agreed that this might be so. All the same, I argued, we should publish the poem. It was vitriolic, but it held truth: it was timely and it was needful that what the poem said should be said. I felt the strong influence of the editorial Edward Bok arguing against any consideration of the poem. The magazine was a woman's periodical; the sentiment in the poem was a slander upon womanhood; thousands of American women would rise in wrath,—and the circulation of the magazine would be seriously injured. All of which came true exactly as the editorial personality had predicted, and for weeks the atmosphere in the magazine's editorial office was, to say the least, tense. But I won out.

The poem was Mr. Kipling's famous "The Female of the Species."

IV

There was a period extending some six months when my own personality was undoubtedly dominant in the conduct of *The Ladies' Home Journal*, and I was personally amazed at the transformation of the contents of the magazine. So were its readers, of whom eighty thousand forthwith discontinued buying or subscribing to the magazine within six months. In an incredibly short time I had given what they deemed a "high-brow" atmosphere to the magazine. I had engaged a corps of writers who had never appeared in the contents; the best and most trenchant of the questions of the day were treated by such pens as former President Eliot, Lyman

Abbott, Jane Addams, Dean Hodges, and others. A weight of authority was given to the periodical which it never had before. The editorials were largely from the same pens,—and the people revolted! They did not expect such material in their magazine; they could find such subjects treated elsewhere, and they would have none of it, they said. It was not long, however, before I felt that unconsciously my real self had lost my grip on the editorial helm, Edward Bok had risen to the surface and I was submerged. The contents went back to its former standard, the circulation leaped forward, and the subscription and advertising departments were happy once more! Edward Bok was in the saddle!

But during the time when I did function I felt no interference from the editorial personality; I was in full sway. Nor was I in the least conscious of the time or the fact when I lost control and was submerged. But for a brief period I had my innings, and did an incredible amount of damage to the circulation. It was exactly as if two different men had been editing, my closest associate told me afterward. He little knew how truthfully he had spoken!

V

I came to the surface again when the idea came to me of publishing, in their full colors, the masterpieces of painting in the private galleries of the United States. This time I did not have full sway. I recall with perfect clearness the battle royal between the two personalities. There was no popular interest in these great masterpieces: the people wanted the more ephemeral art of the modern illustrators, argued the editorial Edward Bok. The pictures I had in mind to reproduce would represent an outlay of at least a quarter of a million dollars, which would be an entire waste, and once embarked on it the series would have to go through to the bitter end, was the further argument. It would be not only a gigantic waste of money, but, in any event, the owners of the pictures, like Mr. Morgan, Mr. Widener, Mrs. Have-meyer, Mr. Freer, Mr. Frick, Mr. Taft, and the others would never consent. And Edward Bok was certainly well supported by the entire editorial staff: not a member believed in my idea. It was impressed upon me that not only would it be a waste of space, but the circulation would be injured. However, I persisted, proved my associates wrong by securing the permission of all the owners of the pictures, printed a series which has never been equalled in any popular magazine and, incidentally, added over one hundred thousand copies to the circulation of the periodical! This time, at least, I proved myself a better editor than Edward Bok.

VI

I was to be submerged, however, before the series reached its end. I had secured the permission of Mr. Freer, of Detroit, then living in New York, to reproduce some of his marvellous early Chinese panels. Knowing these to be the forerunners of western art, I was particularly anxious to have the people see the sources from which the great masters of painting had undoubtedly derived their inspiration. Mr. Freer was reluctant to have his treasures reproduced, being extremely skeptical that the indistinct tones and lines could be brought out by any process. Six artists worked for weeks in Mr. Freer's rooms, and finally results were produced which surprised and pleased even Mr. Freer. But they never reached the public. The editorial Edward Bok had become too strong in his dominance of the situation, and the beautiful reproductions, with their plates all made, rest for aught I know in the archives of the magazine! The early Chinese art proved too much for Edward Bok!

VII

To those who have made a study of dual personality, a recital of incidents such as the above are as old stories. They have again and again been demonstrated as not only possible, but as having existed in hundreds of human lives. It is to those whose minds have never rested on the problem of our dual selves that such "a peek-a-boo state," as one correspondent termed it, seems incomprehensible. The most popular exposition of this fascinating theme is, of course, to be found in Robert Louis Stevenson's *Doctor Jekyll and Mr. Hyde*, but it is to be feared that thousands who read this story accepted it as fiction and not, as it was, based on an actual case in Paris,—exaggerated, perhaps, in the story, but only with that permissible license granted the fictionist.

I remember very well when Richard Mansfield first produced the play based on the Stevenson story. I was with the Scribners, the publishers of the book, in the promotion department. Permission was obtained from the management of the Madison Square Theatre to place a table in the lobby of the theatre and to have the book on sale. I was entrusted to carry out the plan, to see nightly that a circular about the book was placed in each seat and to attend to the sales of the book in the lobby. Naturally, I went into the theatre to see the play, and from that point it was easy to drift "back stage," where, nightly, I saw the play from that point of vantage. I would see Mr. Mansfield come out of his dressing-room, wait at the proper "entrance" for his cue, and when the change would come from "Doctor Jekyll" into "Mr. Hyde," I would witness the transformation in the actor standing just a few feet away before he would "go on" before the audience. Evening after evening I would see this over a period of weeks, the idea kindled my imagination, and I began to read along lines of the different personalities in others, and in some still more pronounced.

VIII

Perhaps no man in the country has given more thought or study to this subject of dual personality than has Doctor Morton Prince, of Boston, whose case of four distinct personalities in the famous instance of "Miss Beauchamp," one of his patients, is known to all who have followed the revelations which have been brought out in studies along this line. Doctor Prince has declared that he has repeatedly had cases of not two, but three, and, in the case of "Miss Beauchamp," four personalities, one sharply distinct and different from the other, and that sometimes these personalities are dominant for hours, again for weeks, and sometimes for years. He has cited one case where one of two personalities has remained dominant for more than twenty-five years, and then became absolutely submerged and did not return.

The explanation for this has sometimes been based on a difference in the activity of the brain-cells involved in each personality, but this is not quite correct. As a matter of fact, very little is known about the cells of the brain, and practically nothing at all has been discovered as to which brain cells are in activity during one mental state or which in another. We have almost nothing to rely upon for a physiological explanation of dual personality. We have, however, much upon which to base a psychological explanation, because we know a great deal more about the mind than we do about the brain. Naturally, in the final analysis, everything, theoretically at least, is brought down to brain-cells, but it is not a question of different brain-cells being involved, but a different combination of those cells. It is very much like music: the same notes are used in "The Star-Spangled Banner" and in a Beethoven symphony, but the difference in the combination of the notes makes the difference in the compositions.

Doctor Prince's simplest explanation is that our different personalities are the expression of different "sides" to our characters; that is to say, different combinations of our traits, each combination being motivated by different instinctive tendencies, such as greed, self-assertion, love, sympathy, and curiosity. The last named tendency, by the way, is the motive which impels in all scientific investigations and the acquisition of knowledge. Our "traits" include our ideals, sentiments, and ambitions. Each combination becoming active produces a different personality. The person then thinks, feels, and acts according to the particular combination of ideals and instinctive tendencies in activity at any particular time, and during that time the other combination or combinations representing sides of the character are submerged.

IX

If Doctor Prince's theory is correct, and it has had abundant substantiation, the case of Edward Bok's dominant personality for almost thirty years passes out of the realm of the unusual. I use the adverb "almost" here because, although I was editor of *The Ladies' Home Journal* for a full period of thirty years, I was constantly aware during the last two or three years of my editorship that the personality of Edward Bok was slowly being submerged, and that, particularly during the period of the Great War, he was very little in evidence in the editorship of the magazine. It was with this growing sense upon me, and of a correspondingly increasing desire to work in other fields, that I felt my time of editorship was over.

X

A very interesting comment on this point was printed in *The Ledger* of Tacoma, Wash., wherein the writer said that a "couple of months ago the editors of the *Atlantic Monthly* received a manuscript submitted for their consideration from one Edward W. Bok. It came from the same address as that used by the author of *The Americanization of Edward Bok*. But this 'W' was something new under the sun. They wrote Mr. Bok asking if he had not made a mistake in putting the 'W' into his name. He replied: "Edward W. Bok is right; that is as I am now; Edward Bok was the chap who edited *The Ladies' Home Journal*, and he is no more. It's the real me now trying to express myself.' And readers of that autobiography had marvelled from the first how its author could so consistently write a whole book about himself in the third person, objectively. His subsequent writings reveal a new being, another self.

"Edward W. Bok is renewing his youth by new service for his fellow-men. For some, literature serves as the medium for the revelation of their other selves. . . . It was a serious-minded and somewhat solitary mathematician by the name of Charles Lutwidge Dodgson who became beloved by all childhood as Lewis Carroll, the author of *Alice's Adventures in Wonderland*.

"Another illustration occurs to us of literature serving to reveal our dual personalities. In Barrie's wholly charming and whimsically serious Rectorial Address delivered at Saint Andrew's University, on May 3, 1922, on 'Courage'—which all of us would be the better for reading—he says:

"'My special difficulty is that though you have had literary rectors here before, they were the big guns, the historians, the philosophers; you have had none, I think, who followed my more humble branch, which may be described as playing hide and seek with the angels. My puppets seem more real to me than myself, and I could get on much more swingingly if I made one of them deliver this address. It is M'Connachie who has brought me to this pass. M'Connachie, I should explain, as I have undertaken to open the innermost doors, is the name I give to the unruly half of myself: the writing half. We are complement and supplement. I am the half that is dour and practical and canny; he is the fanciful half—.' And, near the end of this first and, so he says, last public utterance of his, Barrie adds, concerning M'Connachie: '—he whispered to me just now that you elected him, not me, as your Rector.'

"William Sharp and his feminine other self, Fiona Macleod (sometimes called Wilfion, *i. e.*, William-Fiona), furnish the strangest and most interesting case of dual personality known among the writers of English literature."

XI

It must not be construed for a single moment from what I write, either directly or indirectly, that I belittle the wonderfully constructive piece of work carried out by Edward Bok during his editorship of *The Ladies' Home Journal*. The record of that achievement speaks too loudly to minimize its influence and potentiality. It will always retain a corner of my life close to my heart. It was simply not a work which from its very character I would have chosen to express my real self. There are undoubtedly acute problems which concern themselves with the proper ingredients in cooking recipes, the correct stitch in crocheting or knitting, the most desirable and daintiest kinds of lingerie, and the momentous question whether a skirt should escape the ground by six or eight inches. These are vital points in the lives of thousands of women, and their wisest solutions should be given by the best authorities. But is it too much to say that they are hardly of a nature to develop and satisfy the mental and spiritual nature of a man? At least, not for a lifetime!

XII

William James, of whose doctrines of psychology I am frankly an ardent disciple, has truly said that a process goes on in man's nature whereby, either suddenly or gradually, a self hitherto divided becomes unified, and that a complete division is often established in the twinkling of an eye between the old life and the new. Whatever we may think of the phenomenon itself—it probably only is a phenomenon to our finite senses—the fact stands clear and unassailable, says Professor James, that this process in man creates an entirely new personality. The phrases "a new birth" or "born again" or "twice-born" belong not to the category of rhetorical hyperbole, but reflect actual facts and demonstrated happenings in the physical kingdom.

XIII

A man *can* be twice-born!

TWENTY-SEVEN:

AFTER FIVE YEARS OF "PLAY"

"He is most rich who stops at competence,—
Not labors on till the worn heart grows sere,—
Who, wealth attained, upon some loftier aim
Fixes his gaze, and never turns it backward."

AFTER FIVE YEARS OF "PLAY"

I

THE perplexity which my friends showed when, in full health, I retired from the editorship of *The Ladies' Home Journal* has now disappeared. A period of five years is at least long enough to have demonstrated that I did not disintegrate within that time, as some predicted; that I was not to be puzzled as to what I was going to find to do, as others feared, and that, up to date at least, I have shown no signs of doing a marathon back to the desk, as so many prophesied. On the contrary, much to their surprise, they have witnessed five years of unexampled activity, better health, more vigor at the end than at the beginning, and a satisfaction with life not known before. At the same time, the perplexity of some has not been entirely overcome. Their question has simply changed from "How are you going to keep yourself busy?" to "Just how do you call this prodigious amount of work 'play' as differentiated from the work of five years ago?"

II

The question is not surprising, since "service" activities are as yet so little understood. The past five years have been the busiest and most productive of any similar period in my life. Yet not a single unit of all the activities was planned. I had no idea of what I was going to do after my retirement except that I had promised to put down a record of what I had tried to do in the world up to that time. It was to be solely a record for my family. Not for a moment had I a notion of publishing the material when I had written it. The "record" resulted in *The Americanization of Edward Bok* and in a success which is as bewildering as it has been gratifying. I determined that I would let events take their course, and when a call came that was insistent I would heed it. I had not long to wait. Not for a call, but for calls so many and so-swift-coming as to make the problem not of what but of which to do. This is the first surprise that comes to the man who lays down the reins of business: the many opportunities that have been lying in wait, but which, being busy, he did not see or know of. Not opportunities which are outside of his particular abilities or tastes, but the number which are peculiarly and surprisingly adapted to his previous experience and skill, fitting him with the perfection of a glove. It is really astonishing how many organization presidencies either are open or have a way of opening up, and it is one of the most amusing of problems for a man to conjecture what would actually happen if he accepted them all. There is certainly no basis for the oft-expressed fear on the part of business men that they would not know what to do if they retired. Moreover, they will be surprised how absolutely similar is the particular group of talents called for in the average piece of welfare or civic work to the same talents which they exercised in business, and the absolute congeniality of the work outside the channels of trade.

III

When a man works at a compensated job, he works for himself. When he works at a job for which there is no compensation, he works for others. That sort of work becomes play in the best sense. That is the difference between the man in business and the man retired from business, and just as the distinction is marked in its financial aspect, so equally marked is it in the character of the work, the spirit in which he does it, and that most precious human possession, the sense of freedom in which he comes to it. To the man in business, of practical mind, this explanation may seem like a distinction without a difference; to the man who has experienced it there is a distinction with a marked difference. No one can realize the sense of freedom which is experienced when a man gives up a remunerative job, no matter how congenial it may have been to his tastes, and assumes a position entirely removed from financial compensation. Subtle, of course, it is, but there are subtle factors in life which are tremendously satisfying. The feeling of service from one human to another must be experienced before it can be understood, and even when understood it is difficult of explanation. It is expressed in feelings rather than in words. The day's work may be equally long, the problems as many and as perplexing, the need of careful decision similarly great, the mind as severely taxed to find new avenues for ways and means, but there is an exhilaration in the process that comes not with the problems of the mart and their conduct.

IV

The chief problem which confronts the man who has retired from business is exactly the opposite of what he thinks will be the problem when he contemplates the step. He cannot get away from the insistent question "But what shall I do? How shall I fill up my time?" He will soon be asking "Which of these is it wisest for me to take on? In which direction can I serve best?" In the anxious fear that he may not be busy enough, compared to his former life, his first year or two will be one of mistakes in that at the end of that time he will take an inventory and find he has undertaken more than he can efficiently carry through. This is the mistake which every retired man in the fullness of his health and powers has made. He does not realize that the world outside the channels of trade is so busy, the calls so numerous, the opportunities so many, the work of such magnitude. Of course, it depends on a man's experience and his tastes in which direction he will go, but whatever the direction, his path will be lined with open doors of opportunity.

V

If a man goes along a line of service where his work becomes either of a public or of a semi-public nature, as is very likely in the paths outside of business, his correspondence assumes proportions he dreams not of. The idea he may have of working without secretarial assistance will be shattered. Instead of less assistance, he is likely to need more. If his work is of a nature calling for his taking part in public assemblages, the opportunities offered him will be beyond his calculations. His invitations will exceed the days in the year, and the fastest express train service could not get him from point to point. He will find himself declining ten invitations to every one which he accepts, and finally to do the work which he has set for himself he will, in a short time, decline nearly all if he would conserve his time and strength. He will hear of the most attractive movements in their creation and making that are in the minds of men, and he will be so attracted as to wish that the days were again as long and man's mental and physical endurance five times as great.

VI

It is all so vastly different from what the man before he retires has thought or dreamed. If he has planned for a life of leisure he will have every ounce of his character put to the test to secure even a portion of leisure. I had the most wonderful dreams of leisure time when I would read and study and idle and travel. I would improve my golf and revel in my gardens. I have done none of these. My golf is worse, and my gardens see little of me. Idling comes only when sleep comes, and my chief points of travel lie in the distances between meetings. I have read some and written some, but only by sheer will-power. I have changed the places of my activities: I am freer of foot. I *can* regulate my hours, my comings and goings. The chief gain is an inestimable sense of freedom and a consciousness of service. In that large sense, a retirement from business is a continuous vacation.

VII

The desire to "go back" to business has never entered my mind except at times when offers compelled attention and declination. And I have yet to meet a man who retired from business in the right spirit who has the slightest desire to return. There are men whom necessities of various kinds have compelled to return, often with the very opposite of any desire on their part. There are also those who returned because of mistaken notions of what retirement meant, and have experienced pleasure in their resumption of the reins. These are sometimes cited to "point a moral or adorn a tale." I have personally met and known such men, and in every case, with their own acknowledgment, I have found their natures so steeped and saturated with the excitement of money-making and commercial barter that a mental readjustment was impossible to them, and, as one of them conceded, "I will have to go on, as I began, to the bitter end." And it was a bitter end in this instance,—in a sanitarium. Where inner resources are lacking, the spirit has no chance, and no sight is more pathetic than to see a man who has made himself a slave to business and finally finds himself unable to throw off the shackles, although he is fully conscious that he should. Business, for such a man, is all that there is in life.

VIII

A man of those mental processes confuses the desire for retirement with the need for a vacation. A cessation from the pressure of affairs for a period, be it brief or extended, is all that such a man can "stand": sometimes even this "gets on his nerves," as he will tell you. Such a man can only be pitied. He has made business his god, and he will make it his grave.

I never knew until recently that there is a profession in which a man cannot take a vacation and get away from what he has chosen as his work. I was talking with Frederick Law Olmsted, the landscape expert, and exclaiming upon the singular quality of his work in leaving beauty behind him wherever he went.

"But from which you can never get a vacation," he added.

"How do you mean?" I asked.

"I get exhausted from my work, just as any man does, and when I do, where can I go and forget it? Wherever I go there is landscape, and naturally my mind reverts to work. I begin to move this tree or that, grade this hill or that, open this vista or that," he explained.

"How about the seashore or an ocean trip?" I suggested.

"The best ideas and suggestions for mass formations in landscape work are derived from the formations of the clouds," he added with a grim smile.

IX

Gradually, however, is the American business man learning restraint and wisdom, and the days ahead are certain to see a larger number stepping aside while life still holds out possibilities of enjoyment for them while they afford opportunity for work to younger men. Although many a man fixes the age of fifty as the point at which to slough off or actually retire, there is more in the psychological attraction of the half-century figure than in the actual possibility. Some men, like Herbert Hoover, who began early, can retire at forty; others at sixty. The exact age is immaterial, so long as a man's years when he does retire still assure vitality for performance and capacity of enjoyment. No man, unless physically or mentally incapacitated, has a right to retire from business and fold his hands. Man was created to work and achieve, and the world, particularly at present, is too busy for a man to be idle. If ever the idler was a national liability it is to-day.

X

There was a time, before the Great War, when it looked as if we might develop in the United States a type of American country gentleman,—a man who, having accumulated a sufficiency, when he left business would retire and devote himself to an estate and the pleasures of the land. The English country squire was to find his prototype in the American country gentleman. But the War changed this drift, and, when we are apt to say that the War has left little mark on American thought and character, we forget that, at least, it changed the mental attitude of the man from becoming an American country gentleman into the American man devoted to service. There is no question that a new idea of service was born during the War in the minds of hundreds of American men, and the problems arising out of the War have kindled their imaginations and sharpened their idea of their obligation to their fellow men.

Furthermore, the attitude of the public has altered toward the man of affairs. There is coming into our modern thinking a distinctly healthy element which estimates men by the service they give, outside of business, and of the good they do in the world. There is a growing tendency to appraise the morals of men in their positive rather than in their negative aspects, and to judge courses of conduct by the degree in which they promote human happiness. The day is rapidly passing when a man can live a life unto himself and his pleasures, and hope to retain the respect of his fellow men. A man may have much charm of manner and of temperament, he may be generous of hand, but if his life be one of luxurious idleness, devoted to the sports of the times and not to the problems, he cannot hope, in the future as he has in the past, to stand high among his fellow men. He may receive their pleasant greetings, but not their inner respect. Such a life may be perfectly blameless so far as deportment is concerned, and formerly a man has been judged along that line of reasoning, but with the new consciousness of service has come the feeling that such a life has somehow failed. The world of to-day is beginning to ask of the man who can give service that he shall so live that he shall be missed when he passes on and his place be difficult to fill. Idleness, languor, and an excessive luxury of expenditure upon self and selfish pleasures are rapidly passing into the category of grave offenses to mankind. Instead of a feeling that a life of idleness leads to immorality, there is a growing conviction that such a life *is* immorality.

"I come here to find myself; it is so easy to get lost in the world."

JOHN BURROUGHS

———

"It is a wonderful thing to have a season sometimes with one's self; and sit and watch the world pass by."

RUDYARD KIPLING

———

"Give me, Kind Heaven, a private station,
A mind serene for contemplation."

GAY

"OUT OF TOUCH" IN FLORIDA

I

I BUILT a home in Florida. "There," said the Lady whom I took for better or for worse and got much better than I dreamed or deserve, "there," she said, "we will spend the first three months of each year."

"What!" said my friends, "go away for the three busiest months of the year: the heart of the winter. Madness! You will get out of touch."

And they looked at me regretfully. I was to be "out of touch." What a calamity! What a dismal prospect!

But "out of touch" with what? With the honk of the automobile, or the clang of the trolley? It is really amazing how the nerves will actually bear up with a brief recess from these harmonies of the town.

"Out of touch" with innumerable Committee or Board meetings where, after hours of talk, the end reached is almost the same as the beginning? Some men's patience has a remarkable way of standing the strain of a holiday from these occasions where men excel women!

"Out of touch" with an atmosphere so filled with the smoke of gases of a city's ill-conceived laws that a conifer tree cannot live and a fresh carnation pink wilts before nightfall? The lungs of the human have an astounding vitality to thrive without these cleanly and sanitary accompaniments of city life.

"Out of touch" with dinners in smoke-filled rooms from which one futilely airs one's clothes for twenty things that are and have been and shall be, and that are refreshing and strengthening and broadening to the human mind?

So for a hundred days each year I am "out of touch" in the minds of some of my anxious friends; the same rueful hearts who, when I retired from business now some five years ago, predicted my disintegration within six months and an eager return to the mart within a year. If three months of glorious sunshine in a climate so gentle as to be caressing has put me "out of touch" with some things which in the minds of my friends seem important, is it not possible that I have been permitted to come *in* touch with other things which are vital and likely to be more enriching, more satisfying, and perhaps a bit more deep-reaching?

V

As an instance:

Directly across that part of the peninsula of Florida where Tampa touches the Gulf of Mexico in the West there is a ridge of high land. In the ages ago when what is known now as the land of sunny winters was all water, legend has it that this ridge was the only visible land. It formed an almost inaccessible island, and to it came in the later years a tribe of Seminole Indians who attempted to cultivate the ground, a relic of their effort still standing in an historic seedling orange-tree.

In the centre of this high ridge, directly midway between the two bodies of water, rises the utmost spot of land: the highest point yet measured in peninsular Florida and the highest land within sixty miles of the

Atlantic Ocean or the Gulf of Mexico between Washington and the Rio Grande.   It rises 324 feet, and now forms part of a large private acreage.   From the top of this mount the country sweeps in a gentle decline, and save for the tropical growth of tree and verdure and the cultivated orange groves, with their sweet-scented aroma of orange-blossom as it is wafted to the summit of the mount, the New Englander might feel as if he were looking down on his beloved Connecticut valley or over the foot-hills of beautiful Vermont.   Pine-embowered homes lie beneath; the innumerable Floridian lakes dot an otherwise unbroken panorama of pine-tree and orange grove as the eye looks away over forty or fifty miles of tree-top greenery.

VI

It happened that to this mount there came one day the grandson of a man of the Netherlands who had peopled the island of his home and heart with trees.   As that had proved a haven of rest for the storm-beaten birds of the North Sea, there came to this grandson a vision that this piece of land, the nearest to the sky in Florida, might also be made a haven of cooling rest for those little citizens of the world of wings, which, migrating twice a year between South America or the West Indies and the climes of the North, spend themselves in their flight, and whose weakened little bodies so often meet the search of the observer and lover of birds in the Florida marshes.

As his mind lingered on the exhaustion of the birds, he thought, too, of the humans who exhaust themselves

IX

The timber-man's axe and the speculative mind of the promoter are fast reducing the primitive pine-forests and draining the lowlands of Florida. Your true Floridian thinks of little else than in terms of citrus fruit, and of creating cities where once stood wood and forest. It calls for no long vision to picture the day—not so far off—when "tropical Florida" will exist in storied literature rather than in actuality on the great peninsula of Ponce de Leon, and when a State, now in the making, will be "made" and present a succession of mathematically laid out citrus groves.

To-day it is still possible to find adjacent to miles of cultivated land a tract of tropical jungle exactly as the Indians left it,—too impenetrably tropical and too slow in its transformation for the feverish Floridian to plunge into and change into revenue-producing tracts. But it will not be for long!

X

Thus it happens that within a walk from The Sanctuary there exists a tract of that marvellously virgin tropical jungle into parts of which no human being has perhaps pushed his way for decades. Impenetrable by the undisturbed growth of years, it is with difficulty that the narrowest single trail can be cut even into a hundred feet of the dense jungle underbrush to afford a glimpse of that treasure-house of all tropical lowland: one of those dark mysterious creeks with water as clear as crystal and its bottom growth of mint and wild iris. Fed by springs at the head of the tract, the seemingly dark water wanders along, hampered only by the fallen trees of past generations, each tree trunk a garden of wood-fern, overarched with bowers of wild rose and yellow jasmine. It is easy to picture the Seminole Indians canoeing down the creek for several miles until they reached one of those Floridian lakes that always surprises the Northerner by its miles of width.

No Brazilian jungle on the Amazon could be more densely tropical than this tract of virgin Florida jungle with its marvellous growth of centuries-old live oaks, with their trunks literally dotted with the blooming orchid, and their branches festooned with the drooping grey moss of the tropics. Palms to a height of eighty feet struggle upward to catch a ray of sunlight, their great fan-shaped leaves garlanded and dripping with a shower of jasmine and rose. Trunks of trees rent by ages-old storms have become, with their decayed wood, Nature's own receptacles of exquisite fern, and one walks with noiseless tread on soft carpets made by centuries of fallen leaves and needles of pine. Not a sound breaks the stillness of the jungle: the human eye can detect no living thing, and yet one feels as he walks through the man-made aisle of that tropical forest that thousands of eyes are fastened on him: eyes of the chameleon and of the turquoise-colored beetle which closer scrutiny reveals on fallen trunks. To this refuge, impenetrable to the human, come the bear with her cubs, and the doe with her fawns. The wild-turkey and the heron find here a security which only a state of nature, untouched by man for decades, can give to the wild life of forest and jungle.

TWENTY-NINE:

THE MAN WHO WOULDN'T SELL HIS FATHER

grove of pines, there: every tree counts its years by centuries. Three men with clasped hands can't encircle that live oak yonder. We've tried it."

"How old is such an oak?" queried my friend.

"From eight hundred to a thousand years, sir."

"You have had this in your family, how long?"

"Some seventy-eight years come August," said the cracker.

"Your father bought it?"

"My grandfather, sir. He gave it to father."

"I suppose he didn't pay much for it, did he?" asked my friend.

"Thirty cents an acre, sir," answered the cracker, smiling. "Yes, sir, thirty cents an acre."

"And how many acres are there?"

"One hundred and eighty-five, sir, in the whole plot."

"Fifty-five dollars for the whole. Well, well," said my friend. "And what is land like this worth now?"

"Well, sir," said Tom, "they're selling right up the ridge here now for fifty dollars an acre, and some at a hundred dollars, and none of it as fine land as this."

"Then at the highest price so far paid round here you could sell this plot for $18,500, couldn't you, Tom?"

"If I sold it, yes sir, I fancy I could. It is so beautiful," he said, as his eyes softened and he looked lovingly over the land before him.

"You never thought of selling it?"

"No, sir."

"You are going to build on it yourself some day?"

"No," was the answer, as his honest eyes looked into those of my friend. "I haven't ten dollars to my name, sir. I couldn't build. Reckon I never will, sir. I'm sixty-eight now," and he shook his head ruefully.

"What are you going to do with it?"

"Leave it as it is, sir, as it has been all these years. I like to come up here and look off," he said, as he took off his hat and gazed reverently at the scene before him.

Instinctively we took off our hats.

"Come here often?" asked my friend.

"Almost every day, sir. That's what father did," and his eyes softened.

"He loved it, did he?"

"That's just what he did, sir, he loved it. Why, sir," and his eyes began to sparkle, "father knew every bush on this lot,—every wild-flower. There wasn't a bird-call he didn't know and couldn't answer. He loved every tree on this place. You see, sir, father was a very fine man."

"He must have been," said my friend heartily.

"He was," said the man. "I never met a finer man. He was as near a saint as I guess a man ever gets on this earth. Yes, sir, he was," and Tom seemed lost in contemplation. "That's why I guess I have never done anything with this ground, sir."

"How do you mean, Tom?"

"Well, sir, it's like, well, sort of hallowed ground to me. You see there isn't a foot of sand here, sir," and he looked down to the earth, "on which father's foot hasn't been. There isn't one of these trees on which his couldn't do that, you know. He was too fine for that. Yes, sir," he repeated quietly, "it would be like selling father."

As we rode homeward, my friend was quiet. Not a word had he spoken in the three miles we had ridden. Deep in his coat rested his chin.

Finally, I broke the silence. "You didn't feel as if you could make him an offer?" I asked.

He continued his silence. Then he answered: "No; it would have been profanation." Then he added, "I've put over some deals in my day, large and small, but I've never had an experience like that." He became thoughtful again and, after another silence, he continued, "You're right, but I never saw it before. There are times when money shrinks to something pitiably small, and," he concluded, "unspeakably dirty."

And then, as if speaking to himself, he repeated: " 'It would be like selling father.' What big men God puts in humble places!"

THIRTY:
"IT CAN'T BE DONE"

sity. No professional class has felt more keenly the pressure of higher prices and stationary income than those who think in terms of education and culture, and whose lives are devoted to the spread of knowledge. Along the entire line of education one finds our teachers, our college instructors and professors so underpaid as to preclude their participation, so essential to them, in those events and occasions which are easily within the financial reach of those who have no equal need for them, and who often neither understand nor appreciate them.

II

There is no situation quite so full of sympathetic understanding to me as the case of a college professor who, with a cultured wife and a family of three or four children, finds himself unable to provide his family with those opportunities of light and beauty and color that the world affords. Yet he sees those same opportunities within the comfortable enjoyment of thousands who embrace them, either for some social advantage or that they may, with their new money, be considered as "among those present." He is indeed a strong man whose heart and soul do not become depressed, or whose mind and being do not cherish dissatisfaction with social and economic conditions. It is easy to understand why his impatience with things sometimes voices itself in the classroom.

We have a jocular manner of saying that a prize-fighter receives for one hour's brutal work what a professor cannot earn in a life-time. But this sad fact is not a jocular matter with the professor. The lamentable fact sinks deep into his being. Nor need we take the extreme comparison of the roped arena. The rewards in nearly every line of endeavor exceed those of the man of culture. And yet in the hands of this same underpaid man we place the fortunes, for good or for evil, of our sons and daughters in the most formative and plastic time of their lives.

"It takes me forty years of intensive instruction, with all the vitality there is in me," said a professor, "to earn what is represented here in money at this one football game." A life-time of work, in other words, to say naught of the years of preparation for the work.

It is perfectly natural that a nation of hard-working, prosperous people should be willing to pay huge sums for its sports and amusements. We all crave and need relaxation from the pressure of life. But do we not lose all sense of relations when we contribute with such prodigality to sports and withhold even decent contribution from those who are moulding our future men and women? If we can think of sports in terms of millions, we should think—and we can, if we choose—of education in terms of billions. For while the former is commendable, it must be conceded than an afternoon of sport is fleeting, while an afternoon devoted to the training of a mind may mould or influence a life, or even many lives.

III

It was the consciousness that something must be put into the world which would enable the underpaid professional man to have in his life that which he craved mental quirk, so fatally common, which immediately brushes aside the advantages of an idea and instinctively advances all the objections and obstacles to a plan and clothes them with a pessimism so disconcerting to healthy endeavor. Some of the finest plans born in the mind of man, intended for the benefit of humankind, have been throttled by these obstructionists whose mouths are full of negations and whose souls are empty of affirmations. The great pity is that these shallow minds and warped souls are sometimes listened to, and that thus the world is deprived of something uplifting or beautiful which might set humankind forward a pace. I am unable to give credit to the man who wrote this bit of wise doggerel. But I wish its truth might get down into the consciousness of some of these folks who are always ready to say that a thing "can't be done":

If you think you are beaten, you are;
If you think you dare not, you don't.
If you'd like to win, but you think you can't,
It's almost sure that you won't.
If you think you'll lose, you're lost,
For out of the world we find
Success begins with a fellow's will—
It's all in the state of mind—
Life's battles don't always go
To the stronger or faster man;
But sooner or later the man who wins
Is the man who thinks he can.

V

Despite the wailings of the "can't be dones," the membership list of The Philadelphia Forum was opened, and so rapid was the enrollment that before the list could be closed 4,324 names were received, with a total income of over $56,000. The season began in October, and ended with April, and during this period 76 events were given, so that a general membership ticket represented a cost of approximately 13 cents per event. The first year's events included participation in three concerts of The Philadelphia Orchestra and The New York Symphony Orchestra: a monthly presentation of current events by Vice-President Coolidge, marking the first time that an officer of the United States Government appeared in public to explain what was going on in Washington: the Bach Choir was brought down from Bethlehem for its first visit to Philadelphia; Walter Damrosch was presented in three descriptive talks at the piano; six dances with an orchestra of 20 pieces; William Lyon Phelps was presented in six Bible talks; The Philadelphia Award was bestowed under The Forum auspices; and over 50 of the most prominent speakers were presented in current discussions and in lectures on literature, art, travel, civics, and science. Only on those special occasions when the full membership of The Forum presented itself,—the Academy of Music's capacity is limited to 3,000,—was there a disappointment in store for the last comers who could not be accommodated. But this possibility had been explained at the beginning.

VI

It was thought wise, however, to endeavor to limit the membership of The Forum for the second year to 4,000, and to ensure this the membership fee was in-than is possible where the events are held in a large three-thousand capacity auditorium, and so a series of 25 afternoon events was begun in the Academy Foyer, a beautiful room seating 533 persons. The fee for this series was fixed at $15 for an unreserved seat, and $17.50 for a reserved seat, with the result that almost the entire number of seats were taken on the reserved basis. These events seek to present the more intimate phases of literature, music, drama, and the spiritual life, conducted on the same order as in the evening Forum: a brief hour's talk and a following questionnaire. Again successful was this new departure, and how far this series will expand the desire of the public only can determine.

This year, the fourth year of The Forum, opened even more auspiciously than any previous year in that the entire subscription of 4,000 members has been sold out at an earlier date. The regular members' ticket was kept at $20 for the season, but the reserved-seat price was increased to $50, and the number to 670. Neither increase affected the demand, which before the season opened entirely exhausted the larger number, with a waiting list already formed for the following season. The afternoon series was sold out weeks before the first attraction.

With the 65 or more events in the evening Forum and the 25 events in the afternoon series, it will be seen that a minimum of 90 meetings during a season has thus far developed from out of the three-year experiment,—a record that should convince, if any achievement can, those who predicted that even the first step could not be successfully taken! We, in the East, might, in this respect, learn from the slogan so common in the West,

and so much healthier to good endeavor, of a willingness
to "try anything once!"

IX

I have explained in detail the progress of four years
of The Philadelphia Forum in order to show that the
people of a great city are not only willing, but eager, to
patronize the best form of entertainment if it is presented
within the reach of their purses. They want the best,
but as a rule the best is placed beyond their means. An
audience of The Philadelphia Forum is to-day the most
representative of the professional intelligencia of the
city. It has among its membership over eleven hundred
of the professors, instructors, and teachers of the neigh-
boring colleges; almost the entire roster of the Judges of
the courts (another underpaid profession) is on its books,
while the intelligent class of the public which in their
incomes have not felt the upper reaction of income which
has come to the employer and laborer of the economic
world are for the first time recognized in their desire and
right to have the beautiful things of the world come into
their lives.

What the future holds out for The Philadelphia Forum
no one can foresee. It is an experiment in social eco-
nomics which, having proved successful in Philadelphia,
can be attempted with equal success in every large and
small city, the budget and programme being made pro-
portionate to the needs and means of the community in
which the experiment is made. It forms the most convincing answer possible to the oft-made accusation that
the public will not, in any measure, support the best in

its desire for knowledge and entertainment. The one point to observe in such a Forum is that there shall be a judicious mixture of serious discussion and the arts. Life does not ask us always to be serious and thoughtful. It is just as necessary that we should be taken out of ourselves and away from our every-day perplexities by an evening of laughter, of music, of drama, or of amusement.

X

The problem presented by such a human Forum will not be whether it will succeed, but, as with The Philadelphia Forum, how wisely to limit the number who wish to join in its advantages.

THIRTY-ONE:

WHY

"Go put your creed into your deed."

EMERSON

———

"Public sentiment is everything. With public sentiment nothing can fail; without it, nothing can succeed. Consequently he who molds public sentiment goes deeper than he who enacts statutes or pronounces decisions. He makes statutes and decisions possible or impossible to be executed."

ABRAHAM LINCOLN

WHY

I

I HAVE been frequently asked why several of my latter efforts along the line of public service should have taken the form of monetary awards, the impression undoubtedly being in the mind of the questioner that I laid undue emphasis on material reward for idealistic service. It is perfectly natural that this impression should rest in the mind, since the newspapers find a more dramatic and picturesque quality in the amount of money attached to an Award and the disposition which the recipient is going to make of the sum than they do in the service for which it is bestowed and the value of that service to the people. So the newspaper account "plays up" the money part of the story of an Award, and the reading public accepts the point upon which emphasis is so unworthily placed,—unworthily because we have only to live to realize, with Emerson, that the reward of a thing well done is to have done it, and not the emolument therefor.

II

The idea of public Awards became a study with me when I read some literature explaining the Nobel Prizes, and later when I was asked to associate myself with a group of men in considering the Awards proposed by The Woodrow Wilson Foundation. The monetary fac-

nition of the fact that service stands for something more than self-interest, and is not overlooked by the citizens of a community.

IV

It is an indisputable fact that there has been too much glorification of the man of wealth and of power, and the fact was gradually lodging in the minds of hundreds of young men that this type of man is the only one who in these days was worthy of public notice. It seemed to these young men that the man who believed in service, in working for others, went unnoticed. Usually, that man is of a calibre to which public acclaim does not appeal; he works for the purpose in mind and not for the honors of the world. It is human nature, however, that we all like encouragement; we value recognition of effort, for we realize—and the man who works not for himself realizes it more than any one else—that there is no greater honor in the world than to have the esteem of our fellow men. There were too many young men slowly making up their minds that the only course in life worth while was to amass wealth or power. In fact, many young men had said to me: "What's the use of working for others? Nobody cares whether you do or not; no one encourages that type. That's old stuff." Hence the time was right to bring a concrete idea into being which would show young men that the world *does* care more for the man of service than they imagine, and that henceforth there would be a group of men in Philadelphia who would be watching closely those who did believe that they were their brother's keeper, and were trying to do something to make the world better; to carry out the precepts of Christ and the ideals of mankind. It made no difference in what line of endeavor such service went; the scope was to be as wide as life itself, so long as the purpose of the effort was to benefit others and advance the best interests of the community.

V

Three bestowals of The Philadelphia Award have thus far been made, and it happens that they have been made for signal achievement. It was natural that this should be so, since there are in every community those whose public services are known of all men, and it is logical that such an Award should at least in its first years seek and reward such conspicuous service. But I hope that as time goes on the Award may recognize what will seem to the public some very simple act of service, since in the simplest act we often find the greatest potentiality of service. The outstanding acts of service are, of course, marvellous contributions to the sum total of human happiness, but they are rare. On the other hand, there are acts of service based on the simplest ideals being rendered which contain the germ of happiness for others and for bettering the lives of a people or advancing the interests of a city. Such a service is often the unconscious act of some one working in a modest way; some one of very moderate means who has done something that looks simple, and yet has tremendous potentialities in it; something in which even the man or woman who conceived it did not realize the far-reaching influence for good. It is the tremendous potency of the small thing done in the right spirit that should be recognized in this world: the small seed sown in the right spot and at the right time,—so seemingly small a thing as to cause the public to wonder that so inconspicuous an act should receive so signal a recognition. The Philadelphia Award is in its essence for him whom universities overlook in their recognition: the simple worker at the simple task. He is the man, or she the woman, whom the Award will try to surprise at his or her work; reaching into the smaller and hidden corners of our city life and smoking out, so to speak, the humble server who is almost unknown, whose service is probably unnoticed and yet whose work is full of potentiality for good.

VI

My study into the needs of a city brought to my surprised attention the small interest that existed in a great community in the men who were really more vital to the individual welfare of every citizen than any other: the policemen and the firemen. Here were two classes of men close to the two things which every citizen prizes most: the lives of himself and of his family, and his property. Aside from the mere knowledge that these men were there, and calling upon them with breathless haste when we got into trouble, they counted as for nothing in the thought and consideration of the average citizen. In torrid heat, in zero cold, in rain, in snow, in slush, in cutting winds, in weather when, with gratitude, we are thankful to get into the friendly glow of light and heat, or when, with our families, we escape the torrid heat of the city and go to cool places, these men are either on duty or ready for duty, their families never knowing when they have left their homes in the morning if they will return, or in what condition they may be brought home. "Well," we comfortably argue, "that's their job: that's what they're paid for." But can we really justify an attitude that gives to those public servants less thought and consideration than we bestow thought and consideration on a trusted watch-dog? We, at least, speak to the dog. I have stood on street corners, and watched the attitude of citizens, walking or riding, toward the policeman. The number of those who gave a simple word, a nod of recognition, a smile of consciousness that he was there, was negligible. It scarcely existed. If any human sign was visible, it was that of resentment at his stoppage of their traffic. The more careful the policeman to ensure safety to the rider or walker, the surer was he rewarded with a scowl or the look of impatience! He was in reality regarded in the light of a nuisance by the average person rather than in the light of the best friend of the citizen. As for the fireman, he was never thought of. Out of sight, in his engine-house, he was never given a thought until smoke and fire threatened, and then what a factor he became until after the danger, when we rewarded him with the remark that he inflicted more damage with water than did the fire which he put out! Why are there policemen and firemen, I thought, as I watched these men day after day, when there is returned to them so little in comparison with what they give? But suppose they were not?

VII

I decided to make an effort to bring these important factors in the community life more directly into the consciousness of the people; to make the average citizen mindful of their existence and to give to the men themselves the encouragement that follows when a public becomes conscious of their presence and work. It was not that I wanted to reward conspicuous service; that service is given almost every day by these guardians of life and property. The quality of that service is only one of degree. What I was after was to make the public conscious of these men,—to regard them not as automatons, as mere servants, for how could one really reward the service which these men gave? I wanted to create a human relation between the doer and the man he did it for, and few efforts in service have given me more pleasure and satisfaction than to see the constantly growing human bond between these men and the citizens whom, at the daily danger of their lives, they serve. I created in Philadelphia what is called The Citizens' Award, consisting of as many annual Awards of One Thousand Dollars each to the policemen, the firemen, and the guards of Fairmount Park, as there were outstanding acts of service to warrant their bestowal. For three years now these Awards have been bestowed by the Mayor upon these public protectors in the presence of three thousand of their fellows who are off duty, with the result that the following morning all Philadelphia reads about these men, and the consciousness is driven into the mind of every reader that the policeman and the fireman exist. Nods and smiles and greetings reach out to them from riders and walkers, while at Christmas-time the hand of recognition stretches out to nearly every man on the force. On the other hand, the men who are rendering such important service for order and property realize for the first time that a group of citizens watch what they do all through a year, and are ready to pass out to them the wonderful stimulus of the human "Well done, good and faithful servant!"

Say, as the cynical may: "He certainly seems to be well pleased with his own benefaction." I am,—frankly so; only it is not a benefaction!

VIII

Over thirty years of my life had been spent rather close to the art of the advertisement, and I had also participated in it to some extent. Moreover, I realized that my means had been, and are derived, in large part, from advertising income. It came upon me in the form of a duty to do something to raise the standard of advertising. It had become one of the great American industries, representing a yearly expenditure of hundreds of millions of dollars, and yet, commensurate with its growth, the advertisement had not progressed in originality and effectiveness with the encouragement given it. There, too, hung about the advertisement a legacy of the P. T. Barnum theory of advertising which did not always square so much with the article behind it as it did with a flamboyant manner of presenting the article to the prospective patron. Both in originality and veracity, advertising still left something to be desired.

In the spring of 1923, immediately after the announcement of the Joseph Pulitzer Awards by the Trustees of Columbia University, an editorial appeared in *Collier's Weekly*, stating, in effect, that while these Awards recognized excellence in a play, an editorial, a novel, a biography, a poem, and in other forms of literary and journalistic endeavor, no one had ever thought of creating an Award for excellence in the advertisement. The thought was timely, and it rested with me in fertile soil. I concluded the time was ripe to create a series of advertising awards. Just as it was eminently appropriate that a series of journalistic and literary awards should emanate from Columbia University with its School of Journalism, it was entirely logical that a series of advertising awards should come from Harvard University with its School of Business Administration which includes a course in advertising. To Mr. Ellery Sedgwick, Editor of *The Atlantic Monthly* and a member of the Board of Overseers of Harvard University, I made known my desire to create such a series of awards if Harvard would accept them. The suggestion met with ready favor and immediate acceptance, and, in the autumn of 1923, the Harvard Advertising Awards were announced, the first bestowal to cover the year of 1924 and to be awarded the first week of January, 1925.

The announcement met with universal favor by the interested professions, and there is little doubt that the Harvard authorities will have a wide-spread co-operation in their work. Of course, the efficacy of the Awards is still to be demonstrated.

IX

With the full purpose in mind that the monetary part of the Awards should not constitute the main stimulant, but that the honor conferred by Harvard University upon the recipients should be the chief impulse, the amounts were made of moderate dimensions. There was only one suggestion made to the Dean of the Harvard School of Business Administration, under whose direct auspices the Awards will be conducted: that the Jury of Award should have prominently in mind in their consideration of the bestowals the factor of truth. While the æsthetic note is struck in the conditions, as is also a recognition of the correct use of English, the dominant note back of the Awards is that of a truthful presentation of the subject or article advertised: that veracity of statement shall outweigh even the most artistic conception or beauty of presentation. It is in this respect that the Awards will serve their greatest purpose, as well as call attention to the need of a careful preparation of an advertising campaign with regard to excellence and adequacy of production and efficiency of distribution before it is embarked upon,—a necessity in successful advertising which, in all too many instances, is often ignored, with a resultant waste of effort and appropriation.

X

It was during the period that the Harvard Awards were forming themselves in my mind that I had already worked out the Award which, because of its international scope, was destined so fully to engross the attention of the American public: The American Peace Award.

THIRTY-TWO:

THE AMERICAN PEACE AWARD

No sooner are our children old enough for the play-time of youth than we give them swords and guns and tin soldiers as toys. No sooner can they read than we give them books of battles and wars. We teach a child the sanctity of truth and the necessity for straightforwardness, and then we decorate, with ribbon or medal, the man who most skilfully practices the art of deception in war. We teach a child that it must not be cruel to animal or human, and then we canonize in bronze the man who, in war, inflicts the greatest torture and destroys the largest number of human lives. We teach our children the lessons of creative constructiveness, and then we glorify the man who can conceive and bring into being the most deadly forces of destruction. We bestow distinction upon the mind that can conceive the deadliest poison gas. Our proudest monuments are erected to the heroes of war. Our poetry and our romance breathe forth the spirit of battle. No sooner does peace follow war than the poets begin to sing of battle! We glorify in memorial of bronze the ghastliest destruction of which the human is capable. We lay deep into the mind of each generation that war is inevitable; that man was born to fight and annihilate; that we live in a world of strife, of force, of contention, of battle. We teach that militarism is the ultimate expression of a nation. And to make sure that we shall not be misunderstood we christen a branch of Government "War Department." A decadent people, we preach, is an unmilitaristic people. We even quote the Bible, and take in all its wrongful literalness the injunction that Christ came not to bring peace, but a sword. We shout "huzzas" to the man of iron, and we laugh at the man who says a people may be too proud to fight. Men by the thousands dragged themselves through mud and flame that their sacrifice might end war. We say this reverently, and then we go right on talking war, as if somebody had discovered an ecstacy of the trenches!

We are horrified at the human butchery of a war that reckons a toll of eleven millions of human souls, but we never think of the fundamentals of our own teaching which have brought about such a holocaust of human life.

And, like naïve children, we wonder why peace does not possess the souls of men!

THE AMERICAN PEACE AWARD

I

THE impulse leading to The American Peace Award came directly from the American people.

In the autumn of 1921 I noticed in my correspondence a distinct note of increasing dissatisfaction with national and international affairs. These correspondents were not known to me. They wrote seeking my active interest.

Following the puzzling elections of that year, the note of restless discontent in the letters became more pronounced.

I began to be interested, and tried to find out in a definite way the nature of the disturbing problems. Thus encouraged by my apparent interest, my correspondents either referred me to others who could give me the information I desired, or they induced these to write to me. It was not many weeks before I found myself in correspondence with an impressive number of business men of large contacts who, in turn, induced others of larger contacts to write. Supplementing this increasing correspondence, which soon assumed overwhelming proportions, I began to read the newspapers of other cities, which come to me in large numbers, as well as the magazines or bulletins of large civic, economic and religious organizations. Wherever I went I personally pursued my research by asking and listening.

II

After five months of this extensive research and correspondence, the contents of which I had carefully tabulated as to subjects, I had a reflection of a cross-section of American opinion which surprised me because of its extent and intelligence. Every part of the country was represented: every station in life. I made a retabulation, and finally compressed the material down to the dominating subjects which seemed to be the chief reasons of discontent.

There were several, but overshadowing all others was a general feeling of dissatisfaction that, although it was three years since the ending of the war, practically nothing had been done by the United States Government to avoid another war, or to do its part to achieve and preserve the peace of the world.

From every direction came the opinion that "we should do something": concrete suggestions were few. I was surprised, however, at the intelligence and wide interest shown in regard to international affairs, and very soon I became convinced that the American people wanted to give voice to their opinions as to what should be done. Where a concrete plan was suggested, it generally took the form of the establishment of a newspaper or magazine through which the public could express itself: an obvious suggestion.

III

In almost every letter was the expressed desire, sometimes in the most vehement terms, that there be created some unpartisan and non-political channel through which the people could express themselves on this and other national and international subjects. Literally, hundreds gave vent to this idea of what they called a defect in our system of contact between citizen and Government. They brushed aside the idea of the ballot. "We want to talk, not vote," they wrote. "We want to give expression to our views on these questions—to what we think. We want a direct hand in settling these problems."

When the newspapers were suggested as a channel of expression, they were dismissed as partisan. When Representatives or Senators were suggested, the people replied with an emphatic "No," and then the suggestion: "We want a channel of our own: a direct, open way to Washington, not via the newspapers or the politicians; a way which assures us that our views will be heard and considered, and that our voice will carry to Washington."

There was always a deadly earnestness in this demand; there was a distinct note of impatience with prevailing conditions, and there was a whip-like method of expression, verbal and written, that indicated deep-rooted dissatisfaction with things as they are.

IV

It was the discovery of this widely prevalent note that led straight to The American Peace Award. If the American people were really willing to make these great problems their own, to accept their part in the responsibility of their solution,—all of which I had up to this time doubted,—and they were actually crying aloud for a channel through which they could express themselves, I decided that they should have such a medium, simple and direct.

In view of my other Awards, it was natural that this channel of expression should suggest itself.

V

After taking counsel of persons well-informed on foreign questions with regard to the conditions of the Award, I offered the active conduct of the idea to Miss Esther Everett Lape, with whose previous experience in civic matters I was acquainted and with whom I had been editorially associated.

I suggested to Miss Lape that she should, in consultation with others, form a Policy Committee who, with her in charge, would direct the Award. I was not to assume or to be asked to have any active part in its conduct.

VI

On July 1, 1922, The American Peace Award was announced in the press of the country. It recorded the 60th serious and weighty proposal for organized peace in 617 years of the world's history,—going back to the days of Dante, Erasmus, William Penn, Kant, and Benjamin Franklin.

The Award offered one hundred thousand dollars ($100,000) to the author of the best practicable plan by which the United States might co-operate with other nations to achieve and preserve the peace of the world.

The contest was to be open to every citizen of the United States by birth or naturalization.

It was stated that the Award was offered in the conviction that the peace of the world is the problem of the people of the United States, and that a way can be found by which America's voice can be made to count among the nations for peace as well as for the future welfare and integrity of the United States.

The purpose of the Award was defined to give the American people from coast to coast a direct opportunity to evolve a plan that would be acceptable to many groups of our citizens who, while now perhaps disagreeing as to the best method of international association, nevertheless strongly desired to see the United States do its share in preventing war and in establishing a workable basis of co-operation among the nations of the earth.

It was stipulated that the winning plan should provide a practicable means whereby the United States could take its place and do its share toward preserving world peace, while not making compulsory the participation of the United States in European wars, if any such were, in the future, found unpreventable.

The plan could be based upon the present covenant of the League of Nations or might be entirely apart from that instrument.

The purpose of the Award was twofold: first, to produce a plan; and secondly, to insure, so far as might be, that it would be put into operation.

The Award was, therefore, to be made in two payments: fifty thousand dollars ($50,000) to be paid to

the author of the winning plan as soon as the Jury of
Award had selected it.   The second fifty thousand dollars ($50,000) was to be paid to the author if and when
the plan, in substance and intent, was approved by the
United States Senate; or if and when the Jury of Award
decided that an adequate degree of popular support had
been demonstrated for the winning plan.

The second half of the Award should not be deemed to
have been won unless the conditions mentioned above as
to the approval of the plan should be fulfilled on or before March 1, 1925.

Since the plan finally selected by the Jury might be
a composite of more than one plan, there were also
offered, in addition to the main Award of one hundred
thousand dollars ($100,000), second, third, fourth, and
fifth awards of five thousand dollars ($5,000) each for
any plans or portion of plans used by the Jury of Award
in a composite plan.

If the Jury accepted one plan in full, making no addi-
tions to it from other plans, no subsidiary awards would
be made, which proved to be the case.

Competition for the Award was to close at midnight
on November 15, 1923.

VII

The Policy Committee was announced to consist of
the following members:

John W. Davis, former Ambassador to Great Britain, and
President of the American Bar Association.

Learned Hand, Judge of the United States Court for the
Southern District of New York.

William H. Johnston, President of the International Association of Machinists and executive officer of the Conference for Progressive Political Action.

Esther Everett Lape, Member in Charge.

Nathan L. Miller, former Governor of New York State, State Controller and Judge of the Court of Appeals.

Mrs. Gifford Pinchot, wife of the Governor of the Commonwealth of Pennsylvania.

Mrs. Ogden Reid, Vice-President of the *New York Tribune*, Incorporated.

Mrs. Franklin D. Roosevelt, Vice-Chairman of the New York League of Women Voters.

Henry L. Stimson, former Secretary of War and United States Attorney for the Southern District of New York.

Melville E. Stone, formerly general manager, now counsellor, of the Associated Press.

Mrs. Frank A. Vanderlip, Regional Director of the New York League of Women Voters.

Cornelius N. Bliss, Junior, Treasurer.

VIII

In September, the members of the Jury of Award were announced:

Chairman: Elihu Root, New York, Secretary of War in President McKinley's Cabinet and Secretary of State in President Roosevelt's Cabinet; winner of the Nobel Peace Prize for 1912; member of the Permanent Court of Arbitration at The Hague since 1910; member of the Commission of International Jurists which proposed the plan of the new permanent Court of International Justice, established in 1921; commissioner plenipotentiary for the United States in the International Conference on the Limitation of Armament at Washington in November, 1921.

General James Guthrie Harbord, President of the Radio
Corporation of America; Chief of Staff of the A. E. F. in
France during the organizing period in 1917-18, and
again in 1919. Chief of the American Military Mission
to Armenia in 1919; Deputy Chief of Staff of the
U. S. A. in 1921.

Colonel Edward M. House, personal representative of Ex-
President Wilson to the European governments in 1914–
15–16; designated by President Wilson to represent the
United States in the Supreme War Council at Versailles.

Ellen Fitz Pendleton, President Wellesley College; member
Council for International Federation of University Women; Chairman Committee on International Relations
of American Association of University Women, Senator
of United Chapters of Phi Beta Kappa.

Roscoe Pound, Dean of the Harvard Law School since 1916;
author of a number of works on law, "Readings on Roman
Law," "Readings on the History and System of the Common Law," the "Spirit of the Common Law," etc.

William Allen White, an observer for the American Red
Cross in France, in 1917; delegate to the Russian Con-
ference at Prinkipo in 1919, and editor of The Emporia,
Kansas, *Gazette*.

Brand Whitlock, former Ambassador to Belgium and
formerly Mayor of Toledo, Ohio.

IX

The reaction to the Award from the hundreds of
newspapers which gave to its announcement the importance of a first-page presentation was instantaneously
favorable. There was scarcely an unfavorable note in
the acceptance of the idea. The response from the
public, as expressed in thousands of letters, was equally
favorable to the idea.

Some said, of course, that all the widespread attention given the Award was attracted by the monetary offer of $100,000. Which was true. In fact, that was exactly why the monetary phase was introduced into the Award. Its purpose was to dramatize the idea. It spoke, too, of the serious intent of the founder of the Award. It did precisely what was hoped and intended it should do: it gripped the imagination of thousands who would otherwise not have been attracted, and it focussed public attention upon the Award as no other single factor could have done. It stimulated idealism by the golden spur of self-interest. The same idea of individual emulation lies in the Nobel awards, and in the Woodrow Wilson, Theodore Roosevelt, and Joseph Pulitzer awards. It was also true, however, as was later demonstrated, that hundreds of the plans submitted came, not because of the financial attraction, but because they were asked for and a channel was afforded for their consideration.

I was prepared for the fact that the money phase of the Award would be stressed, and, in some quarters, criticized. But I had also in mind the fact that the men and women who had associated themselves with the conduct of the Award would at once, from their distinction and authority of position, give to the idea its proper place of dignity and solidity. The money was not intended, as the unintelligent and carping were so quick to say, to buy world peace: its purpose was to play its part in making the subject one of widespread thought and discussion, with the result of bringing a united national mind within definable terms.

The monetary part of the Award accomplished this so

completely that at no time during the progress of the Award was it necessary to stimulate the public interest by the usual publicity methods. No propaganda was used in the furtherance of a wide interest: no publicity agent or channels were employed. The Award made its own news, and this was sent out at intervals to the news-papers which seemed anxious to print the information thus furnished. That was all the publicity used in the furtherance of the idea which it was very quickly shown was fully capable of carrying itself.

X

Literally tens of thousands of letters came from those who did not desire to submit plans and yet were anxious to register their opinions as to the method to be pursued by the United States Government in its co-operation with the nations of the world for the prevention of further wars. These opinions were all tabulated and classified, so that the Jury of Award might, when it be-gan its consideration of the plans, have before it, in connection with the plans themselves, a wider sense of the public desire as reflected in the letters.

For the important fact should be borne in mind, which has not always been clear in the public mind, that the work of the Jury was not to consider its own wishes or opinions in any way in the consideration of the plans. With the reflection of the desires of a large cross-section of the American people before it, as indicated in the letters and plans, it was to select that particular practi-cable plan which most accurately reflected the expressed desire of the American people taking part in the Award. It could very well be, as actually proved to be the case, that the plan finally selected might in its content be at direct variance with the personal views held by some members of the Jury.

XI

Plans came in by the hundreds, and later by the thousands. The contents of each were carefully tabulated, and the work of selection and classification went on constantly during the period of time allowed for their submission. In the early autumn, the Jury began its sessions and examination of the plans, in full or by their digests, so that when the last day of submission was reached, at the midnight hour of November 15, 1923, the work was well in hand. The closing day found that 22,165 plans had been received, but as many of the plans were the composite work of organizations, university faculties, and so forth, a single plan often represented the views of hundreds or thousands of individuals.

The plans, as a whole, were found to be of a distinctly high quality. Even a first reading of the plans clearly proved that the Award had enlisted the co-operation of the most intelligent students of foreign affairs, although their identity was, of course, concealed in the sealed envelope accompanying each plan, which was placed in the office safe, while the plan itself went to the Jury. The most careful reading disclosed the fact that approximately 8,000 plans were of the orderly nature to entitle them to further consideration, and with this immense problem the Jury of Award had to deal.

XII

The nature of these plans has been so interestingly set forth, in detail, by Miss Lape in her introduction to the book, *Ways to Peace*, containing twenty of the plans, that this phase of the Award need not be elaborated here except to say that the plans came from every group in American life. Some were obviously from life-long students of history and international law. Some were from persons who had studied little, but who had themselves seen and felt the horror of war—or who are even now living out its tragedy.

However unlike, almost all the plans expressed or implied the same conviction, that this is the time for the nations of the earth to admit frankly that war is a crime and thus withdraw the legal and moral sanction too long permitted to it as a method of settling international disputes. Thousands of plans showed a deep aspiration to have the United States take the lead in a common agreement to brand war in every truth an "outlaw."

Through the plan as a whole ran these dominant currents:

That, if war is honestly to be prevented, there must be a right-about-face on the part of the nations in their attitude toward it; and that by some progressive agreement the manufacture and purchase of the munitions of war must be limited or stopped.

That while no political mechanism alone will insure co-operation among the nations, *there must be some machinery of co-operation* if the will to co-operate is to be made effective; that mutual counsel among the nations is the real hope for bringing about the disavowal of war by the open avowal of its real causes and open discussion of them.

And, finally, that there must be some means of defining, recording, interpreting, and developing the law of nations.

XIII

It was in the last few days of December, 1923, that the Jury of Award reached its decision. On January 7, 1924, the winning plan was published, in whole or in part, in the press of the world.

With the aid of hundreds of newspapers, and ninety-three co-operating agencies, including nearly every prominent civic, religious, economic, and educational organization in the United States, the plan was submitted to a referendum of the American people. Ballots were printed in the newspapers, along with the plan, and accompanied copies of the plan distributed by the co-operating agencies to their members.

When the referendum was closed on March 15, 1924, it was found that approximately 615,000 ballots had been cast, with 87½ per cent in favor of the plan. To some this number of ballots cast was disappointingly small. But when the facts are carefully considered, the number is, on the contrary, very large, and represents, perhaps, the widest and most intelligent plebiscite ever taken on any public question. Speaking personally, the final figure was more than 100,000 in excess of the figure which I had fixed in my mind as a total vote after I had read the plan. It must not be overlooked that the winning plan presupposed a knowledge of the League of Nations and of the Permanent Court of International Justice, which is not even known by that name, but by its more commonly-known title of the World Court,— a knowledge possessed by a small minority of the American people. The people were not asked to vote on a single question, but were asked to read a plan which required a wide knowledge of foreign affairs and foreign relations. Then they were asked to sign a ballot, their name and address, to indicate whether they were voters, to address their own envelope, in the majority of cases, and to supply their own postage. This is all very different from other referendums which ask an answer to a simple question, which do not require the sender to give his name or address, but which simply provide for a postal card with prepaid postage to be returned to an address printed on the card. Such procedure did not seem possible nor wise in the case of The American Peace Award plan. Something more vital and significant was asked of a busy people, deeply engrossed in their own and other affairs. When this fact is taken into consideration, the result was astonishing, while the large percentage of votes in favor of the plan certainly registered a definite opinion.

XIV

In order that this referendum might not be influenced in any way by the identity of the author of the plan, it was wisely decided by the Policy Committee that the name of the winner should not be made public until the plebiscite was well under way or near its completion. The member-in-charge of the Committee was authorized to open the envelope, and counsel the author to silence. Neither the donor of the Award, nor a single member of the Policy Committee or of the Jury of Award, was informed as to the identity of the author of the winning plan. On the evening of Monday, February 4, at a specially arranged meeting at the Academy of Music, in Philadelphia, the Honorable John W. Davis, on behalf of the Policy Committee, announced the name of Doctor Charles Herbert Levermore as the author, and presented him with a check for the first half of the monetary part of the Award.

XV

In order that the public might have a broader idea of the plans submitted, the Policy Committee decided that a book containing nineteen other plans, each of a different nature, in company with the winning plan, should be published. This was done on March 28, 1924, when Charles Scribner's Sons issued a volume entitled *Ways to Peace*, with an introduction by Miss Lape. The varying character of the submitted plans was thus disclosed, as was also the impressive standing of a few of those who contributed to the Award. The envelopes containing these names were opened only after it was decided to include the plans in the book, so that their identity was not known at the time of selection. The authors were:

Professor Edwin Borchard, Professor of Law in the Yale University Law School.

Christian A. Herter, Assistant to the Secretary of Commerce.

William S. Culbertson, Vice-Chairman of the United States Tariff Commission.

Gutzon Borglum, Sculptor and author.

Samuel Peter Wilson, of The American Chemical Society.

Miss M. Carey Thomas, Organizer and former President of Bryn Mawr College.

Charles W. Eliot, President Emeritus of Harvard University.

Ernest Bruncken, former Congressional Reference Librarian.

John McAuley Palmer, Brigadier-General of the U. S. Army: Aide-de-Camp to General Pershing.

David Starr Jordan, Chancellor Emeritus of Leland Stanford University.

Manley O. Hudson, Professor of International Law at Harvard University.

J. Whitla Stinson, of the Bar of the State of New York.

David Atkins, American Institute of Mining and Metallurgical Engineers.

Theodore Stanfield, The American Society of International Law.

Ernest Joseph Howe, The Western Electric Company.

The Right Reverend Charles H. Brent, Bishop of the Diocese of Western New York.

Nathan Isaacs, Professor of Business Law at Harvard University.

Paul H. Arthur, of the Bar of the State of New York.

Charles Herbert Levermore, Secretary of The New York Peace Society.

XVI

It was not to be expected, of course, that the winning plan, no matter what its content, could or would satisfy the divergent views existing on the subject of world-peace. It naturally followed that wide discussion of the merits and demerits of the plan broke loose immediately upon its publication. Some there were who confidently looked to the Award to produce some brilliant and original plan by which the peace of the world was to be brought about, as it were, over night. Many there were who were disappointed at the absence, in the winning plan, of what may be called the emotional idea that only the Golden Rule can bring about peace. The most thoughtful knew that whatever idea was given the Award, bearing always in mind that a practicable or workable plan was asked for, it would follow along prescribed and inevitable lines as a next step. The outstanding fact is that there are only two ways to settle a quarrel: one is to fight it out, and the other is to talk it over. The former, in the case of nations, means war, and that way the people of the United States have certainly, in this Award, shown they want to do away with. What then remains? The alternative method of talking it over naturally connotes a parley or a conference between the parties at variance. This, of course, in the case of nations, logically translates itself into a group, or society, or association, or league of nations, call it what you will, which will assemble around a table and try to find a solution of the difference. What other practicable method is there except through such mutual counsel and co-operation?

The very simplicity of the matter, however, creates its perplexing difficulties, and perplexities always call forth divergent views. Hence, the winning plan in The American Peace Award evoked widespread and often heated discussion. The newspapers took the initiative and argued the plan pro and con,—with a surprising preponderance, however, in its favor. Individuals, clubs, societies, organizations, and every kind of debating club found meat for opinion and discussion. The United States Senate authorized the formation of a select Investigation Committee to examine into the charge of propaganda being used to influence legislative opinion, without reaching any findings.

But no matter what its source, or the intent, the plan was accomplishing its purpose to bring about a wide discussion of peace by young and old.

XVII

One of the strongest points in connection with the winning plan was the paragraph not contained in the plan itself, but written by Elihu Root and expressed by the Jury of Award:

It is the unanimous hope of the Jury that the first fruit of the mutual counsel and co-operation among the nations which will result from the adoption of the plan selected will be a general prohibition of the manufacture and sale of all materials of war.

The fact that six of the most prominent men of the United States, and a woman of outstanding position, were willing to express this sentiment to the world as a practical possibility attracted wide attention and comment. The suggestion was also criticized as being impossible of attainment, but the great majority of the press writers thought otherwise. The editor of the Ironwood, Michigan, *Globe*, in one of the best editorials which appeared on the subject, argued that the world has wars largely because its mental state recognizes the possibility of war, and that the possibility of war being recognized, it is a natural thing to resort to it. Naturally, he argued, if one recognizes a possibility, then it is foolish not to be prepared for it. If military means of determining a question are available, and if nations are prepared to use war for certain decisions, then it is obvious that now and again they will do so. The remedy is to expunge this idea from the human mind.

It ought to be easy, said this writer, to get people to give up something they do not like, since not many men in a regiment really have a good time in battle or a good time in any of the processes of a war. Certainly the people at home do not care for it. Hence why cannot there be a general understanding to give up something which distresses everybody? Any one would give up the toothache or the headache or a broken leg. Why, then, cling to shrapnel wounds? The fact cannot be controverted that one flash of rationality around the world, with everybody agreeing that war is obsolete, and the thing is done.

The trouble is that the human race is perversely illogical. It is contentious. It is full of opinions and prejudices. It loves the idea of fighting. It does not like to get hurt, but it likes to think in terms of fighting. A hundred thousand persons will go to see a prize-fight, and yet on the part of the audience there is no anger in the fight.

It was a significant fact that by far the preponderance of opinion declared it as idle to say that war cannot be outlawed. But, was the unanimous verdict, war must first be outside of the thoughts of men. Then it will be outside their actions.

XVIII

The chief aim of the founder of the Award, which was, of course, an educative one, was thus accomplished far beyond any expections. It is quite within the bounds of conservatism to say that not for a long time, if ever, was a united national mind so concretely fixed upon the question of peace as during the months of the progress of The American Peace Award. Individuals, groups, clubs, organizations, faculties of colleges, entire communities, were, for months, thinking, planning, talking, studying, discussing, and writing peace. Over a quarter of a million of American citizens wrote and asked for the conditions under which plans might be submitted. Hundreds of thousands of American citizens wrote letters to the Award headquarters. Scarcely a newspaper or periodical published throughout the length and breadth of the United States did not print from one to a dozen news articles and editorials touching different aspects of the Award. A group of newspapers and periodicals opened their pages to printing plans sent by their readers. Meetings innumerable were held at which the Award was the sole topic; scores of conventions passed resolutions of endorsement, and pastors of churches, literally by the hundreds, chose the Award as their subject. Ninety-seven of the most powerful organizations of all kinds united themselves with the undertaking, and presented the idea to their memberships through their printed publications. State legislatures passed resolutions commending the idea and the effort. College debates by the scores were held by those who are or within a few years will be the voters of the country.

XIX

Coming as did The American Peace Award out of and from the people, there developed through this discussion a clearer recognition by the people of the United States than could have been brought about by any other method, that they cannot sit placidly by and see Rome burn, that they are a part of the world, and, as such, must play their part in it. No single effort of late succeeded in so fixing the attention of the people of the United States upon our foreign relations, and upon the best methods under which we can live in amity and peace with the nations of the earth, and how far we can go with our contribution to such an end. Librarians from every part of the country reported and still report that there never was such a demand for books dealing with our foreign relations or works on previous peace efforts, and for the records of peace congresses. Booksellers sold more books dealing with the European situation than ever before. The editors of leading American newspapers received letters from individual subscribers and from clubs and organizations, asking that more space be given to foreign news in their papers, in each case crediting their larger interest in the affairs of the world to The American Peace Award. The entire interest of the American people in foreign questions was quickened all along the line.

In all this, there was the awakening, the distinct beginning of an international mind,—a factor in our foreign relations which we so keenly need, and which we must first develop before we can hope to attain an ultimate result.

XX

That essential factor was the chief hope of the realization of The American Peace Award, since it stands to reason that enough people must first think about peace before it can be attained. The hearts of the people must first be set upon having peace. As they have wanted, and have had war, so they can want and have peace. It is, of course, perfectly obvious that peace must be visualized through some system, but, on the other hand, no system or machinery can successfully function unless the spirit and the will of the people are behind it. Peace does not depend upon government except as government is representative of the people. What the attitude of the people is, that must be the attitude of government. What is decreed by unofficial agencies becomes the law of official agencies. As one nation has the power to smash another nation, so likewise has one nation the power to preserve another. Hence, a public conscience must be developed and derived from a personal conscience.

It was the fact that The American Peace Award emanated from the people that gave strength to the idea from the beginning. It was not the size of the monetary award; it was not the publicity accorded it. Important as they were, they were not the determining factors.

XXI

Many said, and said truly, that the means of abolishing war was not a secret: that it was published centuries ago: that it was all contained in the thoroughly practicable admonition "Thou shalt love thy neighbor as thy self." This is true. No one can dispute the truth that no international law or any other kind of law is possible without this supreme law. One may well go further and say that "on these two commandments hang all the law and the prophets": love of God and love of fellow-men. The trouble is to get mankind to remember and follow this golden rule when personal greed and personal anger consume a people and assume national dimensions. It should always be remembered, too, that Christ first laid down the law and the gospels: he spoke first The Sermon on the Mount, and then adjured the people to follow his precepts. So must we humans first lay down certain rules of conduct for nations to follow, and then invoke their enforcement. The rules must come first. They may be born of the spiritual, but they must be laid down for all to read and know. Their observance comes afterward. The spirit of Christ may find a ready and certainly an appropriate place in a treaty or covenant, since it represents all the wisdom of the ages. But we must create and bring into being the covenant and the treaty for guidance of action. Being mortals we must employ the methods of mortals. No peace can ever come about until we write down its meaning and the terms by which it can be had. Then comes not the will to enforce, but the desire to respect peace.

XXII

A distinct achievement of The American Peace Award was the general acknowledgment, which discussion on every hand brought out, that the idea of universal peace had made enormous strides since the curtain of

history unfolded itself. The general feeling was everywhere expressed that we are nearer its attainment than
ever before. Naturally, The American Peace Award
was pointed to as a striking instance of an adventure
which years ago would not have been possible or even
thought of. It is undoubtedly true that the rule of
reason had not yet superseded the rule of force, but the
tendency to substitute the tribunal for the battlefield
was never closer to the desires or the mind and heart of
mankind than it is at the present moment. One needs
only to read history to be convinced of the truth that
where, in ancient days, rulers only thought of the un-
sheathed sword as the instrument for settling disputes,
to-day the mind of the world is thinking in terms of
parleys or conferences. Arbitration has adjusted disputes during the past hundred years which before would
have been provocations for instant warfare. Individuals
have long ago substituted the court for the ring. In
olden days, a tribal feud meant the physical extinction
of a family. To-day such feuds are settled by the courts.
These agencies were the result of education and the resultant enlightenment of the individual. It is along
exactly these lines that states are beginning to act.
Think what we may of the League of Nations or the
World Court, they are functioning and making a distinct
and definite contribution to the growing desire for arbitration. A war is brought about by a cause. A cause is
brought about by a people,—generally by a handful of
persons. With the growing number of educational agencies of peace, mankind is more and more turning to the
conference table and the tribunal. Peace is to-day com-

manding world-wide attention. A significant outcome ot
The American Peace Award which alone made its crea
tion worth while were the other awards for peace made
by The World Peace Foundation for an educational
plan, and by Mr. Edward A. Filene, of Boston, for peace
plans to be submitted by three of the European nations
and Great Britain. Those who say that universal peace
is as far off to-day as it was a century ago are not reading
aright the signs of the times. Never was there a time
when it was commanding the thoughts of mankind as it
is to-day; never did history present a more favorable
time for furtherance of its study, leading straight to an
ultimate adoption.

That fact The American Peace Award demonstrated
in the largest sense with an accuracy true and sure. As
clear as a bell, it showed an expression of what is undoubtedly forming into the will of the American people.
There was a new breadth, a distinct intensity of discussion which no other channel for expression had brought
forth. It represented an increased volume and confidence
in the voice of the people. Again and again were the
words "national obligation" used. There was a new
moral force: a new understanding: a new realization of
a necessity and an awakened popular feeling that is
destined to put a new stimulus into an imperishable
movement.

XXIII

A writer in the Salt Lake City *Deseret News* sees this
trend clearly when he says that there can be little doubt
that the heroic ideals of the past are not the ideals of

the modern world. More and more are men being ad-judged for their honesty, their love of liberty, their de-votion to truth and their service to humanity. To the memory of these men are monuments being erected to-day. It is no longer the man who makes the wounds of the world that is the hero of the people; it is rather the man who heals its wounds, who renders mankind inspiring service which constructs instead of destroys. The people are distinctly changing, says the writer so truly, in all this; they are thinking in different terms. The entire mental attitude of the world is in process of alteration. More emphasis is being laid on the realiza-tion that humanity is one family: that we are all of com-mon blood: that what concerns and is vital to one is of concern and is vital to all. Exploration, travel, the aeroplane, the radio,—all these agencies are bringing peo-ple closer together or face to face. Art and science are reaching out and helping men to feel the brotherhood of man. Our expanding commercial relations are beginning to teach us that one nation cannot be benefited by injur-ing another nation; that the wealth of one is the wealth of all; that the welfare of one is the welfare of all.

These are the facts that the people of the United States are beginning to grasp as fundamental truths. It is a significant fact that not a single plan in all the 22,165 which were submitted to The American Peace Award counselled isolation on the part of the United States. Neither was there a mention of our "splendid isolation" of the past in the hundreds of thousands of letters. In not one instance was the note of "keeping out of Europe" struck. To preserve the sovereignty of the United States, yes: that note was struck, and vigorously so, but not the old idea of going it alone, and the devil take the hindmost. All this was conspicuous for its entire absence from plan or letter. In its place was the opposite: that no permanent gain can accrue to mankind from shedding each other's blood, and that no good thing in this world can come to full fruition save in an atmosphere of humanity and justice.

The American people are to-day feeling more deeply than ever the truth that war is the utter annihilation of that quality of spiritual humanity without which mankind cannot abide.

XXIV

"But surely," so many have asked, "you expected some more definite, some ultimate result, too, did you not?"

No, I expected nothing.

But I had hopes—very deep hopes, and these remain with me. For the fact must be borne in mind that we have by no means reached the end of The American Peace Award. It is at its beginning. The educative stage is passed, but there are other stages. I can see several years of work ahead for the Award organization.

At the same time, I am perfectly free to say that I am so well satisfied with what has been accomplished that, if it were decreed that The American Peace Award should go no further to an ultimate result, I should still feel more than repaid for the effort.

But it does not appear as if it were so decreed.

One of the ranking officials in the United States Government recently wrote me in a letter: "The Award started something that nothing can now stop. The interest is too widespread: the idea has rested too securely and gone too deeply. The Award has planted a seed from which something must come."

XXV

It is only natural that so wide and thorough an awakening of a people usually leads to some result. But when we use the word result we are apt to use it in an immediate sense. The American is by nature impatient. His idea of a result is to-morrow. That cannot be with a question so seemingly complex as that of world-peace. As a matter of fact, the question is, of course, not complex at all: it is amazingly simple, as are all great questions when you strip them of the verbiage with which the human mind persists in clothing them. Accepting, however, the present complexity with which the question has been surrounded, no state of world-peace can be brought about by a single step. As Elihu Root has well said, its consummation can come about only through a series of successive steps, each step a little farther toward the goal.

It is the first step on this road to peace that has been successfully taken through The American Peace Award, —a distinct beginning.

XXVI

It must not be overlooked that the people of the United States stand before the world to-day without any plan of action so far as their relations with the rest of the world are concerned. The views of special groups have lost their force. Besides, that is not what the world asks from the American people. It asks not a foreign policy born of an administration, of a group, or of a political party. It wants an expression of the national will, of the national belief of the people of the United States. The world knows well that without such national support the most carefully worded treaty or agreement becomes a worthless scrap of paper. On the other hand, it is also a fact that world peace can be attained if enough people think of it, and desire it, and say they desire it. The public conscience is derived from personal conscience: the unit becomes the mass.

The nearest approach thus far to the recording of a crystallized national opinion on this question of peace has come through The American Peace Award.

It demonstrated one fact as a certainty:

That the people of the United States are not only ready to take their part in achieving and preserving the peace of the world, but when they were given an opportunity, as in the Award, they let their minds rest on it, and then, by the hundreds of thousands, became vocal, and said so.

That is a distinct step forward, and the importance of a step does not lie so much in whether it is long or short as in whether it is a step in the right direction.

XXVII

Perhaps it is true that the American people may not yet know clearly just where they are going along the road to peace, but that they are distinctly and decidedly on their way admits of little question. No one who had his finger on the public pulse, and heard its beats through the progress of the Award, can doubt this statement for a moment. The people are determined that as they have registered their views through the medium of this Award, they shall now be crystallized into definable terms, and that these views shall be placed before the world. This note of determination was struck in almost every letter. "This must now be carried through" was a common phrase in hundreds of letters, and it was said with a crispness that left no doubt of the determination behind it.

The underlying impulse of the American people toward some form of practical foreign co-operation is strong and irresistible. Partisan politics have beclouded the issue; the absence of a straight and unbiased channel of expression has made it impossible for universal expression. But the moral interest and the moral force of the people are awakened. The American people have had time to think, and they have thought, and the national voice, to a degree, has been heard over the heads of those who have, up to this time, talked to no purpose.

It is idle to say that the time is not opportune; on the contrary, it is distinctly the opportune moment.

XXVIII

We are, as a people, undoubtedly headed for an ultimate result in world-peace, and, of course, we can attain it if we have the mind so to do. When and how we reach it depends entirely upon our will to reach it. It does not matter whether the ultimate result is the adoption of

the winning plan in The American Peace Award.   It
may well be some other plan.   That is a detail.

The main point is that we have started.

XXIX

Ahead of us lies and waits the result!

THIRTY-THREE:

IS IT WORTH WHILE?

That. . .

"continuous moving, the ceaseless becoming which is commonly called Life."

———

"If a man plant himself indomitably on his instincts, and there abide, the huge world will come round to him."

EMERSON

IS IT WORTH WHILE?

I

I HAVE a letter before me which I am asked to answer in this book. It says: "You have now lived sixty years. Do you really believe it is worth while? Are the compensations commensurate with the sacrifices?"

In other words, the old question: Is that wonderful thing which the Lāmas call "the continuous moving, the ceaseless becoming which is commonly called Life,"—is that worth living? To it there can be only the old answer: "Yes, if lived rightly." And rightly, of course, means if the spirit is right.

II

I am free to say that I write here more from observation than from experience,—a point of vantage I venture to say from which most of us write, if we are honest with ourselves and our readers, when we try to deal with this subject. I know I have never learned to live Life rightly. I can truly echo the sentiment of Dwight L. Moody when he said "I have had more trouble with myself than with any other man I have ever met." I have had too distinct a leaning toward looking for and discovering the faults in persons and then of becoming possessed with a mad desire to correct those faults. Naturally, this is fatal to living either calmly or happily with one's self or of cementing the most satisfactory human relations with one's friends. I have never quite learned to after he had met him as many times as there were days in the year. A human being is so complex that we cannot wisely or truly judge him until we have known him for a considerable time.

IV

Life as given to us is of itself very simple, and every attribute is given to us with Life to meet its tasks. It is a mistaken notion that we are sometimes asked to carry more than we can bear; no load ever given to man is too heavy for the spirit given to him at the same time. This is difficult of belief in times when the cross of disillusionment or of disappointment, of sorrow or of loss, is laid upon us to carry, but that is only because our finite penetration stops this side of Divine laws.

V

It is for us to decide whether we keep Life simple or make it complicated. Most of us do the latter. But one fact is absolute: that happiness was intended as a normal gift, just as good health is a normal condition. It is we ourselves who change the normal to the abnormal, and then we ask "Is Life really worth living?" It is. But we must live it as it is given to us to live and intended that we should live it. If we begin, however, to introduce a quality of wrongly appraising others, of attributing a wrong instead of a right motive, of creating distrust and turmoil within ourselves where it was intended that the peace of confidence and faith should rule, it follows, as night follows the day, that we create unhappiness, and Life begins to take on a sombre hue.

Life itself is always firm and true. It is we who make it seem changeable. It offers the highest mental reactions or the dullest of impacts, exactly as we choose.

It all comes back to the spirit,—the spirit in which we ourselves live our own lives, not alone for their own expression as it concerns us, but in the manner in which our lives touch the lives of others. We cannot live by ourselves and for ourselves. Our human relations must be right. I care not how efficient a man may be in his work in the world; he fails of a well-lived life if his human relations are not true.

VI

I have in mind, as I write, a man who sits high in the councils of his peers. In any list of the ten great Americans he invariably finds his place. His ability, farsightedness, remarkable vision, and integrity of purpose none can question. His work has made and will leave its mark upon his generation. Respected by his fellows, his name the signal for approval in any gathering of his countrymen, he is a type of successful man whom the young American admires and would emulate. He counts his means by the millions. It would seem as if he has everything that may be desired by men. And he has,— except one priceless gift, and that is happiness. The one inner quality that transcends his almost super-human abilities, he lacks. And all because he has never taken the trouble to keep right his human relations. Things mean more to him than people; accomplishment more than friendship. The world is closer to him than is his family, and yet he is a devoted husband and a careful there is always one real factor in Life, and that is Truth. As Confucius has so well said: Truth is the law of God. It is the beginning and end.

IX

To take as one's motto the saying of Captain Bill McDonald, of the Texas Rangers: "No man in the wrong can stand up against a fellow that's in the right and keeps on a' comin'."

Then Life *is* worth living.

THIRTY-FOUR:

WITH WHICH I CLOSE

children to give to parents, and even a greater heritage for them when they become parents to give to their children.

III

There is a rule of life to which there is no exception: that a gentleman has only one code of manners, no matter what may be the station in life of the one addressed or dealt with. Too often is the opposite found in the young, particularly in the case of those boys who come from homes where opportunities are many and from which the world may reasonably expect the right attitude. No two persons are born so unequal that the same coin of human courtesy cannot be current between them. The woman who circumstances have decreed shall seemingly play a lowlier position in the world is very often of infinitely finer grain and more worthy of consideration than her sister whom some good—or ill— fortune not of her own making has raised to a position which the world regards as superior. At least, there can be no two codes of manners where a woman is concerned, no matter in what position in life she may have been chosen by God to play her part. A young man should never lose that vital sense of relation in personal conduct, —and as he goes on and preserves that attitude he will realize how important it is in getting straight his sense of relations to everything else, particularly in maintaining an attitude of gracious consideration toward all. For in the code of the gentleman there is always included the rare quality of consideration which does so much and goes so far to sweeten life in all its avenues and activities.

IV

I want to say it carefully when I state that theological doctrines are not of supreme importance. It is only the narrow and unthinking who will say that without them one is deprived of the essentials of religious training. Years of repeated declaration are not necessary for a belief in a Divine regulation of our lives and in a belief in that help which comes from that communion with the inner self which we call prayer. Not the prayer for specific things or for concrete advantages, but that supplication for help and for courage which, when it is sought in the right spirit and is thus vouchsafed us, fills and bathes our souls with a restful quietude and steels our hearts with a calmness and strength that nothing else can bring.

As one goes along in life the truth is borne in upon him that in speaking of one's soul instead of thinking of it as something he possesses, *man is a soul*. This is the great lesson that Socrates taught humanity. The soul is the conscious self of a man living in a world of realism, and that is why man is so rarely satisfied. He must live in the realm of idealism. His route may be along the ways of materialism, but his destination, his goal, must be something else than the realistic: something higher, finer, deeper, and more satisfying.

Belief in the existence of a God within us needs no explanation nor calls for any defense. Its presence is too manifest in every act of our lives and in every thought of the mind. "There are no tricks in plain and simple faith." The man who has lived needs no argument in.

books. Of little reading, Jesus Christ revolutionized man and re-created a world. Only two books belonging to Shakespeare have ever been found, and the authenticity of both has been challenged. All this is not saying that man should not read; but it points to the truth that where he substitutes Life for the book he is by no means to be ignored.

It is interesting as one goes on to see how unconsciously he eliminates from all that he has read, and finds himself leaning heavily on a few sources. It is a favorite game with some to choose the ten greatest authors or the one hundred best books. But I have come to the point where I find about all I need is in the Bible, Shakespeare, and Emerson, and I think I would add William James. There is not much in life that is not said in those three or four inspired sources. And all of James is in Emerson, and all of Emerson is really in Shakespeare, and all of Shakespeare is in the Bible. Whenever the need is strong for something more modern, as seemingly adapted to our every-day need of the present, I turn to a copy, always on my desk, of Kipling's "If,"—perhaps the most searching poem in the realm of recent English literature. Actually, there are only a few vital truths, and they are all in the Sermon on the Mount and in the book of Proverbs. Latter-day writers only reiterate, revise, and say the same truths in different ways. Beaten down, life resolves itself to a very few things, which, if a man has them at his command, cause his existence to flow gently on and to come very close to the Divine, as Marcus Aurelius so well said.

VII

The effort to achieve right living is not as difficult as some make it out to be. It is not a game, of course, but neither is it a battle. It is an undertaking which, if kept simple, resolves itself into a minimum of anxiety. Wordsworth summarized it well when he spoke of Life as "a few strong instincts and a few plain rules." One finds, too, I think, the truth of Carlyle's dictum that "one's instinct is truer than one's thought."

It is the ways of men which most perplex,—their self-revelations in their acts. Every human being has some blind spot; each is full of shortcomings. These are not visible at first, but further acquaintance with any one reveals the inevitable weaknesses where at first strength only seems to be present. This should never surprise. It will perplex, and often cruelly disappoint. We naturally want those we esteem to respond ever to the best. But none can,—always. Therefore, it is wise to accept people at their best, and believe in their best and not lay too much emphasis on their lesser selves. There is a wonderful sentence of two words which I have always regarded as the greatest text in the Bible: "Judge not." All life, it sometimes seems to me, is in that marvellous dictum. Let the imagination play with that injunction and it becomes a gospel of life in itself in its far-reaching potentialities. It is so easy to counsel others to "judge not"; so very hard for us to do it ourselves. It is so easy to write it here; I have found it so hard to do. It is always human nature to attribute the worst motive for an act,—never the best. It is so easy to think of evil import; so hard to believe in the good intent. Yet the good is infinitely more universally present in action than the evil,—when we understand and are patient enough to look under the surface. But that patience also is a difficult quality to exercise. Patience seems so difficult of attainment, yet it is such a vital branch of justice. Time, if permitted a chance, inevitably makes clear what at first seems indisputably wrong. "Time makes more converts than Reason." To be kindly of judgment and slow of appraisement of another's acts is a quality hard for man to master, but in it nevertheless lie the seed of our own happiness and the justice that we owe to others.

VIII

One of the teachings which a young man will find it most difficult to practice is thoroughness, because he will meet on every hand a lack of it. He will meet men who go round in circles, who leap from topic to topic in conversation (if there *is* any left in the world, as he grows older), who jump from one thing to another in their daily lives, who go from one meeting to another absolutely forgetful at the last of what transpired at the one before; men who in all that they do will remind one of the song of the Persian poet:

> "Myself when young did eagerly frequent
> Doctor and saint, and heard great argument
> About it and about; but evermore
> Came out by the same door where in I went."

We meet men whose orbit is pitifully small; whose horizon is contracted and whose vision reaches not beyond the day or the circle in which they move, those of whom Hannah More so well said:

"In men this blunder still you find:
All think their little set mankind."

In each case the absent ingredient is that of thoroughness,—the lack of will to think a problem through, to think before action, to deliberate before decision, to attain a larger horizon.

But by just so far as a young man will meet so much that lacks the thorough touch will his own thoroughness stand out the more clearly for men to see. He will learn for himself how fundamental is this need of thoroughness, even in the smallest deed. He will discover that the man who is indifferent to it is the man whose carelessness in deed makes him also confused of word and rambling of thought. Thoroughness is always born of an orderly mind, and such a mind can accomplish with apparent tranquillity the purposes that to others would appear impossible. The acts of man should be constructive, and most of man's undertakings have some permanent achievement in view. But what permanence can there be that is not born of thoroughness? Acts done haphazardly usually return to their maker for accounting, like a duty shirked that one meets as he turns a corner a little further along. We are asked to do certain things only once; we are permitted to go through life only once; the place we are at to-day we shall never see again. To-day is all we have, since yesterday is gone and to-morrow is but a hope. What we do, therefore, with only the present and one chance given us admits of none but the finished rule that governs every act, remembering that often it is the smallest act, seemingly trivial at the time, by which we are judged and our character is measured. We have all the time there is to do what we are called upon to do; hence whatever we do should be of our best and according to our best. For we little know by what act we are appraised or how we are judged by the seemingly inconsequential thing that leaves our hands.

There is not one of us who is not an example to some one else. Often our actions are watched by some one, and are accepted as a standard for some other life. We may consider ourselves the humblest and the most obscure, but always is there some one else who considers himself humbler and more obscure, and looks to another for precept and example. The most unthought-of saying of ours may be the seed that drops on fertile soil; the smallest action, in our eyes trivial and inconsequential, is an example which is observed and followed by another. Our influence may fall in the most unlikely places:

> "This learned I from the shadow of a tree,
> Which to and fro swayed o'er my garden wall:
> Our shadow-selves, our influence, may fall
> Where we can never be."

Every faculty we have is preserved and strengthened and increased by the thoroughness which we manifest. It is only the great man who appears to know how to do the smallest thing with thoroughness. He surmounts difficulty with care, and regards an obstacle not as something to shirk or avoid, but simply as a difficulty to be overcome. In the face of his thoroughness the insurmountable often melts like snow under a spring sun. The man who has accepted thoroughness as his gospel in life is a hard man to beat. He is well-nigh unconquerable.

IX

If the sons learn from the father, as they grow, it is also true that the father learns from the sons. Parenthood is not any more one-sided in its benefits than any other blessing in life. If anything, it seems to me as if children, rightly taken, educate the parent more than the parent educates the children. I am living over again my boyhood years with my sons. I have known every step of the way they are taking. Again and again has the impulse been strong with their mother and me, as we saw one of them headed straight for the wall of experience, to step in and spare the impact. We had to learn a great deal of restraint not to flag them on their path, every instinct in the parental nature prompted, but Experience came in, rapped at the door of our common-sense and counselled "Hands off. None learn except from me." We learned, too, from them the great parental lesson to put aside our own pet desires, to modify our own comfortable ways, and to realize that they had the right of way in our lives; not to weaken them, but to strengthen ourselves and make us better fitted for the discharge of the fullest parenthood. And children's needs can be insistent, as every parent finds out, and always at the moment when the parents have plans of their own which it seems so necessary to be carried out, or personal desires which seem so pleasant to realize. These often call for an entire and not always a simple mental readjustment and an alteration in fixed plans and habits, but parenthood is an exacting master and has little regard for personal inclinations. Whenever the responsibility is discharged in this spirit the reward is usually assured, but not always. In the main, however, the result can be gauged by the effort. The child is, generally speaking, the true reflection of its parents and the result of its training.

X

The lives of those who are now young will be lived during one of the most wonderful centuries in the history of the world. They will think in terms that we dream not of. The dimensions of Life are growing larger and larger, and they will grow with them. Accomplishment will enlarge as vista after vista is opened for the achievement of man. The world is to be made into a great community, with its present farthermost reaches brought into easy communication. No one dare say what the result of this closer relation will be, but one thing is certain: achievement will assume proportions of which this generation knows not. It is the brave man to-day who ventures to say that any accomplishment is impossible: we stand daily in the presence of what a few years ago was deemed outside the realm of possibility. What will be unattainable in the coming generation if this be true now? We each work with the tools available at the present; we strive within the limits of our generation; our accomplishments are adapted to our times and confined within the extent of our knowledge. We have so worked for our time. Our sons will work for their time. But theirs will exceed the present in the penetration of man's scrutiny and his discovery, and proportionately the field of human endeavor will enlarge itself. Hence, while the fundamental principles of life are immutable and will remain, the scope of endeavor will be so widened that those who are part of it will deal with measures that would stagger present belief. It will be a greater and a fuller world in which to work, and yet more closely related and in touch: whether it will be a better world remains for the generation to prove by what it puts into it and what the people of that time will stand for and insist shall prevail. The distance to which one can project a radio message, or across what vast space one can pick it up, is not half so important as the content of that message. It is what we do with and how we use the marvellous inventions of the day that count. But service will be more universal, and proportionately greater will be the good which men can render to mankind.

XI

Those who were born under favorable conditions should be the leaders of men and the doers of things, provided they take their America right and see its people truly. Riddled with faults and shortcomings as is American life, it has within its people qualities as titanic as they are potential. The need is to brush away the America of the superficial; the America that spends itself in wasteful extravagance; that wastes itself in mean-

ingless amusement, and talks in terms of putrid cabaret
psychology; that sings itself in meaningless verse and
paints itself in grotesque pictures. The batik hound is
not American any more than is the smoking divorcée. I
am one with the writer, Bart Haley, who sees the real
American as being he who, stone by stone, and girder
by girder, makes a marvellous building of thirty or more
stories stand safe and secure on the rock of the earth; the
man who makes it possible for us to walk across waters
and ride under the beds of rivers; the man who can bur-
row under the earth to build and then operate great
railroad systems in tiers, and build on top of them great
buildings; the man who with wire, steel, and canvas constructs a mechanism that equals and bewilders the eagle
in its flight; the man who defies the accepted laws of
time and space; who matches his physical strain and
stress against the machine of steel and iron which he pro-
pels and compels to do his bidding; the man whom we
call a workingman, a laborer, but who is really an artist
far greater than he who paints on canvas or chisels in
marble. He is an artist with a concentrative power: an
imagination and a capacity to match himself against
the forces of the Infinite that open the door of science;
that unlock the secrets of Nature and that enrich the
thoughts and lives of his fellow men. This is not the
America of material achievement,—it is the America of
the man who dreams with his imagination, who dares
with his courage, and who does with his spirit of endurance. That is America at its greatest. It is an America,
too, that will grow greater and firmer and more substantial as time goes on and as the achievements of men teach

her that cardinal lesson which, once learned, will make of her the greatest nation in the world.

But——

Thoroughness first; then speed.

XII

If doing what are judged to be the big things of the world fall to a young man's lot, he will learn a lesson in their doing that few people discover and realize: that the big things of life are the easiest to do. It is the little things,—the small, obvious tasks, or the keeping of our human relations right that are difficult to do. Those are really the tests of a man and his character. It seems sometimes as if in the doing of what the world calls big things God adds His strength to that of the doer, probably knowing that man cannot do them alone, and thus He adds Himself to the power of man. But in the little things, little only because they seem so, and not because they are really so, He leaves man to himself, so as to fit him for the problems of daily life and of his contacts with his fellow men. And left to ourselves, it is then that we get our feet all tangled up, our minds become confused, our judgments get warped, and we do not appear quite so large and so competent in the doing.

There was a wonderful woman in the Great War; a figure that stood out among womankind. With plenty of means, she organized her own ambulance corps, founded two wonderful hospitals, and organized the personnel of each with unerring efficiency: with her own hands she nursed back to life and cheered literally hundreds of buddies who had practically given up. Her work resulted so wonderfully that she became one of the great figures at the front, sought at every point, and finally decorated with every medal that could be given her by foreign governments. And yet as a friend in her private circle, as a wife to her husband, and as a mother to her children, she was a deplorable failure. She could organize, she could lead, she could make new soil for uprooted people, she could give new hope and aspiration to others, she could do the seemingly big thing with a positive genius. But when it came to the seemingly small things of life, which of course were in her life the greatest, she failed, and her life after the War came to a point of absolute ruination for herself and her family.

XIII

And so I see those who are still young as part of a great world, a greater world and yet a more closely united world, and from the manner in which they begin so will they be a distinct part of it, doing a work that men will see and seeing will respect the doers; a work conceived in the spirit that does rightly, pursued with that breadth of character and depth of sincerity which means security of foundation and the co-operation of the best of our fellow men, with that disregard for fame which is ephemeral. Then will a young man prove to himself and to others the truth of Woodrow Wilson's searching epitomization of the only worth-while work of man: "Do you covet distinction? You will never get it by serving yourself. Do you covet honor? You will get it only as a servant of mankind."

Honors will be theirs because they will not seek them;

distinction will be theirs because the work of the hand will bear the hall-mark of that quality. A son will hold up with credit the name he bears in proportion as he holds himself in respect, taking his work and not himself seriously, believing always that nothing counts so much as character and nothing succeeds like the action born in truth.

THIRTY-FIVE:

THE BOOK OF THE PAST AND THIS BOOK

"What do you read, my lord?
Words, words, words!"
                                    SHAKESPEARE

———

"Knowledge comes, but wisdom lingers."
                                    TENNYSON

THE BOOK OF THE PAST AND THIS BOOK

I

THE poet sings of "old pages for memories," and humanely fails to indicate the quality of the memories. But he who is an author knows. By accident or design he finds himself turning over pages yellow with age and reading what he wrote fifteen or twenty years ago. And, oh! the sinking of the heart! How was it possible to have written this and that? He turns back to the title or to the end to be sure that his name is signed to what he is reading, and there is the horrible confirmation. It is sad enough to realize that he wrote it, but how did it ever get printed? And, printed, how did the public accept it? Or did this kindly public simply put its tongue in its cheek, shrug a shoulder, and keep a polite silence? We say sometimes of a public that it is cruel and that its criticism is harsh, but is it not also long-suffering? Is it more considerate than we have given it credit? Or, being powerless to do otherwise than to read or not to read, does it merely accept all that is offered, dismissing what it likes with an approving nod and passing what displeases with a shrug or a frown?

II

That we insistently and grievously fail to give praise where praise is due and where a word of simple commendation would be so welcome admits of no doubt. It is

part of human nature perhaps more quickly to condemn
than to commend. We take what pleases us for granted.
We think of the author who writes a successful book, of
the actor who successfully interprets a part in a play,
the statesman who notably achieves,—all as inundated
with letters of praise and surrounded by flattering satel-
lites, when the truth of the matter is that these same people are sometimes the loneliest persons in the world.
We say to ourselves "He receives so many letters he does
not care for any word from me" or "She has the world
at her feet; what will she care about a word of mine?"
with the result that everybody says the same thing, no
one carries out his impulse, and often abject loneliness
is the lot vouchsafed the supposed recipient of all these
imagined attentions. So many of the successful men
and women have sadly spoken to me of this erroneous
conception of the public concerning the imaginary show-
ers of praise which come to them, two Presidents of the
United States among them. Not that those men and
women work for praise,—they would not achieve if
praise were their goal. But is there anything more satisfying than to receive the commendation of one's fellow-
men? If so, I know it not, and it is neither egotism nor
conceit that makes the word of commendation so valued!

III

I remember some years ago when the country was
cast in economic gloom, Walter H. Page, then editor of
The World's Work, published an "Uplift Number" of
his magazine. It was like a rift in the clouds that hung

low and dark over the horizon. He put the note of optimism—justifiable optimism—on every page and in every article; and men read his message of cheer with relief and refreshment.

We were lunching together shortly afterward when I mentioned the issue, and remarked upon the good it must have done. "I was going to write you and tell you so," I added, "only I didn't want to add to the hundreds of letters you must have received."

"Why didn't you carry your impulse into action?" he sadly asked. "You speak of the hundreds of letters; I received just one. Just another slap on the back would have meant so much," he concluded.

There and then we formed a society of two, called "Say-the-Word Club" which since has been augmented by other members. We agreed that henceforth when any man or woman did a thing that pleased or helped us, we would immediately, before the impulse left us, write a brief note of commendation. During all those war days while Ambassador to the Court of Saint James's, Page kept to his agreement, and this generation has produced no greater letter-writer! Sometimes we exchanged the answers we would receive,—some from the great and others from those who had achieved without fame—but invariably the same was the keynote in every reply: "You don't know what your word meant to me. It is one of the few times any one has thought to write the voluntary word of 'Well done, good and faithful servant.'"

I wrote to Page once and commended him. "I see you are practising our doctrines on me. Thanks, old man, thanks muchly, and many times. God knows I need it."

We all need it!

IV

I suppose not all writers are dissatisfied with their past work, except to the extent of having that healthy dissatisfaction which they should have concerning any work that might have been better done. Fortunate is that writer who can look back with pleasure to his work of the past and be satisfied with it. I had that pleasant experience just once.

One day I received in the mail two short essays. I liked them immensely. With a great satisfaction I commented to myself: "There! why don't more authors write like that? An editor's life would be worth living, and magazines would be worth reading." I wrote to the "author"—a woman—telling her of my unqualified pleasure with her work, and waited in vain for an acknowledgment or the submission of the additional manuscripts I suggested she might send me. Then I published one of the essays. The magazine had not been out more than two days when I received a letter from a reader asking if we had exhausted new material and were forced to fall back on published articles, enclosing the same article from my "newly-found author" published eighteen years before and signed with my own name! I looked up the other manuscript, and soon found the second article in a file of the same magazine, also signed by myself! And this is the work I had so satisfyingly commended to myself!

A line to the "author" brought back an immediate answer with my unused check, sent a year before, and the explanation that she had wagered with a man-friend that she could catch an editor napping, and I had been selected as the somnolent subject!

In two cases, therefore, I could not only look my past work in the face, but actually pay for it! But never have I been granted a similar exhilaration. If I am not ashamed of most of my earlier writings, neither am I proud of them.

V

Not that I have the slightest doubt or misgiving as to my position in the world of writers. I had that position very plainly fixed for me not so long ago. It was by a woman of unquestioned intelligence, who was also the editor of a well-known magazine. She had taken the pains, unnecessarily I thought, to read "everything" I had written, and had come to the conclusion that I had written nothing that was really worth the attention of any intelligent person; in fact, she went so far as to say that she marvelled that what I had written for other editors and publishers had ever reached print. She was very careful to explain that she had never printed anything from me in the periodical of which she was editor nor would she give space to anything that I could or would write. Naturally, to receive such a flaying went deep, and I began to ponder over the position in which I found myself. I was along in years, and if I was to extricate myself from the position given me by my editorial critic, it was time I got busy. I did. With due regard for the "pitiful neglect of careful workmanship," "the entire absence of technique," and "the glaring violations of grammar and elementary rhetoric" which she said characterized my writings, I wrote an article, only to discover when I finished it that it was exactly like all my other work. I felt inclined to admit that the unenviable position accorded me was fixed. I determined, however, to let the lady herself fix it for me once more. So I enclosed the article in an envelope and sent it to her, asking for publication. Within a fortnight I received a courteous note in the lady's own handwriting, not only accepting the article and enclosing a check for a most generous amount, but asking if I would "favor" her with future contributions.

My only regret when I received her gracious note was that I had not sent the manuscript over my own name. For you see, after all, the incident settled nothing!

VI

Then, what of this book?

Tolstoi said to a friend: "I almost never read over my printed works. But if for some reason I have to do so I invariably say to myself, 'That ought all to be written over. It should be put this way.'" That is true. Every writer has this experience, but it usually applies more to style than to content. A writer may lack force in what he says, and yet have a message which will carry to the heart of mankind. The technique of writing is not all there is to the art of conveying meaning. It is much, and fortunate is he who possesses it, but it is not the Alpha and Omega of the writer.

This does not mean that any one with a message should or can become a writer. Something more than the mere message is necessary, and that something more is the experience of living, touching Life at its manifold contacts, and an inner conviction that what we believe is true. It is all-too-common a belief that any one can "become an author," as the phrase goes. All too lightly does the public view the capacities necessary for authorship. We have often laughed at the stock story of the man who, when asked if he could play the violin, answered "I don't know, I never tried." But when we ask if one has ever tried to write a book, and the same answer is given, we do not laugh: on the contrary, we are apt to urge the person "Why don't you try?" as if the art of writing a book were less of a feat than the playing of a violin. Only those who have lived and suffered and gone through the birth-pangs of writing a book,—I mean now an earnest book, a real book,—know what it means; what Joseph Conrad so aptly called "experiencing the fearful pangs of book-birth." That feat has again and again cost many an author—as in Conrad's own case— a year or more of health. It was Tolstoi who said: "No one ought to write unless he leaves a fragment of his flesh in the ink-bottle every time he dips the pen."

How will what I have written here appear to me in content ten or fifteen years hence? Will I read what has gone before with the same misgivings, with the same feeling as if the heart is about to miss a beat or two? Does the writer finally reach a point where what he says and the way he says it remain with him as the limit of his

capacities and make a favorable appeal to his judgment?
It seems the best now possible.

VI

One should have arrived somewhere at sixty!
But——

THIRTY-SIX:

BUT——

"The man of wisdom is the man of years."

YOUNG

"To-morrow, and to-morrow, and to-morrow,
Creeps in this petty pace from day to day
To the last syllable of recorded time,
And all our yesterdays have lighted fools
The way to dusty death.   Out, out, brief candle!
Life's but a walking shadow, a poor player
That struts and frets his hour upon the stage
And then is heard no more: it is a tale
Told by an idiot, full of sound and fury
Signifying nothing."

SHAKESPEARE

"Of cheerful yesterdays and confident to-morrows."

WORDSWORTH

BUT——

I

BUT——

If Mr. Beecher was correct, as I feel that he was, in his contention that the age of wisdom begins only when a man has lived the circle of twice thirty years, then all the deductions in the foregoing pages go for naught; they are only lessons learned, but not capable of expression in soundness of judgment. I may have discerned, but I have not penetrated. I may have scratched the surface of Life, but I have not plumbed its depths. I may have learned prudence, discretion, caution, even balance! But wisdom,—that is something different! As the flower is to the bud, so is wisdom to learning.

II

To-morrow, however,——

To-morrow I open the door to the golden age of wisdom: that calm and sane period when, as the play says, humor takes the place of anger and forbearance displaces criticism,—that period of life which the young call old age; when all judgments shall be sound; when all decisions shall be wise; when there shall be no gropings for the best means or the best ends, but when, with clearsightedness, they will be made manifest; when in divination I shall be skilled and in judgment I shall be true; when, from a background of experience absorbed and of lessons learned, granting, of course, that I have learned aright, I shall draw, as water is drawn from a reservoir, the lessons of Life and apply them in clear comprehension and with unerring judgment to the affairs of life and of conduct.

In that golden period, I may hope to be equable, impartial, unperplexed, clear-headed, far-sighted, and possessed of unwarped judgment. Because of such is the true quality of wisdom!

What a reward for having lived and learned for a span of twice thirty years! For what has Life to offer that is greater than the power to decide everything rightly for one's self and to lead others aright? What an equipment for service!

A road straight and clear!

III

I wonder——

" And what is writ, is writ—
Would it were worthier."

BYRON

———

By the Same Author:
To Be Published in 1954:
THRICE THIRTY

EDWARD WILLIAM BOK

BIOGRAPHICAL DATA

1863: Born, October 9, at Helder, Netherlands.

1870: September 20: Arrived in the United States.

1870: Entered public schools of Brooklyn, New York.

1873: Obtained first position in Frost's Bakery, Smith Street, Brooklyn, at 50 cents per week.

1876: August 7: Entered employ of the Western Union Telegraph Company as office-boy.

1882: Entered employ of Henry Holt & Company as stenographer.

1884: Entered employ of Charles Scribner's Sons as stenographer.

1884: Became editor of *The Brooklyn Magazine*.

1886: Founded the Bok Syndicate Press.

1887: Published Henry Ward Beecher Memorial (privately printed).

1889: October 20: Became editor of *The Ladies' Home Journal*.

1890: Published *Successward*: Doubleday, McClure & Company.

1894: Published *Before He Is Twenty*: Fleming H. Revell Company.

1896: October 22: Married Mary Louise Curtis.

1897: September 7: Son born: William Curtis Bok.

1900: Published *The Young Man in Business*: L. C. Page & Company.

1905: January 25: Son born: Cary William Bok.

1906: Published *Her Brother's Letters* (Anonymous): Moffat, Yard & Company.

1907: Degree of LL.D. of Order of Augustinian Fathers conferred by order of Pope Pius X, by the Most Reverend Diomede Falconio, D.D., Apostolic Delegate to the United States, at Villa Nova College, Villa Nova, Pennsylvania.

1910: Degree of LL.D. conferred, in absentia, by Hope College, Holland, Michigan.

1912: Published *The Edward Bok Books of Self-Knowledge;* five volumes: Fleming H. Revell Company.

1913: Founded, with others, The Merion Civic Association, at Merion, Pennsylvania.

1915: Published *Why I Believe in Poverty:* Houghton, Mifflin Company.

1916: Published poem, *God's Hand,* set to music by Josef Hofmann: Schirmer & Company.

1916: Became the "anonymous donor" whereby the deficit of the Philadelphia Orchestra would be insured for five years upon condition that before the end of that period an endowment fund of $1,500,000 should be raised to insure the permanence of the Orchestra.

1917: Vice-President Philadelphia Belgian Relief Commission.

1917: Member of National Y. M. C. A. War Work Council.

1917: State chairman for Pennsylvania of Y. M. C. A. War Work Council.

1918: Member of Executive Committee and chairman of Publicity Committee, Philadelphia War Chest.

1918: Chairman of Philadelphia Y. M. C. A. Recruiting Committee.

1918: State chairman for Pennsylvania of United War Work Campaign.

1918: August-November: visited the battle-fronts in France as guest of the British Government.

1919: September 22: Relinquished editorship of *The Ladies' Home Journal,* completing thirty years of service.

1920: September 20: Upon the 50th anniversary of arrival in the United States, published *The Americanization of Edward Bok:* Charles Scribner's Sons.

1921: Created the Philadelphia Award of $10,000 a year to the citizen of Philadelphia or vicinity who, during the preceding year, shall have performed, or brought to its culmination, an act or contributed a service calculated to advance the best and largest interests of Philadelphia.

1921: Founded the Philadelphia Forum at Philadelphia.

1921: Elected President of the Netherland-American Foundation at New York.

1921: Awarded, by Columbia University, the Joseph Pulitzer Prize for the best American biography published during the year 1920.

1921: Awarded the Gold Medal by the Academy of Political and Social Science at New York.

1922: Published *Two Persons*: Charles Scribner's Sons.

1922: Created, on the highest point of land in Florida, "The Sanctuary" for humans and birds, at Mountain Lake.

1922: Created The Citizens' Award of $1,000 to be awarded, each year, to each of the six policemen, firemen, and park guards of the city of Philadelphia who shall have performed an outstanding act of service or contributed to the efficiency of the service during the preceding calendar year.

1923: Published *A Man From Maine*: Charles Scribner's Sons.

1923: Degree of LL.D. conferred by Rutgers College, New Brunswick, New Jersey.

1923: Degree of Doctor of Humane Letters conferred by Tufts College, Massachusetts.

1923: Edited series of *Great Hollanders*: Charles Scribner's Sons.

1923: Created The American Peace Award of $100,000 for the best practicable plan by which the United States may co-operate with other nations to achieve and preserve the peace of the world.

1923: Created The Harvard Advertising Awards bestowed by The School of Business Administration of Harvard University for raising the standard of advertisements in American and Canadian periodicals and for the intelligent conception and execution of plans for advertising.

1924:   Decorated by Her Majesty, Wilhelmina, Queen of the Netherlands, with the Cross of the Knight of the Netherland Lion.

1924:   Donated a window in The Niewe Kerk, at Delft, Netherlands, commemorative of the 25th anniversary of the coronation of Her Majesty, Wilhelmina, Queen of the Netherlands.

1925:   Published *Twice Thirty*: Charles Scribner's Sons.

INDEX

INDEX

Alcott, Louisa May, 121; autograph of, 123.
Alice's Adventures in Wonderland, 381.
America, 129; autographed, 132, 133.
America, road-building in Netherlands and, 274; Netherlanders in orchestras of, 278; Dutch origin of institutions of, 279–281.
American Peace Award, the, 445; establishment of, 449–453; conditions of, 452–454; purpose of, 453; Policy Committee of, 454, 455, 462, 463; Jury of Award of, 455, 456, 458, 459; public attitude toward, 456 ff.; plans submitted to, 459 ff.; winning plan of, 461 ff.; results of, 468 ff.
Americanism, 253–257.
Americanization of Edward Bok, The, 3, 7, 17, 139, 264, 371, 380, 388.
Americans, 505 ff.; confidence of women in men, 239, 240; the "hyphenated," 253, 254; pride of, in Dutch ancestry, 257.
Amsterdam, 275, 276; Bank of, 285; Symphony Orchestra of, 277.
Antje, 21 ff.
Argonne, 325.
Armaments, Conference for Limitation of, 267, 279.
Arthur, Paul H., 464.
Atkins, David, 464.
Atlantic Monthly, The, 380, 444.
Awards, 435 ff.; the Philadelphia, 427, 437–440; the American Peace, 445, 449 ff.; the Nobel Prize, 435, 437, 457; the Woodrow Wilson Foundation, 435, 437, 457; the Pulitzer, 436, 457; the Citizen's, 442; the Harvard Advertising, 444, 445, 449 ff.; the Theodore Roosevelt, 457.

Babes in the Wood, The, 232–235.
Bach Choir, the, 427.
Barbara Frietchie, autographed, 120.
Barnouw, A. J., 263.
Barrie, James M., 381, 382.
Basle, 259.
Battle Hymn of the Republic, autographed, 124.
"Beauchamp, Miss," 378.
Beecher, Henry Ward, 104, 108, 523; Edward Bok and, 4–6; autograph of, 100.
Belgium, 272.
Bell, Alexander Graham, 194.
Bell Telephone Company, the, 194.
Ben-Hur, 111; autographed passage from, 109.
Bennett, Fillmore, 128, autograph of, 134.
Bible, the, 498.
Birkenhead, the Earl of, 429.
Bismarck, Count von, 31–34.
Bliss, Cornelius N., 455.
Boerhaave, 284, 285.
Bok, Cary William, 3; ancestry of, 17; choice of a college by, 162.
Bok, Edward W., Henry Ward Beecher and, 4–6; at age of wisdom, 5–10, 523; simplicity in writing of, 8; birth of, 16; in France, 20, 38; and his governess, 21, 22; and his aunt, 23–25; good health of, 25–26; curiosity of, in infancy, 30–32; Count von Bismarck and, 31–34; collection of autographs by, 33, 85–89, 97–135; fearlessness of, 34, 37 ff.; father's illness, 35–37; call of, on President Hayes, 39; King Kalakaua and, 40, 41; office boy in Western Union Telegraph Company, 41, 49, 50; determination of, to be successful, 42, 43; extra money

533

MR. BOK'S OTHER BOOKS